Customizing Materials Management Processes in SAP® ERP Operations

 PRESS

Martin Murray
SAP MM – Functionality and Technical Configuration
2008, 588 pp.
978-1-59229-134-2

Martin Murray
SAP Warehouse Management: Functionality and Technical Configuration
2007, 504 pp.
978-1-59229-133-5

Michael Hölzer and Michael Schramm
Quality Management with SAP
2009, 632 pp.
978-1-59229-262-2

Rajen Iyer
Effective SAP SD
2007, 365 pp.
978-1-59229-101-4

Akash Agrawal

Customizing Materials Management Processes in SAP® ERP Operations

Galileo Press

Bonn • Boston

Galileo Press is named after the Italian physicist, mathematician and philosopher Galileo Galilei (1564–1642). He is known as one of the founders of modern science and an advocate of our contemporary, heliocentric worldview. His words *Eppur si muove* (And yet it moves) have become legendary. The Galileo Press logo depicts Jupiter orbited by the four Galilean moons, which were discovered by Galileo in 1610.

Editor Meg Dunkerley
Copyeditor Jutta VanStean
Cover Design Jill Winitzer
Photo Credit Image Copyright Deborah Reny, 2008. Used under license from Shutterstock.com.
Layout Design Vera Brauner
Production Editor Kelly O'Callaghan
Typesetting Publishers' Design and Production Services, Inc.
Printed and bound in Canada

ISBN 978-1-59229-280-6

© 2010 by Galileo Press Inc., Boston (MA)
1st Edition 2010

Contents at a Glance

Contents

Acknowledgments

A book of this proportion would not have been possible without the continuous support of family and friends. A very special thanks to all of my family and especially to my parents for their continuous follow-up to finish this book. Thank you also to my wife and son for their support in the creation of this book.

In addition, I would like to especially thank Meg Dunkerley of SAP PRESS for her trust and hard work in releasing this book.

Furthermore, this book would not have been possible without the help of my friend Yogesh Pampattiwar. Yogesh has extensive experience in procurement and materials management and he has shared his knowledge to make this the best reference book possible.

Finally, a special thanks to financial accounting guru Alok Agrawal. Due to his wide industry and SAP experience, Alok is an expert in financial accounting and he helped with writing the text on the various materials management-financial accounting integration areas.

Preface

Welcome to the first edition of *Customizing Materials Management Processes in SAP ERP Operations*, a compilation of business processes and configuration techniques. During my work on various materials management (MM) implementation projects, I always wished for a good resource that could help offer quick solutions and easy-to-follow guidance. With the completion of this reference book that wish has come true. This book will enhance your knowledge of MM by providing process steps and configuration details for essential business processes.

Who Needs This Book

The main purpose of this book is to explain the various industry best business processes used in MM. As such, it is a reference book for MM consultants, which they can use during their SAP implementation, rollout, and support projects. This book will help consultants find quick solutions for their clients.

This book is also useful if you are an end user who wants to become familiar with common MM functionalities. If you are working on SAP Sales and Distribution (SD), for example, this book will help you understand MM-SD integration by covering intercompany stock transfers via SD, inventory management for goods issue to customers, special stock handling, and more. Similarly, if you are working on SAP ERP Financials Financial Accounting, this book will offer you a greater understanding of MM-Financial Accounting integration. Topics covered in this area include automatic account determination and general ledger account posting during various business transactions.

How to Use This Book

Each chapter in this book focuses on business processes, explaining the business scenario and the step-by-step procedures — supplemented by screenshots — needed to execute the scenario in SAP.

Here's a brief overview of what is covered in each chapter.

Chapter 1

This chapter starts with the importance of an ERP system and SAP. It explains the SAP system landscape, which is very important for every SAP professional. It will also give you an overview of how different functional areas of SAP software are integrated.

Chapter 2

This chapter explains the various elements of an organizational structure and provides you with in-depth knowledge of all possible organizational structure scenarios.

Chapter 3

This chapter describes the importance of master data and how different master data such as material master, vendor master, and purchasing info records are maintained at different organization levels. Various important elements of master data, such as material type and vendor account group are covered in detail.

Chapter 4

This chapter is the heart of the book because it covers various procurement processes across industry verticals. You will obtain in-depth knowledge of procurement processes and their configuration.

Chapter 5

This chapter explains the inventory management functionality. It also explains the inbound and outbound process in inventory management and describes various stock types in inventory management and physical inventory processes.

Chapter 6

This chapter explains different invoice processing scenarios and the general ledger account postings in each scenario.

Chapter 7

This chapter starts by explaining the importance of inventory valuations and then explains various methods of stock valuation. It also describes the functionality of split valuation and how this can be used in different industry scenarios.

Chapter 8

This chapter describes the pricing procedure and automatic account determination functions in SAP. It also explains the step-by-step configuration of these key areas. In addition, this chapter explains the release strategy and version management functionality configuration for various purchasing documents.

Chapter 9

This chapter explains the importance and use of the classification technique and how this is used for material classification. It also describes the step-by-step process to classify materials.

Chapter 10

This final chapter reviews the content covered in each chapter and provides you with lessons learned.

Let's get started. In the next chapter, you'll get an overview of SAP ERP and MM.

ERP applications are no longer optional for enterprises. They play a vital and essential role in business operations, from running day-to-day transactions to providing informative reports and analysis. SAP is the hottest topic in ERP software, and the subject of this chapter.

1   Introduction

ERP stands for *enterprise resource planning*. It is the concept of planning, executing, and reporting across multiple business functions or business units. To manage various functional areas within the enterprise, you need to have an appropriate system or application. Different ERP systems (software products) are available from various vendors. The term ERP originally referred to how a large organization planned to use organization-wide resources, and, in the past, was only used in reference to larger industrial organizations. Today, however, the concept of ERP is extremely comprehensive and can be applied to any type of business, large or small.

Today's ERP systems can cover a wide range of functions and integrate them into one unified database. Originally, ERP systems were used to control only human resources; supply chain management, customer relations management, financials, manufacturing, and warehouse management were all single, stand-alone software applications, usually housed with their own database and network. Today, however, they all fit under one umbrella: the ERP system.

In this chapter, we'll provide you with a brief overview of SAP ERP, an introduction to materials management (MM), and a description of the SAP system environment.

1.1   Overview of SAP ERP

SAP ERP is the world's leading ERP software, developed by SAP AG. SAP AG was founded by five German engineers in 1972, and SAP is an acronym for "Systeme,

Anwendungen, Produkte in der Datenverarbeitung." In English this translates to "Systems, Applications, and Products in Data Processing."

SAP ERP is integrated ERP software, which means that all functional areas fall under one umbrella, allowing information to be shared among functional areas.

Figure 1.1 shows some of the functional departments within an enterprise. Each functional department needs information from other departments, which is made possible by an integrated system. For example, the Sales and Distribution department is responsible for marketing and collecting customer orders and therefore generates a demand for finished goods in the Production Planning department. Similarly, raw materials are procured by the Purchasing Department based on requirements from the Planning Department and kept in inventory and maintained by the Plant Maintenance department. Then, on orders from the Shop Floor Control department, the raw materials are issued to the shop floor. Of course, many of these processes and transactions involve money and must be recorded by the Finance and Controlling department. From just these few examples, you can see how the different departments are dependent on each other and how transaction information flows to multiple departments.

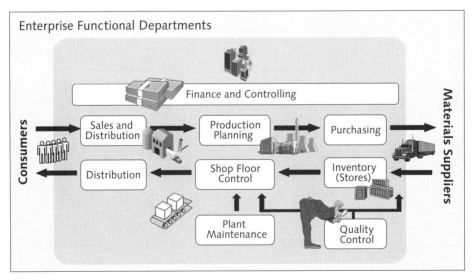

Figure 1.1 Various Functional Departments in an Enterprise

SAP provides an integrated solution for all functional departments of an enterprise by offering a specific component for each. The following are the most commonly used components of SAP ERP:

▶ SAP ERP Financials Financial Accounting (which we'll refer to as Financial Accounting for short)

▶ SAP ERP Financials Controlling

▶ HCM: Human Capital Management (human resources)

▶ PP: Production Planning

▶ PS: Project Systems

▶ SD: Sales and Distribution

▶ MM: Materials Management

▶ QM: Quality Management

▶ PM: Plant Maintenance

SAP has also developed additional products to meet customer requirements. These new products are also called *new dimensional* products that can be implemented alone or in integration with SAP ERP (or any other ERP) products. The following are examples of these new dimensional products:

▶ SAP SRM: Supplier Relationship Management

▶ SAP SCM: Supply Chain Management

▶ SAP CRM: Customer Relationship Management

▶ SAP BW: Business Warehouse

Aside from the core components and new dimensional products, SAP also provides industry-specific solutions, including the following:

▶ SAP for Retail

▶ SAP for Banking

▶ SAP for Mill Products

▶ SAP for Aerospace and Defense

▶ SAP for Media

▶ SAP for Automotive

▶ SAP for Healthcare

- SAP for Service Providers
- SAP for Utilities
- SAP for Oil and Gas
- SAP for Engineering & Construction
- SAP for High Tech & Electronics
- SAP for Consumer Products
- SAP for Insurance
- SAP for Public Sector
- SAP for Telecommunications
- SAP for Chemicals
- SAP for Pharmaceuticals

SAP software is highly customizable, and it can be altered to meet almost any enterprise requirement. It was originally developed using Advanced Business Application Programming Language, fourth generation (ABAP/4) language, which was used up until the release of SAP 3.1. When SAP 4.0 was introduced, the name of the language was changed to simply ABAP. ABAP is basically the same as ABAP/4, but contains several improvements and features that make it an object-oriented language. In general, you do not need to know ABAP to use SAP software, but SAP does provide an ABAP-development workbench for customer-specific enhancements. This workbench includes all of the tools necessary to develop and design programs, screens, and more.

1.2   Overview of Materials Management

MM is a key area within Logistics with SAP. Logistics is the most extensive area of the SAP application, and contains the largest number of components, as follows:

- MM: Materials management
- PP: Production planning
- PM: Plant maintenance
- PS: Project system

- QM: Quality management
- SD: Sales and distribution

MM is a very important component of logistics because it's tightly integrated with all of the other components of SAP Logistics. MM consists of the following components:

- MM-PUR: Purchasing
- MM-IV: Invoice verification
- MM-IM: Inventory management
- MM-CBP: Consumption based planning
- MM-EDI: Electronic data interchange
- MM-IS: Information system

Purchasing includes operations such as request for quotation, quotation comparison, outline agreement with vendors, order monitoring, and so on. Invoice verification is important from an accounting perspective because it allows for vendor payment, and incorrect postings may cause financial loss for the enterprise. Inventory management is required in every step of supply chain management and is responsible for stock tracking, issuing materials, and receiving materials. Inventory management also verifies the system stock and physical stock at regular intervals and ensures that both records match. Consumption based planning (CBP) is used to plan the quantity of raw materials to be procured; using CBP is optional. Electronic data interchanges (EDI) are required only when you want to send messages—such as purchase orders—to a vendor in electronic format. Electronic format has many advantages over physical format—such as fax and printouts—because it saves communication time and also the cost of paper and printing. Information systems contain different reports for management to analyze day-to-day business operations and to help take appropriate strategic decisions. Information systems also provide flexibility to customize reports for customer-specific requirements.

This book deals specifically with materials management in SAP ERP Operations. However, before we can get to that, you must understand some basic information about the SAP system environment.

1.3 SAP System Environment: Development, Quality, and Production Clients

It's extremely important for everyone involved in SAP implementation, support, rollout, or upgrade projects to understand the SAP system environment. A *system environment* is referred to as a *client*. For example, the development, quality, and production environments are respectively known as:

▶ Development Client

▶ Quality Client

▶ Production Client

> **Note**
>
> The use of the word "client" here can sometimes cause confusion because the word can also be used to refer to SAP customers.

SAP developed the client concept to use single SAP instances for development, quality testing, and production. Customers can create different clients within the same SAP instance (a single SAP server). For example:

▶ Client 100: Development

▶ Client 200: Quality/Testing

▶ Client 800: Production

Transactional and master data are differentiated based on client number, which form a composite primary key for most of the database tables. When you log on to the SAP system, you enter the client number in the first screen, as shown in Figure 1.2. When you perform any transaction, the data is saved in a database header table and item table. For example, the header table EKKO, which is used for purchase orders header data, contains a composite primary key that includes the client number and purchase order number (Figure 1.3). If you create a purchase order for Client 800 (the production client), it's saved with a client number and purchase order number and forms a composite primary key. This particular document will only be used for the production client. This is how SAP separates the production, development, and testing data in a single SAP instance. (These tables are also called *client-dependent tables*.)

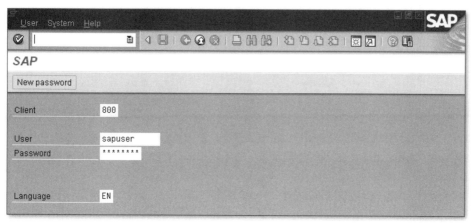

Figure 1.2 SAP Logon Screen: Client Number

Data Browser: Table EKKO Select Entries 200

Table: EKKO
Displayed fields: 20 of 76 Fixed columns: 2 List

	Client	Purchasing Doc.	Company Code	Doc. category	Document Type
	800	4151504103	1000	F	NB
	800	4151504104	1000	F	NB
	800	4151504105	1000	F	NB
	800	4151504106	1000	F	NB
	800	4151504107	1000	F	NB
	800	4151504108	1000	F	NB
	800	4151504109	1000	F	NB
	800	4151504110	1000	F	NB
	800	4151504111	1000	F	NB
	800	4151504112	1000	F	NB

Figure 1.3 Purchase Order Header Table EKKO: Client-Dependent

While configuring the SAP system, you might get a warning stating that a table is *cross-client* (Figure 1.4). Cross-client tables are client-independent tables, and any changes made in these tables are applicable for all clients. Figure 1.5 shows an example of a client-independent table. Table T682 (access sequence table) is a cross-client table; therefore, the client number is not involved in the primary key.

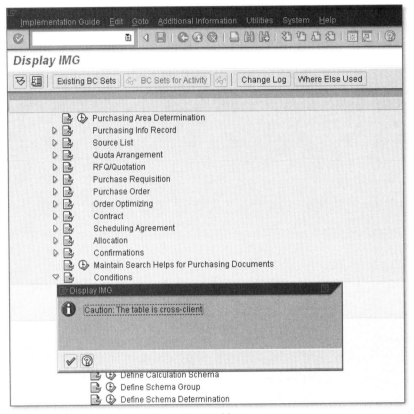

Figure 1.4 Warning Message: Cross-Client Table

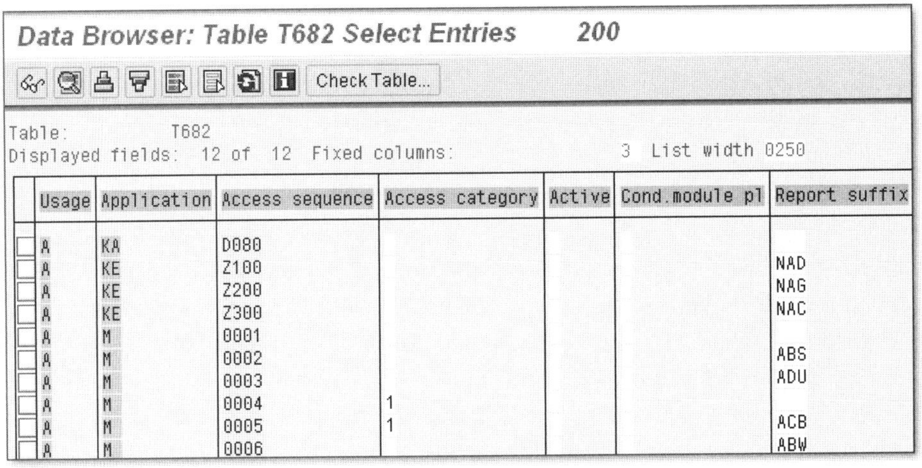

Figure 1.5 Database Table for Access Sequence: Cross-Client Table

The majority of SAP customers use separate servers for each client, which are hosted on separate physical boxes.

In the following sections, we'll discuss the different types of clients and the process of moving objects from one client to another.

1.3.1 Client Descriptions

Each client is created for a specific purpose, and the system landscape is decided based on customer requirements, complexity, and data safety. The system landscape varies for each customer but will always have a minimum of three clients: Development, Quality/Testing, and Production (Figure 1.6).

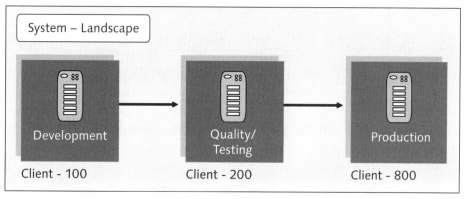

Figure 1.6 System Landscape

The development client is where the customization and development work take place. After the development work is completed, the customization object creates a transport request in the development client, and the object is transported to the quality/testing client. Finally, after it has been tested and found satisfactory, the object is moved to the production client. It's the production client that end users interact with; day-to-day operational transactional data is entered here. Because the production client is used for real time data, it's very sensitive. Any test transaction posted in the production client is posted in a real time business transaction of the customer; therefore, you must be very careful while working on the production client.

Some SAP customers create two separate clients (a sandbox client and a golden client) instead of one development client. A *sandbox* client is mainly used for configuration ideas and development, and is also where system design work takes place. When you are comfortable with your configuration solution in the sandbox client, you must reconfigure your solution in the golden client. If the configuration in the sandbox client isn't appropriate, it isn't reconfigured in the golden client. Sandbox clients may contain many additional customizations that haven't been reconfigured in the golden client. The golden client is configured only for approved designs; therefore, it's always a clean system.

The golden client is also known as the configuration client. Ideally, no transactions or testing takes place in the golden client; therefore, it doesn't have any master or transactional data. The golden client is used only for configuration and to transport the configuration to the testing/quality and production clients.

1.3.2 Transport Requests

Transport requests are the means by which your configuration settings are moved from one client to another client, and are created automatically when you make any changes to configuration tables or programs. When a transport request has been created, it can be moved to another client only if it's released. Basis consultants are responsible for transporting transport request from one client to another.

There are many transaction codes in SAP software to manage transport requests. You can use Transaction SE10 to view and manage transport requests. This transaction allows you to select the request types and statuses you want to display (Figure 1.7). After you click on the Display button, the system displays the list of transport requests (Figure 1.8). Transport requests with a status of Released can't be changed. Transport requests with a status of Modifiable can be changed. You can select the same transport request number when saving configuration changes so that the changes are updated in the same transport request. However, if the transport request isn't modifiable, you can't select it for changes; instead, you need to create a new transport request for the changes.

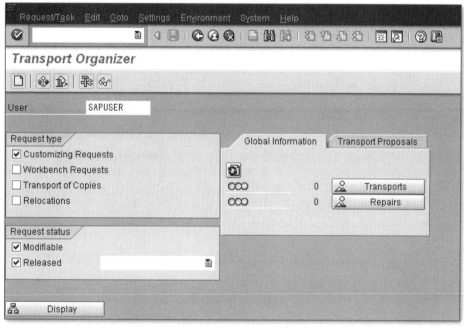

Figure 1.7   Transport Organizer: Transaction SE10

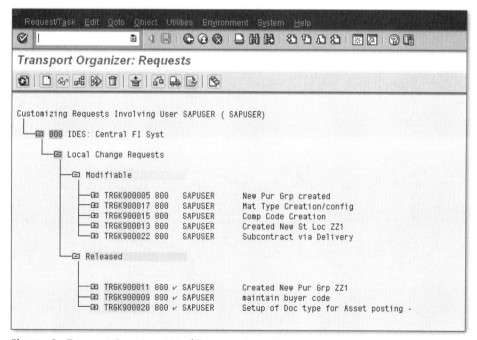

Figure 1.8   Transport Organizer: List of Transport Requests

To release the transport request, select the transport request number and click on the Transport button (or press F9). First, release the reference Customizing tasks, which you will find under the transport request. Then, release the transport request. After a successful release transport, the request is changed to a status of Released and can't be modified.

> **Note**
>
> If you have multiple transport requests for the same Customizing table, you need to ensure that the transport requests are transported in the appropriate sequence. Otherwise, you may miss the configuration settings in the target client properly due to overlapping transport requests (because the last configuration settings can be overwritten by the previous configuration settings).

1.4 Summary

This chapter has provided you with an introduction to ERP and an overview of SAP as a whole. It also outlined the basic components of materials management within SAP ERP Operations. Most importantly, this chapter described the SAP system landscape, and the significance of each system environment: the development, quality, and production clients.

In the next chapter, we'll discuss the organizational structure used in SAP systems.

The organizational structure is the key for a successful SAP implementation. To achieve flawless execution of business processes, it's extremely important that the organizational structure is accurately mapped in the SAP system.

2   SAP Organizational Structure

Configuring an accurate organizational structure is the key to a successful SAP implementation. From the materials management perspective, purchasing organizations, plants, storage locations, and purchasing groups are important elements of an organizational structure. In this chapter, we'll review what organizational structures are and how they're used in SAP systems. We'll also provide the configuration steps for the various possible organizational structures available in the SAP system. You'll learn about many different elements of organizational structures available in industries and how to map these elements into the SAP organizational structure.

2.1   Introduction to Organizational Structures

For any successful implementation project, you need to ensure that you correctly understand your customer's organizational structure and that you map this organizational structure in a way that meets all of the business process requirements. To do this, it's very important that you understand the essential terminology used in an industry and in the SAP organizational structure.

As shown in Figure 2.1, the different functional departments of an organization are mapped into SAP software using organizational units. *Organizational units* are responsible for a set of business functions. An enterprise or corporate group is mapped into SAP software as a *client*, and different companies or subsidiaries of an enterprise are referred to as the *company code*. Clients and company codes are two types of organizational units that are found at highest level in the SAP organizational structure.

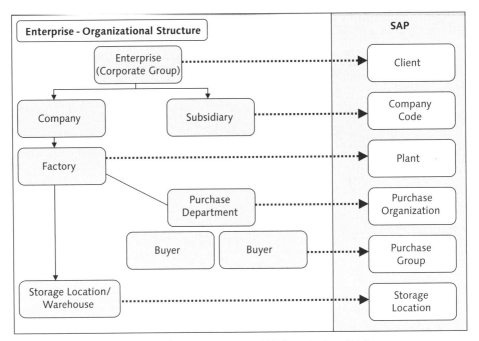

Figure 2.1 Mapping of Functional Departments into SAP Organizational Units

> **Note**
>
> In an SAP system, the word *client* has a specific meaning, and it's important to have a clear understanding of what's meant when this word is used. In general language, "client" means the customer to whom you are providing services. In an SAP system, however, "client" is used to refer to a corporate group, which is the highest organizational element. Client is also used to differentiate among real-time data, test data, and development data (as discussed in Chapter 1).

2.1.1 Levels of an Organizational Structure

Client is the highest element in the SAP organizational structure, but there are many other levels (Figure 2.2). A client may have one or more company codes assigned to it; each company code may have one or more plants assigned to it; and each plant may have one or more storage locations assigned to it. Furthermore, each company may have set of purchasing groups. A *purchasing group* is a buyer or group of buyers and is defined independent of the organizational structure. Therefore it isn't assigned to a purchasing organization or company code. Detailed definitions of client, company code, plant, storage locations, and purchasing groups are provided in the following sections.

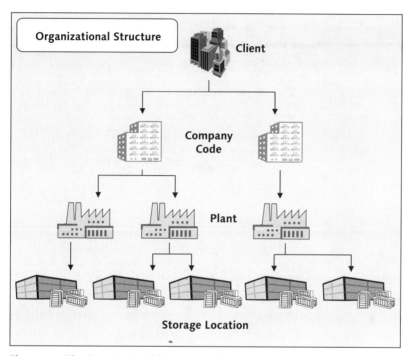

Figure 2.2 The Organizational Structure in SAP Systems

Client/Company

As the highest organizational unit in an SAP system, the client can be a corporate group and can represent a company or a conglomerate of companies. For example, consider a fictional corporate group called ABC Corporation, which has companies such as ABC Steel, ABC FMCG, and ABC Pharmacy. If ABC Corporation wishes to implement SAP software for all of its companies in a single instance, then it should be represented as a client. On the other hand, if the different companies install the SAP software individually, then each company will have one SAP instance and the individual companies will represent the client.

Company Code

The company code is the smallest organizational unit for which you can have an independent accounting department within external accounting. For example, a corporate group (a client) may have one or more independent companies, all of which have their own SAP general ledger (G/L) account, balance sheet, and profit and loss (P&L) account. Each of these independent business entities needs to be created in the SAP system as separate company codes.

Plant

In industry terminology, a manufacturing facility is called a plant. In an SAP system, however, a plant can be a manufacturing facility, sales office, corporate head office, maintenance plant, or central delivery warehouse. In general, the plant can be any location within a company code that is involved in some activity for the company code.

Storage Location

A storage location is a place within a plant where materials are kept. Inventory management on a quantity basis is carried out at the storage location level in the plant, as is physical inventory. Physical Inventory is the process of verifying physical stock with the system stock. If any differences exist in stock quantity, system stocks are updated with actual physical stock quantity. Physical inventory is carried out at each storage location level.

Purchasing Organization

In industry terminology, the purchasing department deals with vendors and is responsible for all procurement activities. The purchasing department is mapped as a *purchasing organization* in the SAP system. Purchasing organizations negotiate conditions of purchase with vendors for one or more plants, and are legally responsible for honoring purchasing contracts.

Purchasing Group

A purchasing group is a term for a buyer or group of buyers responsible for certain purchasing activities. Because a purchase order is a legal document, the purchasing group is represented on a purchase order or contract. The purchasing group can also play an important role in reporting various purchasing transactions. In an SAP system, a purchasing group isn't assigned to purchasing organizations or any other organizational units. Purchasing groups are defined at the client level and can create purchasing documents for any purchasing organization.

Now that you have a good understanding of the various organizational units, let's move on to learning how to create an organizational structure based on business scenarios.

2.1.2 Business Scenarios and Organizational Structure

The organizational structure needs to be designed and configured in the system based on the different business scenario requirements of the enterprise (client). An SAP system's organizational structure is very flexible and there are a variety of possible combinations. We'll address these in the following sections.

Scenario 1: Plant-Specific Purchasing

You may come across a scenario where your customers have separate purchasing departments for each plant, and each purchasing department is responsible for negotiating with vendors, creating contracts, and issuing purchase orders. This scenario is called a *plant-specific purchasing organization*. In this scenario, you need to define a purchasing organization for each plant in the SAP system, and then assign these purchasing organizations to their respective plants.

For example, in Figure 2.3, the client has two different company codes, and each company code has plants assigned to it. Company Code-1 has two plants, and Company Code-2 has one plant. Additionally, for each plant, there is a separate purchasing organization. Purchasing Organization 1, Purchasing Organization 2, and Purchasing Organization 3 are assigned to Plant-1, Plant-2, and Plant-3, respectively.

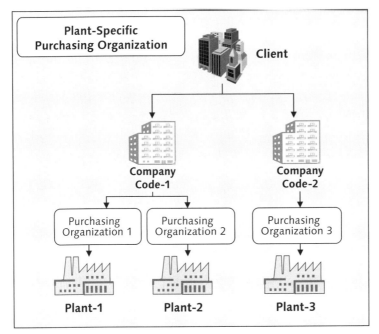

Figure 2.3 Plant-Specific Purchasing Organization

Scenario 2: Cross-Plant Purchasing

Some customers may have a scenario where a single purchasing department is responsible for procurement activities for more than one plant. In this case, you need to create a purchasing organization that's responsible for more than one plant in the same company code.

For example, in Figure 2.4, the client has two different company codes, and each company code has plants assigned to it. Company Code-1 has two plants, and Company Code-2 has one plant. Purchasing Organization 1 is assigned to Plant-1 and Plant-2 because it's responsible for both of the plants in Company Code-1.

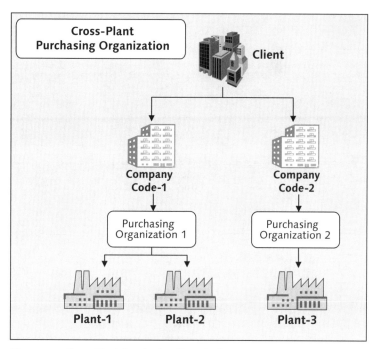

Figure 2.4 Cross-Plant Purchasing Organization

Scenario 3: Cross-Company Code/Corporate Group Wide Purchasing

Some customers have just one purchasing organization for the procurement activities of multiple plants in different company codes. In Figure 2.5, the client has two different company codes, and each has plants assigned to it. Company Code-1 has two plants, and Company Code-2 has one plant. Purchasing Organization 1 is assigned to Plant-1, Plant-2, and Plant-3 of Company Code-1 and Company Code-2.

Example

One of the world's leading producers of printing papers, headquartered in Germany, has over 15 company codes and 50 plants—and all of the plants are assigned to a single purchasing organization. This was done so that this purchasing organization controls all vendor negotiations, making them responsible for high-volume orders, which increased their negotiation power. Using a single purchasing organization also makes it easier to maintain and track long term contracts with vendors.

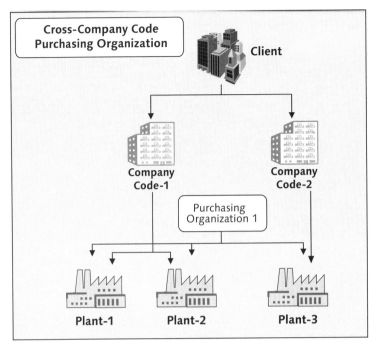

Figure 2.5 Cross-Company Code Purchasing Organization

Scenario 4: Reference Purchasing Organization

Some customers may have a scenario where they have one centralized purchasing department at the corporate group level responsible for the negotiation and creation of global agreements. These agreements are used by local purchasing organizations to create purchase orders. This business scenario helps companies negotiate better prices due to high volume purchases. In an SAP system, such a purchasing organization is referred to as a *reference purchasing organization*.

For example, in Figure 2.6, the client has two different company codes and each company code has plants assigned to it. Company Code-1 has two plants, and Company Code-2 has one plant. For each plant, there is a separate purchasing organization: Purchasing Organization 1, Purchasing Organization 2, and Purchasing Organization 3, which are assigned to Plant-1, Plant-2, and Plant-3, respectively. Purchasing Organization 4 is assigned to Purchasing Organization 1, Purchasing Organization 2, and Purchasing Organization 3.

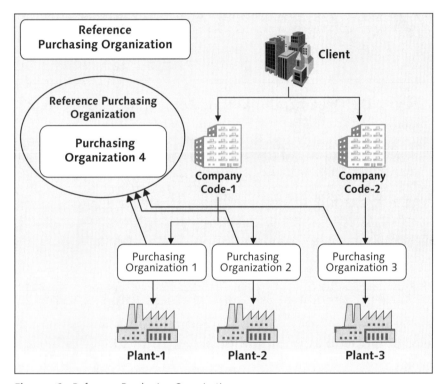

Figure 2.6 Reference Purchasing Organization

Purchasing Organization 4 is the reference purchasing organization. The reference purchasing organization can negotiate with vendors and create global outline agreements (contracts and scheduling agreements). Plant-specific purchasing organizations (i.e., Purchasing Organization 1, Purchasing Organization 2, and Purchasing Organization 3) can issue purchase orders to vendors with reference to these global agreements.

Scenario 5: Standard Purchasing Organization

SAP also provides a *standard purchasing organization*, which is used to create automatic purchase orders. In the automatic purchase order creation process, the system needs to find the purchasing organization. The system gets the plant code from the purchase requisition and, from the plant code system, determines the standard purchasing organization (because the standard purchasing organization is assigned to the plant). Finally, a purchase order is created.

Now that you have a thorough understanding of the different organizational structure elements and how to apply these elements to different business scenarios, let's move on to the actual steps needed to set up organizational structures.

2.2 Setting Up Organizational Structures in an SAP System

Configuring organizational structures in a sequence with the correct steps is very important. Without the correct configuration, your business transactions will end up posting wrong entries. In this section, you'll learn step-by-step procedures to correctly configure an organizational structure.

2.2.1 Creating Company Codes

In general, we recommend that when creating a company code, you copy a company code from an existing company code. In a standard system, company code 0001 is provided by SAP for this purpose. When you copy company codes, the system also copies the company code-specific parameters. If necessary, you can then change the specific data in the relevant application. This is less time consuming than creating a new company code.

To copy the company code from an existing company code, go to SAP IMG • ENTERPRISE STRUCTURE • DEFINITION • FINANCIAL ACCOUNTING • EDIT, COPY, DELETE, CHECK COMPANY CODE.

Click on the company code Copy option, and then on the Copy Organization Objects button. As shown in Figure 2.7, enter "0001" in the From Company Code field (Company code 0001 is SAP AG) and enter the code you want to create into the To Company Code field. The company code can be a maximum of four digits long and it can be alphanumeric.

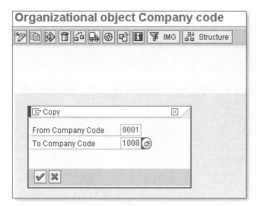

Figure 2.7 Company Code Creation via the Copy Function

After you click on the OK button, a popup window asks whether you want to copy the G/L account company code data. Click on Yes. This brings you to a message about changing the local currency; select the appropriate currency.

You'll now see a message that outlines the completed activities. From here, you can edit the data in your newly created company code by going to the navigation path SAP IMG • Enterprise Structure • Definition • Financial Accounting • Edit, Copy, Delete, Check Company Code • Select Edit Company Code Data. By selecting your company code and clicking on the Details button, you can change the company name, city, country, currency, and language.

2.2.2 Defining Valuation Levels

Stock materials can be managed in inventory on the basis of quantity, value, or both. This depends on the material type of the material master record. For each material type, you can configure whether inventory management is on a quantity basis, a value basis, or both. In a standard system, raw material (material type code ROH) is managed on a quantity and value basis. If the stock is managed on a quantity basis, this means that every stock movement such as goods issue or goods receipt is noted in inventory management and stock quantities are updated. Similarly, if stocks are managed on a value basis, the stock value that is material value is updated in the financial book of accounts during every goods movement transaction such as goods issue or goods receipt. When you procure valuated materials (managed on a value basis), the stock value is updated into stock G/L accounts. The valuation of stock materials can be done at the plant or company code level. Based on the customer requirements, you need to define the value area for the valuated materials.

To access or define the valuation level, follow the navigation path SAP IMG • ENTERPRISE STRUCTURE • DEFINITION • LOGISTICS-GENERAL • DEFINE VALUATION LEVEL.

You'll have two options available as follows:

▶ Valuation area is a plant

▶ Valuation level is a company code

The valuation area/level is simply the level at which you want to valuate your inventory. If you define valuation at the plant level, you need to define a separate valuation area for each plant and stock materials will be valuated separately for each plant.

SAP recommends setting the plant as a valuation area, which is necessary if you are using SAP Production Planning, Costing, or SAP for Retail.

> **Note**
>
> Once set, it's not possible to switch the valuation level from plant to company code, or vice versa.

2.2.3 Creating Plants

To create a plant, follow the navigation path SAP IMG • ENTERPRISE STRUCTURE • DEFINITION • LOGISTICS-GENERAL • DEFINE, COPY, DELETE, CHECK PLANT.

You'll see three activity options, as shown in Figure 2.8, and listed here:

▶ Define plant

▶ Copy, delete, check plant

▶ Define plant for cross-system goods flow

It's best to copy a plant from an existing one, and then make the required changes (just as we discussed with company codes). This copies all of the dependent table entries into Customizing; otherwise, you would need to maintain these manually.

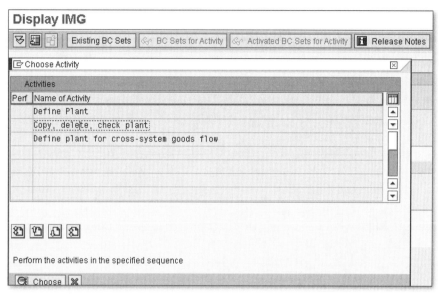

Figure 2.8 Plant Creation

To create a plant via the copy function, select Copy, Delete, Check Plant. On the next screen, click on the Copy Org Object button and enter the From Plant and To Plant codes, as shown in Figure 2.9. Finally, click on OK.

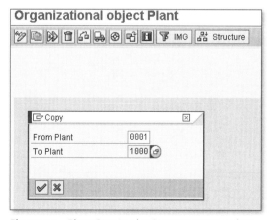

Figure 2.9 Plant Creation by Copying Existing Plant

To see the completed activities, enter the existing plant (from which data will be copied to your new plant) in the From Plant field, and enter the new plant code in the To Plant field.

After this, select Define Plant, select the plant and either click on Details or use the combination of Ctrl + Shift + F2 to define the plant's address, factory calendar, telephone numbers, and so on. The language can be set by clicking on the Address icon. If you are working for a U.S.-based customer, you might have to define the tax jurisdiction code, which is used for determining tax rates.

2.2.4 Assigning Plants to Company Codes

After you've created a company code and plant, you must assign the plant to the company code. To do this, go to the menu path SAP IMG • ENTERPRISE STRUCTURE • ASSIGNMENT • LOGISTICS-GENERAL • ASSIGN PLANT TO COMPANY CODE and click on New Entries. Enter your company code and plant and click on Save, as shown in Figure 2.10.

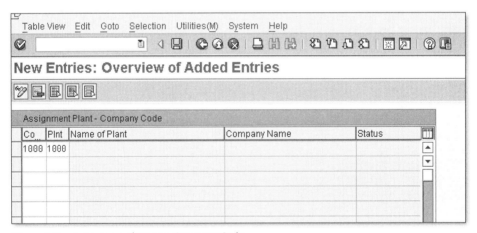

Figure 2.10 Assigning a Plant to a Company Code

2.2.5 Creating Storage Locations for Plants

Storage locations are created under the plant. Because of this, you can reuse the same storage location code for other plants. The menu path for a storage location is SAP IMG • ENTERPRISE STRUCTURE • DEFINITION • MATERIALS MANAGEMENT •

MAINTAIN STORAGE LOCATION. Enter the plant number for which you want to create a storage location.

From here, click on the New Entry button, and enter the storage location number and description, as shown in Figure 2.11.

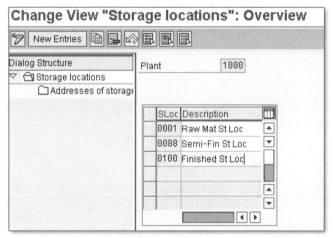

Figure 2.11 Storage Location Creation

Storage locations are always created for a plant. You can also maintain an address for a storage location. To define the address, select the storage location and click on Addresses in the left hand menu. Enter the address data and click on Save.

2.2.6 Creating Purchasing Organizations

A purchasing organization is responsible for procurement activities, and creating a purchasing organization in the system is important for the purchasing cycle. To do this, follow the menu path SAP IMG • ENTERPRISE STRUCTURE • DEFINITION • MATERIALS MANAGEMENT • MAINTAIN PURCHASING ORGANIZATION. From here, you can click on New Entries and enter the purchasing organization code and description, as shown in Figure 2.12. When finished, save the entries.

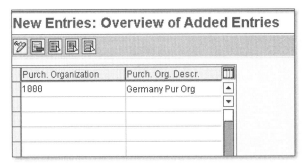

Figure 2.12 Purchase Organization Creation

2.2.7 Assigning Purchasing Organizations to Company Codes and Plants

After you have created the purchasing organization, plants, and company codes, you need to appropriately assign everything to complete the organizational structure. To assign purchasing organizations to company codes or plants go to SAP IMG • ENTERPRISE STRUCTURE • ASSIGNMENT • MATERIALS MANAGEMENT, as shown in Figure 2.13. Based on the business scenario, various options are available for assigning purchasing organizations.

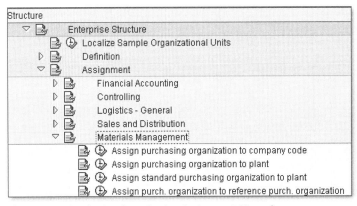

Figure 2.13 Purchasing Organization Assignment Menu Screen

The steps outlined next need to be taken to understand each assignment option and configuration step.

Assigning Purchasing Organizations to Company Codes

To configure the scenario where a purchasing organization is responsible for the plants of one company code only, follow the path SAP IMG • ENTERPRISE STRUCTURE • ASSIGNMENT • MATERIALS MANAGEMENT • ASSIGN PURCHASING ORGANIZATION TO COMPANY CODE, as shown in Figure 2.14.

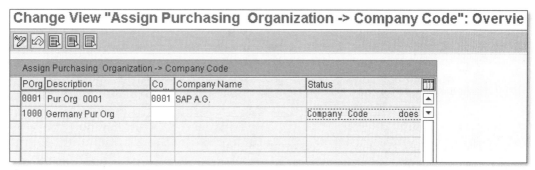

Figure 2.14 Assigning a Purchasing Organization to a Company Code

Remember that in a cross-company code purchasing organization, you don't assign the purchasing organization to a company code. A cross-company code purchasing organization is the purchasing organization responsible for procurement activities for plants and that belongs to different company codes.

Assigning Purchasing Organizations to Plants

Assigning a purchasing organization to a plant is mandatory. If you don't assign a purchasing organization to plant, you can't create purchase orders for that plant. You can assign one purchasing organization to one or more plants by following the menu path SAP IMG • ENTERPRISE STRUCTURE • ASSIGNMENT • MATERIALS MANAGEMENT • ASSIGN PURCHASING ORGANIZATION TO PLANT, as shown in Figure 2.15.

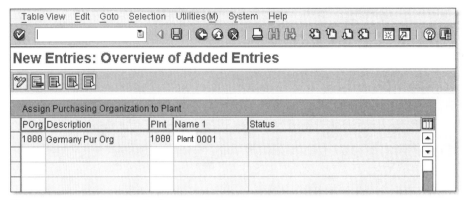

Figure 2.15 Assigning a Purchasing Organization to Plants

As previously discussed, you can assign one purchasing organization to one or more plants. You have the following options:

▸ One purchasing organization procures for one plant (plant-specific purchasing)

▸ One purchasing organization procures for several plants (cross-plant purchasing)

▸ Several purchasing organizations procure for one plant (a combination of plant-specific purchasing organization, cross-plant purchasing organization, and cross-company code purchasing organization)

2.2.8 Assigning Standard Purchasing Organizations to Plants

If several purchasing organizations procure for a certain plant, you can define one of them as the standard purchasing organization for the pipeline procurement, consignment, and stock transfer scenarios. The standard purchasing organization is used by the system in case of source determination for stock transfers and consignment. In the case of goods issues of pipeline materials, the purchasing information records of the standard purchasing organization are read.

To assign the standard purchasing organization to a plant, use the following path: SAP IMG • ENTERPRISE STRUCTURE • ASSIGNMENT • MATERIALS MANAGEMENT • ASSIGN STANDARD PURCHASING ORGANIZATION TO PLANT. As shown in Figure 2.16, you can define one standard purchasing organization for each plant, and this purchasing organization is automatically proposed and selected by the system while creating automatic purchase orders.

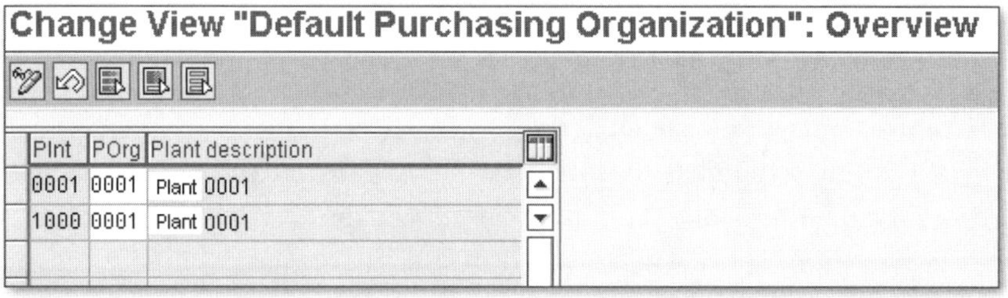

Change View "Default Purchasing Organization": Overview

Plnt	POrg	Plant description	
0001	0001	Plant 0001	▲
1000	0001	Plant 0001	▼

Figure 2.16 Assigning a Standard Purchasing Organization to Plants

2.2.9 Assigning Purchasing Organizations to Reference Purchase Organizations

In an enterprise, you may have a scenario where one purchasing department wants to refer to the purchasing terms and conditions of another purchasing department. In SAP terminology, the referred purchasing department becomes the reference purchasing organization. Thus, when a purchasing organization is assigned to a reference purchasing organization, it can make use of the already-negotiated terms of purchases such as rate per unit, discount based on volume, payment terms, and so on.

To set this up, follow the path SAP IMG • ENTERPRISE STRUCTURE • ASSIGNMENT • MATERIALS MANAGEMENT • ASSIGN PURCHASING ORGANIZATION TO REF PURCHASING ORGANIZATION (Figure 2.17).

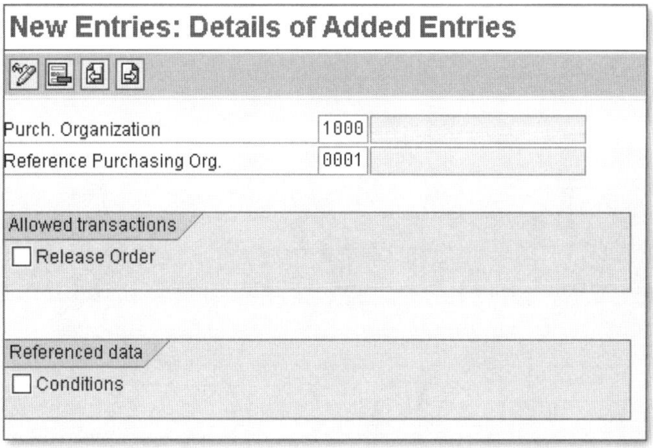

New Entries: Details of Added Entries

Purch. Organization	1000
Reference Purchasing Org.	0001

Allowed transactions
☐ Release Order

Referenced data
☐ Conditions

Figure 2.17 Assigning a Reference Purchasing Organization to a Purchasing Organization

As shown in the Figure 2.17, in addition to the assignment, the following two settings need to be configured:

▶ **Allowed Transactions – Release Order**
In a scenario where a purchasing organization is allowed to create contract release orders from the contracts of the referenced purchasing organization, check this box.

▶ **Referenced Data – Conditions**
In a scenario where a purchasing organization wants to refer only to conditions from the contracts of the reference purchasing organization, check this box.

In a scenario where a purchasing organization wants to refer conditions and create contract release orders from contracts of a referenced purchasing organization, check both boxes.

2.2.10 Creating Purchase Groups

The purchasing group can be an individual or a group of individuals responsible for performing procurement activities such as the creation of purchase orders or contracts.

In an SAP system, the purchasing group is an independent entity, so it's not assigned to any purchasing organization. To create a purchasing group, follow the path SAP IMG • MATERIALS MANAGEMENT • PURCHASING • CREATE PURCHASING GROUPS. Click on New Entries, and enter the purchasing group, description, telephone number, and fax number, as shown in Figure 2.18. Save the entries to create the purchasing group.

Change View "Purchasing Groups": Overview

New Entries

Purchasing Groups

Pu	Desc. Pur. Grp	Tel.No. Pur.Grp	Fax number	Telephone	
001	James Harrison	06227/341285			
002	George	06227/341286			
003	Martin	06227/341287			

Figure 2.18 Creating and Editing Purchase Groups

2.3   Summary

In this chapter, we've reviewed the basics of organizational structures, including the process of setting them up in an SAP system. Configuring accurate organizational structures is the key to a successful SAP implementation.

You are now able to:

▸ Define an organizational structure based on business processes and operational scenarios in an enterprise.

▸ Understand and configure various units in the SAP organizational structure.

▸ Make assignments based on your knowledge of how the units in MM organizational structures are related to each other.

Let's move to the next chapter to understand the different master data used in materials management. We'll also learn how to define master data, and how to configure various master data elements.

Master data is the source of centrally maintained information and is available for retrieval when required during transactions. This helps maintain consistent information enterprise-wide and eliminates repetitive data entry.

3 Master Data

In the first part of this chapter, you will learn about master data, including how to configure it and how it relates to the organizational structure. In the second part of the chapter, you will learn about the different master data required by MM in SAP ERP Operations, and what its advantages and usages are.

Master data is a collection of frequently-used data records that don't change often; master data is static in nature. There are many different categories of master data in an SAP system, such as customer master data, vendor master data, and G/L accounts master data. The master data categories specific to MM are as follows:

▸ Vendor master

▸ Material master

▸ Purchasing info records

▸ Source list

▸ Quota arrangement

▸ Service master data

The most important of these is material master records. Material master records are used in almost all materials management transactions, including purchase orders, goods receipts, and invoice receipts. In the following sections, we'll discuss these categories in more detail. Before we get into the individual master data details, however, let's explore how master data is maintained at different organizational levels such as client, company code, plant, purchasing organization, and so on.

Master data is created at the client level, but specific department data (also known as *functional* department data) is maintained at the department level. By creating the material master record at the client level, you ensure that it has a unique material code and that every plant and department doesn't create the same material with a different material code. The department-specific data in the record will then be maintained by various departments such as purchasing, sales, and production.

> **Note**
>
> Data maintained at a higher level is inherited by the lower level of organizational unit. For example, a material number and description maintained at the client level is inherited by plant and storage location.

3.1   Vendor Master Records

Vendor master records are maintained by both the purchasing and accounting departments, as illustrated in Figure 3.1. As a vendor is crediting business partners in the company, the purchasing department maintains purchase-related data such as payment terms, and the accounting department maintains vendor G/L account information such as bank account details.

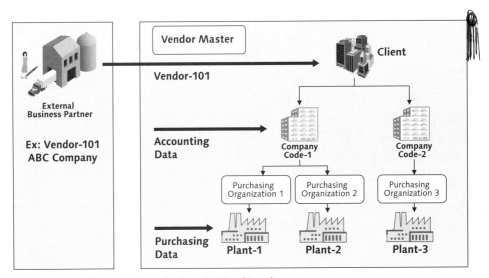

Figure 3.1 Vendor Master Data by Organizational Level

The vendor master record consists of three sections: general data, accounting data, and purchasing data, as follows:

▶ **General Data**
General data is maintained at the client level because this data is common for all the lower-level organizational units. Examples of general data include vendor address, contact phone numbers, and so on.

▶ **Accounting Data**
Accounting data is maintained by the accounting department and is created at the company code level. To maintain accounting data, use Transaction codes FK01, FK02, and FK03.

▶ **Purchasing Data**
Purchasing data is maintained by the purchasing department and is created at the purchasing organization level. To maintain purchasing data only, use Transaction codes MK01, MK02, and MK03.

If you create a vendor centrally, it means you want to maintain accounting data and purchasing data together; in this case, use Transaction codes XK01, XK02, and XK03.

In the following sections, we'll discuss the vendor account group and the four main characteristics this group controls.

3.1.1 Vendor Account Group

The vendor account group plays an important role in vendor master data because it has many controlling functions. It's used to categorize vendors, and vendors similar in nature are grouped together (such as one-time vendors, domestic vendors, overseas vendors, employee vendors, and so on). While creating vendor master data via Transaction XK01, you need to select vendor account groups, as shown in Figure 3.2.

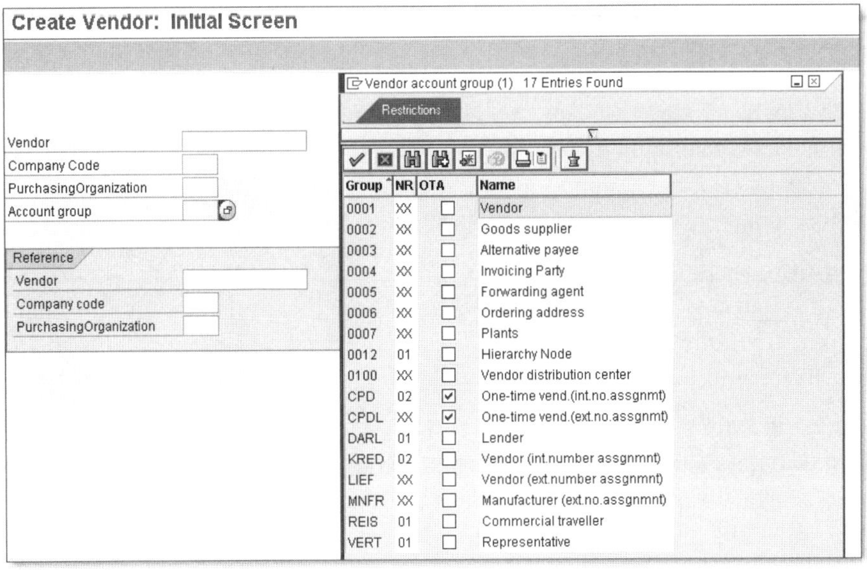

Figure 3.2   Vendor Account Groups

Predefined vendor account groups are available in the SAP system, but you can also create additional account groups based on customer requirements. To configure a new account group, go to SAP IMG • FINANCIAL ACCOUNTING (NEW) • ACCOUNTS RECEIVABLE AND ACCOUNTS PAYABLE • VENDOR ACCOUNTS • MASTER DATA • PREPARATIONS OF CREATING VENDOR MASTER DATA • DEFINE ACCOUNT GROUPS WITH SCREEN LAYOUT (VENDORS) (Figure 3.3). In the screen that displays, you'll see a list of existing account groups. Create a new account group by copying an existing account group and making the required changes in the new account group. You can also create a new account group from scratch, but it's faster to use the copy function.

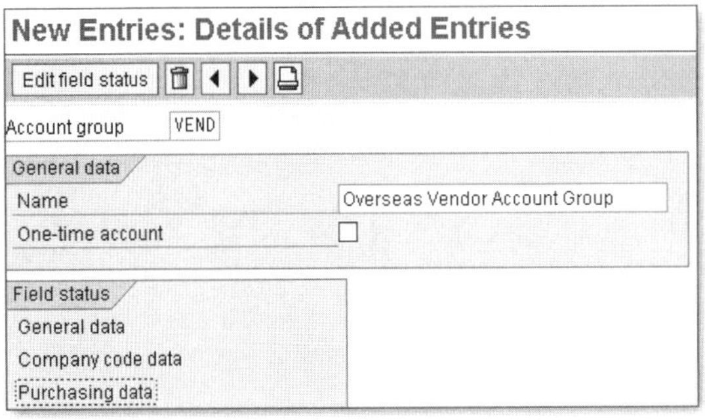

Figure 3.3   Vendor Account Group Creation

If you are creating an account group for a one-time vendor, select the One-Time Account checkbox under General Data. This functionality is discussed in detail in Section 3.2.4.

The account group controls four specific characteristics:

▶ **Field Selection**
Enables you to control the fields in various screens. You can, for example, make certain fields required fields, and suppress others.

▶ **Number Interval**
This can be either an external number range (manually assigned) or an internal number range (system-assigned).

▶ **Vendor Status**
The account group determines whether the vendor is a one-time vendor.

▶ **Partner Schema**
Determines which partner schemas are valid.

We'll discuss these characteristics in more detail in the following sections.

3.1.2 Field Selection

Under General Data, Company Code Data, and Purchasing Data (found in the Field Status box), you can configure different fields such as Suppress, Required Entry, Optional Entry, or Display, as shown in Figure 3.4. Let's go through the meaning of each of these options.

▶ **Suppress**
This field will not be displayed when creating vendor master data for your account group.

▶ **Required**
This field will be mandatory when creating vendor master records.

▶ **Optional**
This field will be displayed when creating vendor master data, and you can either enter a value or leave the field blank.

▶ **Display**
This field cannot be edited when creating vendor master records.

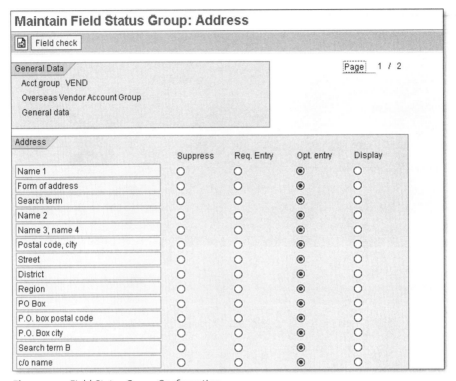

Figure 3.4 Field Status Group Configuration

The field status in the vendor master data can be controlled by account group, company code, and activity (transaction code). The respective menu paths for these are:

▶ SAP IMG • FINANCIAL ACCOUNTING (NEW) • ACCOUNTS RECEIVABLE AND ACCOUNTS PAYABLE • VENDOR ACCOUNTS • MASTER DATA • PREPARATIONS OF CREATING VENDOR MASTER DATA • DEFINE SCREEN LAYOUT PER COMPANY CODE (VENDORS)

▶ SAP IMG • FINANCIAL ACCOUNTING (NEW) • ACCOUNTS RECEIVABLE AND ACCOUNTS PAYABLE • VENDOR ACCOUNTS • MASTER DATA • PREPARATIONS OF CREATING VENDOR MASTER DATA • DEFINE SCREEN LAYOUT PER ACTIVITY (VENDORS)

However, SAP recommends controlling screen layout via the account group only. In some exceptional cases, you can control field status via Activity, for example, if you want to allow entries in the Reconciliation Account field in create mode (Transaction XK01/FK01) and don't want to allow entry in the Reconciliation Account field in change mode (Transaction XK02/FK02). In this case, you need to define the field status of the Reconciliation field as required by the activity.

> **Note**
>
> If the field status has been defined in different ways by various modes, the final field status is determined based on the highest priority, as shown in Figure 3.5. The highest priority is Suppress, followed by Display, Required, and Optional.

Field Selection Priority in Vendor Master

Priority	Function	Character
1.	Hide	–
2.	Display	*
3.	Required	+
4.	Optional	•

Example with Results

Control Level	Field-1	Field-2	Field-3	Field-4
Account Group	Hide	Required	Required	Optional
Transaction Code	Required	Display	Optional	Optional
Company Code	Display	Optional	Optional	Optional
Result	Hide	Display	Required	Optional

Figure 3.5   Field Selection Priority in the Vendor Master

3.1.3   Number Interval

Each vendor account group will have a type of number assignment. This can be either an *internal number assignment* or an *external number assignment*. Each assignment will also have a *number range* (such as 100000 to 199999). When creating vendor master data based on the type of number assignment and the allowed number range, the vendor code will be generated.

You have assigned an internal number assignment and number range 02 to vendor account group "KRED –Vendors." The number range 02 has a starting number of 200000 to 299999. While creating the vendor master for the KRED account group, the system won't allow you to enter an external vendor code because it has been configured for internal number assignment. The system will create vendor code 200000 for the first vendor, 200001 for the next vendor, and so on.

Defining Number Ranges for an Account Group

To create a number range, go to SAP IMG • FINANCIAL ACCOUNTING (NEW) • ACCOUNTS RECEIVABLE AND ACCOUNTS PAYABLE • VENDOR ACCOUNTS • MASTER DATA • PREPARATIONS OF CREATING VENDOR MASTER DATA • CREATE NUMBER RANGES FOR VENDOR ACCOUNTS (Figure 3.6). To create the number ranges for the vendor account, specify the following under a two-character key:

▶ A number interval from which the account number for the vendor accounts should be selected.

▶ The type of number assignment (internal or external).

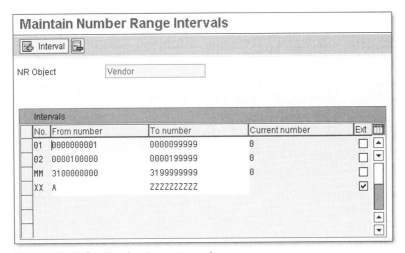

Figure 3.6 Define Number Range Interval

Click on Insert Interval, and enter the values in the To and From fields. If you're working with an external number range, select the Ext checkbox; for internal number generations, leave it unchecked.

The next important step is to assign number ranges to the account group.

Assigning Number Ranges to an Account Group

To assign a number range to an account group, go to SAP IMG • Financial Accounting (New) • Accounts Receivable and Accounts Payable • Vendor Accounts • Master Data • Preparations of Creating Vendor Master Data • Assign Number Ranges to Vendor Account Groups.

In this step, you allocate the number ranges that were created (in the previous step) to the account groups for vendors. You can use one number range for several account groups, as shown in Figure 3.7. Select the number range for your account group, and click Save.

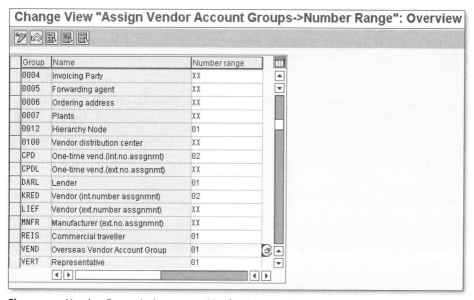

Figure 3.7 Number Range Assignment to Vendor Account Group

3.1.4 Vendor Status (One-Time Vendor)

You can create a vendor master record for one-time vendors with the one-time vendor account group. A *one-time account* records transaction figures for a group of vendors with which you conduct business once or rarely. Certain vendor data (such as address and bank details) isn't entered in the master record but rather in a transactional document (such as a purchase order). This vendor master data will be used in purchasing documents when you are working with a one-time vendor.

In the standard system, the vendor account groups "CPD – One Time Vendor with Internal Number Assignment" and "CPDL – One Time Vendor with External Number Assignment" are preconfigured for one-time vendors. However, you can also create your own vendor account group, if required, as discussed in Section 3.1.1. To configure the one-time account group, select the One Time Account checkbox, as previously shown in Figure 3.3.

3.1.5 Reconciliation Accounts for Vendor Master Records

When you create vendor master records, you have to maintain a reconciliation account. The reconciliation account is a G/L account in SAP ERP Financials Financial Accounting (which we'll refer to as Financial Accounting).

Your company or client may have many vendors (perhaps thousands), which increases the size of financial reports and makes it difficult to maintain separate G/L accounts. To resolve this, SAP provides subledger accounting for vendors. A reconciliation account is a G/L account used for multiple vendors, and each vendor will have a subledger account number and that is vendor code.

When you create a vendor master record, you need a unique number for the vendor. Depending on the account group, either the system assigns this number automatically, or it's assigned manually. This vendor number is also used as the subledger account number in Financial Accounting).

When entering invoices for the vendor, the system uses the reconciliation account from the vendor master records and posts the accounting entries into a reconciliation or G/L account. Because the same reconciliation account can be used for many vendors, it maps a company's liabilities towards several vendors in a single G/L account. For example, as you can see in Figure 3.8, two different vendors (Vendor 1001 and Vendor 1002) have the same reconciliation account. While posting an invoice for each of the vendors, the invoice amount is credited to their subledger account separately, but, in Financial Accounting, it's posted into one G/L account (the reconciliation account).

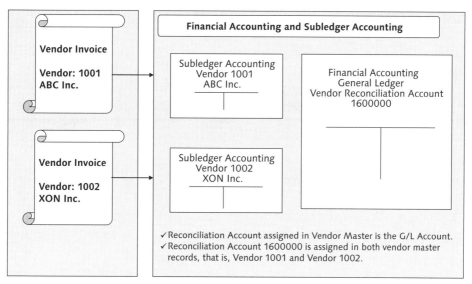

Figure 3.8 Subledger Accounting

3.1.6 Partner Schemas

In purchasing, you have contact with various business partners such as vendors or carriers. For each account group, you can define which roles these business partners may assume. For example, you can specify that certain vendors may function as ordering addresses only and not as invoicing parties. You can use partner roles to define relationships within a corporate group as well as with independent external partners.

For example, Steel Inc. is a corporate group with two companies: South West Steel Inc. and North East Steel Inc. In this scenario, South West Steel Inc., located in California, can be listed as the ordering address, whereas North East Steel Inc., located in New York, can be listed as the goods supplier. Additionally, another enterprise called ABC Carriers can be listed as the goods delivering partner. These different assignments—ordering address, goods supplier, and goods deliverer —are the roles of the different partners.

Configuring Partners

Let's now look at how to configure the partner function.

1. **Define Partner Roles**

   The first step in using partner functions is to define the partner role. Go to menu path SAP IMG • MATERIALS MANAGEMENT • PURCHASING • PARTNER DETERMINATION • PARTNER ROLES • DEFINE PARTNER ROLES, as shown in Figure 3.9.

Funct	Name	NoTpe	Unique	HigherPar.
$$	Area	0	☐	
$1	Created by	US	☐	
01	Shipping point	VS	☐	
1A	Customer hierarchy 1	KU	☐	1B
1B	Customer hierarchy 2	KU	☐	1C
1C	Customer hierarchy 3	KU	☐	1D
1D	Customer hierarchy 4	KU	☐	
2A	Vendor hierarchy 1	LI	☐	2B
2B	Vendor hierarchy 2	LI	☐	2C
2C	Vendor hierarchy 3	LI	☐	2D
2D	Vendor hierarchy 4	LI	☐	
AA	SP Contract rel. ord	KU	☐	
AB	Department resp.	0	☐	
AD	Additionals	LI	☐	
PE	Con.pers.fresh prod.	AP	☐	
SP	Sold-to party	KU	☑	
AI	IS-PAM: Cert. owner	KU	☑	

Figure 3.9 Define Partner Role

For the partner role, enter an alphanumeric key—which may consist of up to two characters—and some descriptive text. After you've entered the partner role, you need to specify the partner type, which is an identifier indicating the kind of partner involved (e.g., a vendor, which is abbreviated as VE).

Please note that you cannot edit partner types. You can only choose the partner types that are provided by SAP. You can, however, define the higher-level role that's used in purchasing (as of Release 4.0). This can be done for any partner role.

2. **Maintain Language-Dependent Key Reassignment for Partner Roles**
   Maintaining the appropriate language-dependent key reassignment for part-
   ner roles is important. The menu path for this is SAP IMG • MATERIALS MAN-
   AGEMENT • PURCHASING • PARTNER DETERMINATION • PARTNER ROLES • MAIN-
   TAIN LANGUAGE-DEP. KEY REASSIGNMENT FOR PARTNER ROLES, as shown in Figure
   3.10.

Change View "Language-Dependent Key Reassignment

Partner function	Name	Lang-spec.part.func.
AD	Additionals	AD
AF	Con.pers.fresh prod.	PE
AG	Sold-to party	SP
AP	Contact person	CP
BA	Ordering address	OA
DP	MRP controller	DC
EK	Buyer	BU
EN	Enduser for F.Trade	EU
HS	Manufacturing plant	MN
LF	Vendor	VN
LW	Delivering plant	DP
Q1	QtyCertRec/shpTo pt	Q1
Q2	QtyCertRec/soldTo pt	Q2
RE	Bill-to party	BP
RG	Payer	PY
RS	Invoicing Party	PI
SP	Forwarding Agent	CR

Figure 3.10 Language-Dependent Key Reassignment

In this step, you can change the identifiers for the predefined partner roles to
identifiers in your language. For the standard settings, separate identifiers are
supplied for all languages, such as the following:

▶ German: Lieferant = LF

▶ English: Vendor = VN

3. **Define Permissible Partner Roles per Account Group**
   In Step 1, we assigned partner roles. Now, we need to assign these partner roles
   to the vendor account group. Only assigned roles will be available for selection

when creating the vendor master record. To assign partner roles, go to SAP IMG • MATERIALS MANAGEMENT • PURCHASING • PARTNER DETERMINATION • PARTNER ROLES • DEFINE PERMISSIBLE PARTNER ROLES PER ACCOUNT GROUP, as shown in Figure 3.11.

Funct	Name	Group	Name
2A	Vendor hierarchy 1	0001	Vendor
2A	Vendor hierarchy 1	0012	Hierarchy Node
2B	Vendor hierarchy 2	0001	Vendor
2B	Vendor hierarchy 2	0012	Hierarchy Node
2C	Vendor hierarchy 3	0001	Vendor
2C	Vendor hierarchy 3	0012	Hierarchy Node
2D	Vendor hierarchy 4	0001	Vendor
2D	Vendor hierarchy 4	0012	Hierarchy Node
AD	Additionals	0001	Vendor
AD	Additionals	KRED	Vendor (int.number assgnmnt)
AD	Additionals	LIEF	Vendor (ext.number assgnmnt)
AZ	A.payment recipient	0001	Vendor
AZ	A.payment recipient	0003	Alternative payee
AZ	A.payment recipient	0100	Vendor distribution center
AZ	A.payment recipient	KRED	Vendor (int.number assgnmnt)
AZ	A.payment recipient	LIEF	Vendor (ext.number assgnmnt)
0A	Ordering address	0001	Vendor

Figure 3.11 Permissible Partner Roles per Account Group

In this step, you can assign the allowed partner roles for each account group. Vendors created for the account group will be allowed to assume only assigned partner roles. For example, if you have assigned the ordering party partner role to Vendor account Group 0001, then vendors created for this account group can be an ordering party only, not an invoicing party.

Partner Settings

In this section, we'll explain how to define partner determination schemas and assign them to account groups. Partner schemas consist of groups of partner roles that are assigned to vendor account groups at three different levels: purchasing organization, vendor sub range, and plant. While creating the vendor master record, you need to select the account group. Based on the account group and level, the system will determine the partner schema. All of the allowed partner roles of the partner schema will be copied (defaulted) in the vendor master record. Follow these steps:

1. **Define Partner Schemas**

   The first step is to define the partner schemas, which allows you to group various partner roles. You can specify that certain roles in a schema are mandatory (i.e., cannot be changed after entry).

   Go to the menu path SAP IMG • MATERIALS MANAGEMENT • PURCHASING • PARTNER DETERMINATION • PARTNER ROLES • DEFINE PARTNER SCHEMAS, as shown in Figures 3.12 and 3.13.

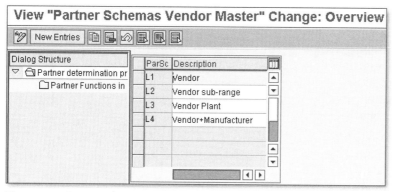

Figure 3.12 Partner Schema – Vendor Master

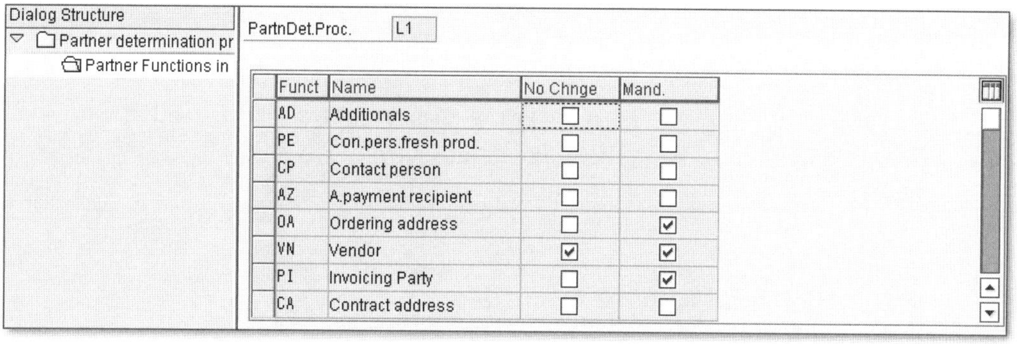

Figure 3.13 Partner Functions in Partner Schema

You can define different partner schemas at different data retention levels within the vendor master record. For example, you can have a different ordering address at the purchasing organization level than you do at the plant level.

2. **Assign Partner Schemas to Account Groups**

   In this step, you assign partner schemas to account groups. Go to SAP IMG • MATERIALS MANAGEMENT • PURCHASING • PARTNER DETERMINATION • PARTNER ROLES • ASSIGN PARTNER SCHEMAS TO ACCOUNT GROUPS, as shown in Figure 3.14.

Change View "Assignment of Partner Schemas to Account Groups":

Group	Name	PS EKO	PS VSR	PS Plt
0001	Vendor	L1	L2	L3
0002	Goods supplier			
0003	Alternative payee			
0004	Invoicing Party			
0005	Forwarding agent			
0006	Ordering address			
0007	Plants			
0012	Hierarchy Node			
0100	Vendor distribution center			
CPD	One-time vend.(int.no.assgnmt)			
CPDL	One-time vend.(ext.no.assgnmt)			
DARL	Lender			
KRED	Vendor (int.number assgnmnt)			
LIEF	Vendor (ext.number assgnmnt)			
MNFR	Manufacturer (ext.no.assgnmnt)	L4		
REIS	Commercial traveller			
VEND	Overseas Vendor Account Group			

Figure 3.14 Assign Partner Schema to Vendor Account Group

In this section, you've learned about the essential characteristics and functions in vendor master records. In the next section, we'll move on to discussing material master records.

3.2 Material Master Records

Material master records are the key element of MM. In this section, we'll discuss how material master records are created at different organizational levels and how different department-specific data is maintained in different views. We'll also discuss the main controlling elements of material master records such as material type.

Material master records are a company's main source for material-specific data. The transaction codes for material master records are as follows:

► Create material: MM01

► Change material: MM02

► Display material: MM03

Material master data has different views for each department, which are the same as tab pages. For example, the purchasing view is used for ordering, the accounting view is used for material valuation, and the MRP view is used for planning (Figure 3.15).

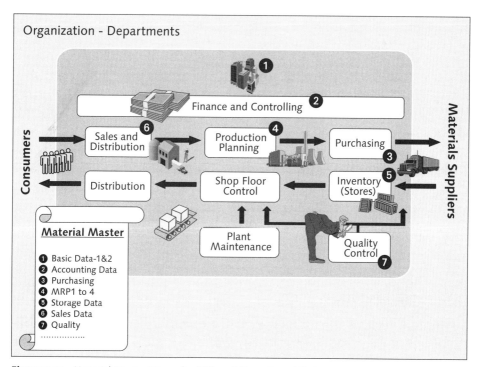

Figure 3.15 Material Master Views for Different Department Data

The material master code is created centrally, and each department can maintain department-specific data in the material master record (just as with the vendor master record). This concept is illustrated in Figure 3.16.

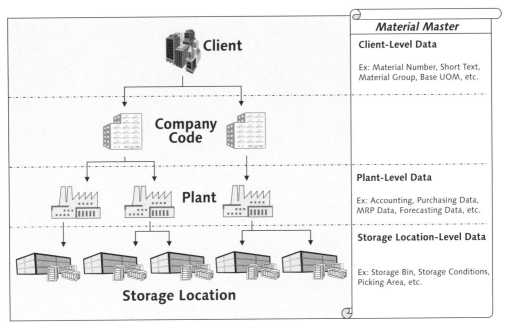

Figure 3.16 Material Master Organizational Level Data

General data that's valid enterprise-wide is stored at the client level, and plant-relevant data is maintained at the plant level. Similarly, data that's valid for a particular storage location is maintained at the storage location level.

In the following sections, you'll learn about the main attributes and configurations of material master data.

3.2.1 Main Attributes

The main attributes of material master data are the material number, industry sector, and material type, as shown in Figure 3.17.

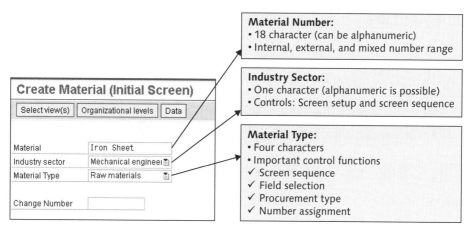

Figure 3.17 Main Attributes of Material Master Data

The *material number* is a unique 18 character field. It can be entered manually, or be created automatically by the system, based on the type of number assignment. For external number assignment, you can enter the material number manually, and for internal number assignment, the system will create the material number automatically when you save the material master record.

The *industry sector*, as shown in Figure 3.17, controls the screen setup and screen sequence. The SAP system includes predefined industry sectors, but if any specific requirement doesn't match with these predefined sectors, you can create your own.

Material types have many controlling functions, including the following:

▶ Number assignment

▶ Number range

▶ Procurement type

▶ Screen setup (i.e., allowed views, field selection, and screen sequence)

▶ Price control

▶ Account determination

▶ Quantity and value updating in plants

SAP provides preconfigured material types, but you can also create your own by copying the standard material types and making the required changes. Some of the SAP-provided material types are:

▸ ROH: raw material

▸ HALB: semi-finished material

▸ FERT: finished material

3.2.2 Configuring a New Material Type

To configure a new material type, go to SAP IMG • LOGISTICS-GENERAL • MATERIAL MASTER • BASIC SETTINGS • MATERIAL TYPES • DEFINE ATTRIBUTES OF MATERIAL TYPES (Figure 3.18).

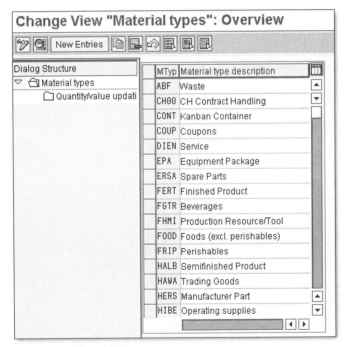

Figure 3.18 Material Types

Here, you can either make changes to an SAP-provided material type (such as DIEN, HALB, or FERT), or you can create a new one. To do the latter, either click on the New Entries button, or copy an existing material type and make the required changes.

For additional settings, select the Material type and click on the Details button. You will see the details of the selected material type as shown in Figure 3.19.

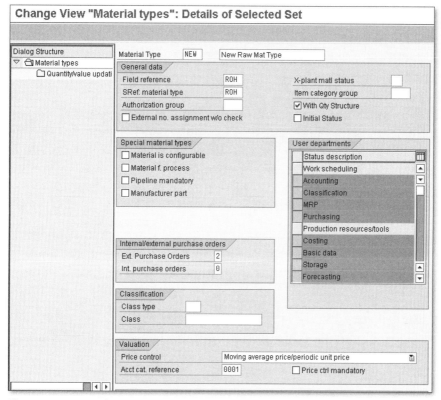

Figure 3.19 Material Type Creation

The following are the key settings in material types (Figure 3.19):

▶ **Field Reference Key**
This determines the field status such as Required, Hidden, Display, and Optional.

▶ **Views (User Departments)**
User departments such as purchasing, sales, and production are referred to as views in the material master. This determines which views can be selected for the material type. For example, a sales view is essential for finished goods because you need to maintain sales department-specific data to sell the materials.

▶ **Pipeline Allowed/Mandatory**
This determines whether pipeline handling is possible or mandatory. It also determines whether it's possible to set external and internal purchase orders, as well as quantity and value updates.

▶ **Type of Procurement**
This determines whether internal procurement, external procurement, or both are allowed.

▶ **Price Control**
You can select Standard Price or Moving Average Price for a material type, as shown in Figure 3.19. The selected price control is copied (defaulted) when you create a material master record, but you can change price control from Standard Price to Moving Average Price and vice versa. If the checkbox Price Ctrl Mandatory is activated, the price control method selected in the material type cannot be changed while creating a material master record.

After you've selected the material type, click on the Quantity/Value Updating folder (on the left side of the screen). As Figure 3.20 illustrates, you need to select Quantity Update and Value Update in each valuation area. The significance of these fields is as follows:

▶ **Quantity Update**
Specifies that the material is managed on a quantity basis in the material master record for the relevant valuation area.

▶ **Value Update**
Specifies that the material is managed on a value basis in the material master record for the valuation area concerned. The values are updated in the respective G/L accounts at the same time.

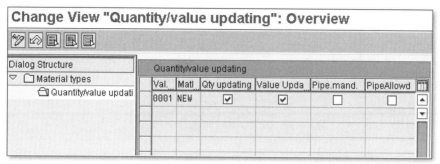

Figure 3.20 Quantity/Value Updating for Material Type and Valuation Area

3.2.3 Defining a Number Range for a Material Type

In this step, you define the type of number assignments and the number of range intervals for material master records. When creating a material master record, you must assign it a unique number. There are two ways of doing this:

1. **Internal number assignment**
   In this case, a number within the defined number range is assigned by the SAP system.

2. **External number assignment**
   In this case, you can assign a number within the defined number range interval. You can define the intervals for external number assignments numerically as well as alphanumerically.

You can also define both an internal and an external number range interval for the material type.

To configure a number range for material types, go to the menu path SAP IMG • LOGISTICS-GENERAL • MATERIAL MASTER • BASIC SETTINGS • MATERIAL TYPES • DEFINE NUMBER RANGE FOR EACH MATERIAL TYPE. (Figure 3.21).

Click on Maintain Group to maintain a new group for the new number range, as shown in Figure 3.21. In the top screen menu, go to GROUP • INSERT (shown in Figure 3.21), the result of which is shown in Figure 3.22. Enter the group Text (the group name) and a new number range in the From Number and To Number fields, and then click Save.

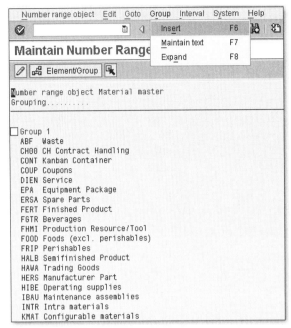

Figure 3.21 Number Range for Material Types

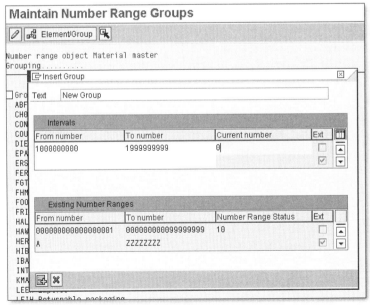

Figure 3.22 Number Range and Number Range Groups for Material Type

3.2.4 Defining Field Selections

The field status of a field in material master data is controlled by the following:

▸ Material type

▸ Transaction code

▸ Industry sector

▸ Plant

▸ Procurement type (internal/external)

Similar fields are organized under different groups called *field selection groups*. For example, Field Selection Group 1 contains two fields, Base Unit of Measure, and Unit of Measurement Text, as shown in Figure 3.23.

A field reference key is assigned to each of the different controlling units such as material types, transaction codes, industry sectors, plants, and procurement types. For example, Field Reference keys DIEN and MM03 are assigned to the Service material type and the Display Material transaction, respectively.

Maintain the field status for the combination of Field Selection Group and Field Reference Key, as shown in Figure 3.23.

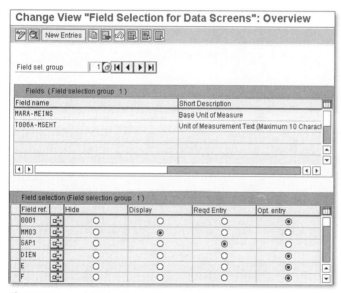

Figure 3.23 Field Selection in Material Master

It's important to know that SAP recommends the following:

▶ The field status of a field selection group for the field reference key prefixed with "SAP" must not be changed.

▶ The field reference key for transaction codes and procurement type (E – internal procurement, and F – external procurement) are already configured and cannot be changed.

▶ New field reference keys must begin with Y or Z.

▶ New field selection groups, if required, can be taken from those that aren't pre-configured. For example, 206 through 240 are available.

▶ The system determines how the field status should be set, as follows:

  ▶ The field status "Hidden" has the highest priority, followed by "Display," "Mandatory," and "Optional," in that order.

  ▶ As shown in Figure 3.23, while in Transaction code "Display Material (MM03)", all fields in field selection group "1" have a status of "Display."

3.2.5   Defining Material Groups

You can define different material groups to distinguish various materials. For example, an enterprise that manufactures computers can classify computers as desktops, laptops, and servers; each of these would be its own group. To define material groups, go to SAP IMG • LOGISTICS – GENERAL • MATERIAL MASTER • SETTINGS FOR KEY FIELDS • DEFINE MATERIAL GROUPS, as shown in Figure 3.24.

Change View "Material Groups": Overview

Matl Group	Material Group Desc.	Grp.	D...	Description 2 for the material group
01	Material group 1			
02	Material group 2			
DESKTOP	Desktop Computer			
LAPTOP	Laptop Computer			
SERVER	Server			

Figure 3.24 Material Groups

You have now seen how material master data is maintained by different departments at different organizational levels, and we've gone through the main attributes and configurations of material master data. In the next section, we'll move on to discussing info records.

3.3 Purchasing Info Records

In vendor and material master records, you maintain vendor- and material-specific information. In purchasing info records, you maintain information about the relationships between vendors and their material. For example, each vendor may have specific terms and conditions of purchase for each material—it's this information that's stored in purchasing info records.

As shown in Figure 3.25, purchasing info records contain the information for material and vendor combinations. This information is defaulted (copied) during the purchase order creation.

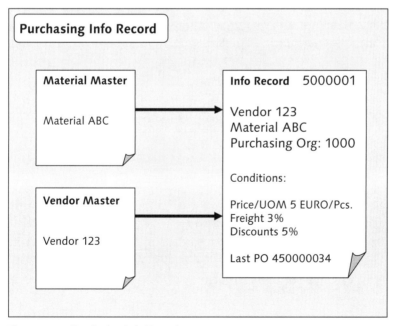

Figure 3.25 Purchasing Info Records

You can maintain the following data in purchasing info records:

- Current and future prices and conditions (gross price, freight, and discounts)
- Delivery data (planned delivery time, and tolerances)
- Vendor data (vendor material number, vendor material group, etc.)
- Texts

In the standard system, two types of text are available. First, there is internal info memo record text, which is used for internal comments only. Internal comments will be copied into purchase orders (POs), but shouldn't be copied to output such as print, fax, or email. Second, there is the PO text, which is used to describe PO items or materials copied into the PO *and* to the output. In addition to these standard types of text, any other type can be configured as well.

The data maintained as described is populated automatically by the system while creating POs. Purchasing info records save time and provide consistent data.

3.3.1 Structure

Info records are maintained at different organizational levels, as shown in Figure 3.26. Examples include Client Level, Purchasing Organization Level, and Plant Level.

As shown in Figure 3.26, purchasing info records have General Data, Purchasing Organization Data, and Plant Data. General data being maintained at the client level is common to all purchasing organizations and plants.

When you create a PO, the system searches for the valid info record for the Purchasing Organization/Plant combination. If there are no such info records, the system searches for the purchasing organization only.

In addition, purchasing info records are created for a type of procurement, also called *info category*. When you create an info record using Transaction ME11, you need to select the info category, as shown in Figure 3.27. You need to create separate info records for each type of info category.

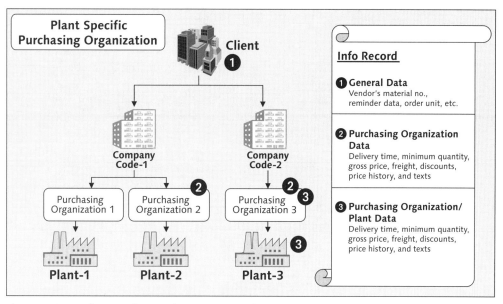

Figure 3.26 Purchasing Info Record – Organizational Levels

Create Info Record: Initial Screen

Vendor	V100
Material	SPLIT VAL
Purchasing Org.	0001
Plant	0001
Info Record	

Info category
- ⦿ Standard
- ○ Subcontracting
- ○ Pipeline
- ○ Consignment

Figure 3.27 Info Record – Info Type

There are four info records categories, as follows:

▸ Standard info record for a standard procurement type.

▸ Subcontracting info record for a subcontracting procurement type.

- ▶ Consignment info record for a consignment procurement type.
- ▶ Pipeline info record for a pipeline procurement type.

In a special scenario of consumables materials with no material number, purchasing info records are crated based on the material group.

Regular Vendor

The regular vendor is used by the system during source determination. This is a vendor from whom you regularly buy a particular material. You can set the indicator for regular vendor in the general data of a purchasing info record, as shown in Figure 3.28. This can be set for only one purchasing info record for each material. If in Customizing the use of regular vendor is permitted and is configured for a specific plant, the regular vendor will always be suggested during source determination.

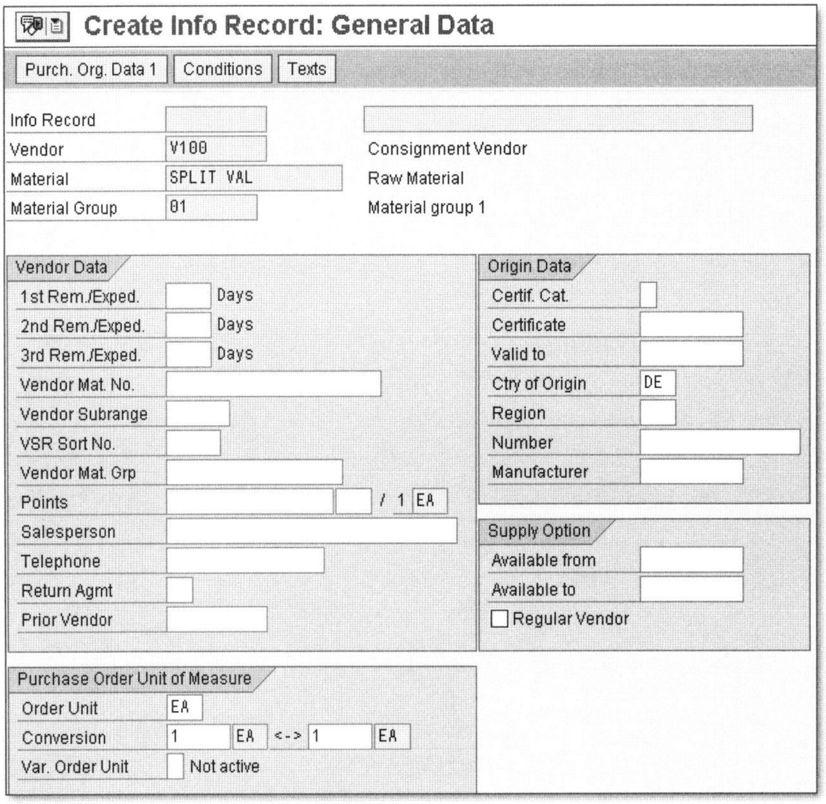

Figure 3.28 Info Record – Regular Vendor

3.3.2 Creation

Purchasing info records can be created manually, or they can be created automatically when you create POs or outline agreements (Figure 3.29).

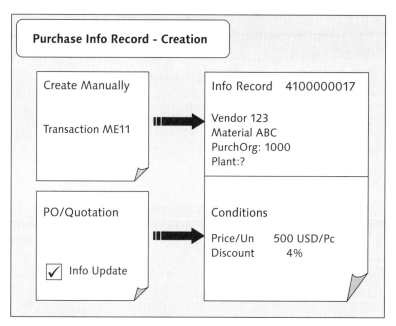

Figure 3.29 Info Record Creation Ways – Manual or Automatic

Manual Creation

Purchasing info records can be created manually for a purchasing organization and/or plant via Transaction code ME11. Transaction code ME12 can be used for updating already-created purchasing info records.

Automatic Creation

Purchasing info records can be created or updated automatically by setting the *info update* indicator while maintaining a quotation, PO, or outline agreement. Furthermore, the type of purchasing document determines what updates are triggered by the info update indicator, as follows:

▶ **Quotation**
Time-dependent conditions are copied into the purchasing info record.

▶ **Purchase Order/Contract Release Order/Scheduling Agreement**
Conditions are never created or updated. The purchasing info record is updated with the document number in the last document number field.

▶ **Contract**
If purchasing info records already exist, they aren't updated. If purchasing info records don't exist, they're created with time-dependent conditions from the contract.

Let's now move on to the configuration settings required for purchasing info records.

3.3.3 Configuration

How prices are stored in purchasing info records for each plant can be defined in the system. Let's go through the configuration settings for condition control in purchasing info records.

Condition Control at the Plant Level

For each plant, you can define how prices and conditions are stored. To do this, go to SAP IMG • MATERIALS MANAGEMENT • PURCHASING • CONDITIONS • DEFINE CONDITION CONTROL AT PLANT LEVEL, as shown in Figure 3.30.

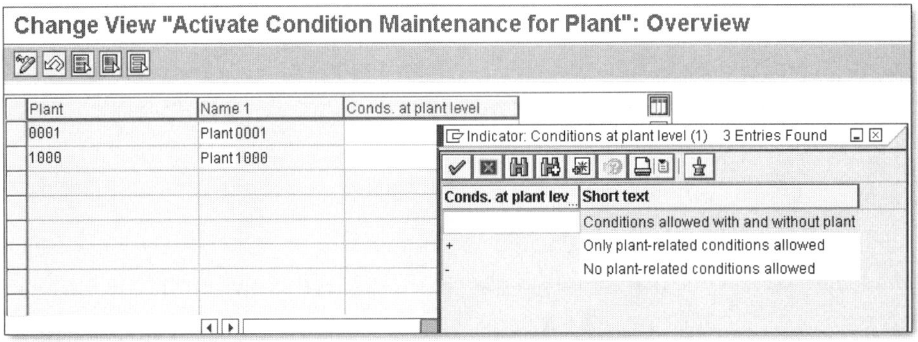

Figure 3.30 Configuration for Condition Control at the Plant Level

For each plant, you can select any of the following options:

▸ **Only Plant-Related Conditions Allowed**
In this case, you must create purchasing info records and contract items at the plant level. Therefore, centrally-agreed contracts cannot be created.

▸ **No Plant-Related Conditions Allowed**
In this case, you may not create any purchasing info records or contract items at the plant level.

▸ **Conditions Allowed with and without Plant**
In this case, you can create purchasing info records either at the plant level or at the purchasing organization level.

Activate Regular Vendor per Plant

For each plant, you can define whether using the regular vendor is permitted. To do so, go to SAP IMG • MATERIALS MANAGEMENT • PURCHASING • SOURCE DETERMINATION • DEFINE REGULAR VENDOR. Select the Reg. Vendor checkbox, as shown in Figure 3.31.

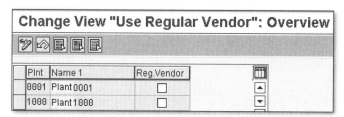

Figure 3.31 Regular Vendor

3.4 Source List

The source list is a type of master data. It contains a list of allowed sources of supply for a material in a specific plant and for a certain period of time.

3.4.1 Structure

The source list is used for the following:

▶ Maintaining a fixed source of supply.

▶ Limiting the selection of sources of supply during the source determination process.

▶ Blocking a source of supply.

A source list contains the following information for a material-plant combination, as shown in Figure 3.32.

▶ **Validity period**
The period during which the source of supply is valid.

▶ **Sources of supply**
These can be purchasing info records, supplying plants, or contract and scheduling agreements.

▶ **Blocked indicator**
If you wish to block a particular source of supply, you can set the Blocked indicator in the source list. If you wish to exclude material from external procurement, enter the validity period only. Don't enter a source of supply and set the Blocked indicator.

▶ **Fixed indicator**
If you wish to set a certain source of supply as the default, set the fixed source of supply indicator in the source list. However, note that the fixed indicator is ignored during the planning run.

▶ **MRP indicator**
If you want a particular source of supply to be considered during the planning run, set the MRP indicator to "1." This will allow the system to understand that it's relevant for MRP. If you want to generate schedule lines during the planning run, the indicator has to be set to "2."

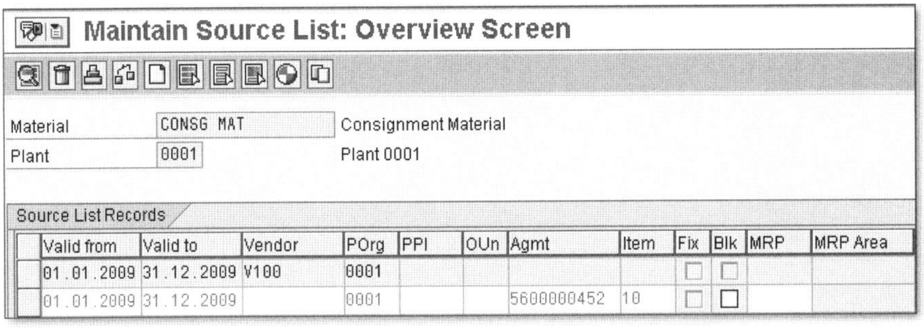

Figure 3.32 Source List Overview

3.4.2 Creation

The source list can be created manually or it can be generated automatically. To create a source list manually, use Transaction code ME01, as shown in Figure 3.32. A source list can also be created from a purchasing info record and an outline agreement.

In a purchasing info record, select EXTRAS • SOURCE LIST. The source list will be generated for all of the plants for which the purchasing organization is responsible. You can limit the plants by selecting GOTO • PLANT.

In an outline agreement, select ITEM • MAINTAIN SOURCE LIST. If a plant isn't maintained for this item, one has to be entered in the source list. In material group contracts, the material-specific source list can be created in a similar fashion. Here, you can also either include entered materials or exclude them from the subject contract.

Alternatively, a source list can be generated for a material or group of materials in a plant. This is done via Transaction ME05. However, note that this is a mass generation program and, as such, should be used judiciously.

3.4.3 Configuration

If you want to make a source list mandatory for a material, you can set the Source List Required indicator in the material master record of that material. If you wish to make the source list mandatory for all materials in a plant, go to SAP IMG • MATERIALS MANAGEMENT • SOURCE LIST • DEFINE SOURCE LIST REQUIREMENT AT PLANT LEVEL, as shown in Figure 3.33.

Plnt	Name 1	Source list
0001	Plant0001	☐
1000	Plant1000	☐

Change View "Source List/Plant": Overview

Figure 3.33 Defining the Source List Requirement at the Plant Level

You now know the purpose of source lists and the various settings associated with them. Let's move on to the subject of quota arrangement to discuss how the different sources of supply can be used in purchasing.

3.5 Quota Arrangement

In an enterprise, you may have different sources of supply for the same material. If you wish to distribute POs among these sources of supply in a systematic manner, you can use the quota arrangement function of MM with SAP ERP Operations.

3.5.1 Elements

Quota arrangement consists of various elements:

▶ **Validity period**
Quota arrangement for a material is maintained for a specified time period.

▶ **Procurement type**
This can be either internal or external procurement.

▶ **Special procurement type**
This can be consignment, subcontracting, or third-party procurements.

▶ **Procurement plant**
This can be a supplying plant which acts as a vendor.

▶ **Quota**
This is the number that specifies which portion of a requirement should be procured from a given source of supply. For example, if there are three sources of supply for a material and you want requirements to be evenly distributed among all three sources, enter "1" as the quota. The quota per vendor will be automatically converted to 33%.

▶ **Quota base quantity**
The quota base quantity is treated as an additional quota-allocated quantity. You can use this to regulate the quota arrangement without actually changing the quota, if, for example, a new source of supply is included in the arrangement. Otherwise, if not set manually, let the system determine this.

▶ **Quota allocated quantity**

This is the total quantity from all purchasing documents such as requisitions, orders, contract release orders, and planned orders. The quota-allocated quantity is updated automatically for each order proposal to which the quota arrangement is applied.

▶ **Quota rating**

This is used by the system to determine the source of supply. The system calculates quota rating as follows: quota rating = (quota − allocated qty + quota base qty) / quota.

You can maintain the quota arrangement via Transaction MEQ1, as shown in Figure 3.34.

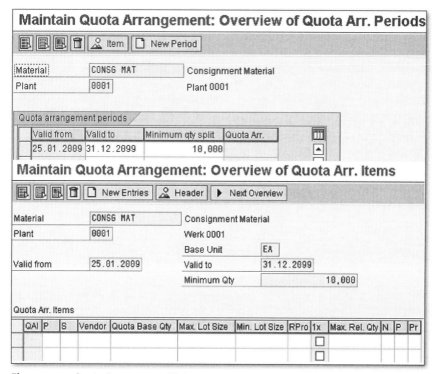

Figure 3.34 Quota Arrangement Maintenance

Configuration

If you want to use quota arrangement for a material, it has to be set in the purchasing view of a material master record, as shown in Figure 3.35.

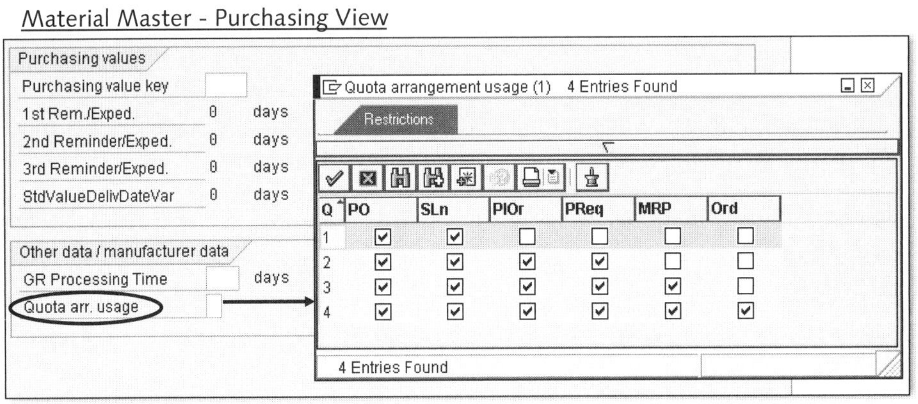

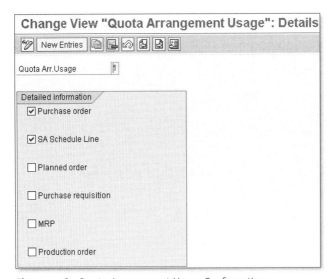

Figure 3.35 Quota Arrangement Usage Indicator in a Material Master Record

The quota arrangement usage indicator can be set, as shown in Figure 3.36. To do so, go to SAP IMG • Materials Management • Purchasing • Quota Arrangement • Define Quota Arrangement Usage.

Figure 3.36 Quota Arrangement Usage Configuration

> **Note**
>
> Service master records are used only for the procurement of services. This is discussed in Chapter 4, Section 4.6.2.

3.6 Summary

In this chapter, we reviewed how to configure master data with your business processes in mind. You should now understand the significance of the various organizational levels in master data, and be able to decipher the different types of master data required in MM. We've also reviewed how to configure master data based on various business scenarios.

Let's now move on to the next chapter to discuss procurement processes. There, you'll learn about the application of various types of master data in procurement processes.

Procurement processes are an extremely important part of MM, and learning about the various elements and aspects involved in these processes is an essential part of effectively using this application.

4   Procurement Processes

Procurement processes are an important function within an enterprise. In response to a need for a system of best practices, SAP has created a set of predefined procurement processes that can be customized to suit specific customer requirements.

The procurement cycle typically starts with the requirement of a material or a service, and ends with processing payment to the supplier. In industry terminology, this is called the *procure to pay* (P2P) cycle. In this chapter, we'll discuss the following:

- ▶ Direct material procurement
- ▶ Indirect material procurement
- ▶ Services procurement
- ▶ Consignment procurement
- ▶ Subcontracting procurement
- ▶ Third-party procurement
- ▶ Outline agreements
- ▶ Stock transfers
- ▶ Intercompany procurement

All of the procurement processes are similar in nature in that they start with a requirement and close with payment processing. However, depending on what and how you're procuring, they can be distinguished from one another. The SAP system uses the item category to determine what can be procured and how procurement can be carried out. Therefore, before we move on to describe each business process in detail, you need to understand the concept of item category. We'll look at this next.

4.1   Item Category

In SAP procurement, a very important basic concept common to all procurement processes is the *item category*. As mentioned previously, the SAP system uses the item category to determine what can be procured and how procurement can be carried out. It determines the type of procurement process, and is defined in the procurement documents. The item categories provided by SAP such as Standard, Limit, Consignment, and so on, are illustrated in Figure 4.1.

Change View "Item Categories": Overview

ItmCat (int.)	ItmCat (ext.)	Text item category
0		Standard
1	B	Limit
2	K	Consignment
3	L	Subcontracting
4	M	Material unknown
5	S	Third-party
6	T	Text
7	U	Stock transfer
8	W	Material group
9	D	Service

Figure 4.1 Item Categories

You select the appropriate item category in a purchasing document based on the type of procurement, and the item category available depends on the document type. For each document type, the allowed item category can be configured; this topic will be covered in Chapter 8, Key Configuration in Materials Management.

As shown in Figure 4.1, item categories are defined from 0 to 9. They cannot be changed or modified, however, their external representation and text can be changed if needed. For example, Item Category 2 is represented externally by K and its description is Consignment. You can change the external representation K to C (or any other letter that's not used by another item category) and you can also change the description, if required.

> **Note**
>
> Item categories are predefined by SAP and you cannot change the internal representation of an item category between 0 and 9. The only aspects of item categories that you can edit are their descriptions and external representations. To do so, the menu path is SAP IMG • MATERIALS MANAGEMENT • PURCHASING • DEFINE EXTERNAL REPRESENTATION OF ITEM CATEGORIES.

As illustrated in Figure 4.2, the item category controls the Account Assignment, Goods Receipt, and Invoice Receipt.

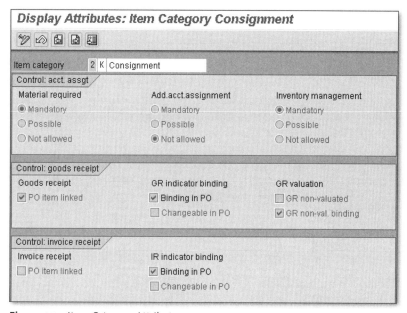

Figure 4.2 Item Category Attributes

For example, Item Category K represents the consignment procurement process, entailing, among many other controls, that material and inventory management are mandatory. We'll discuss each item category control when covering the different procurement processes.

Now that you understand the concept of item categories, we can go into more detail about the P2P cycle. We'll begin with an introduction to P2P, and then discuss each of the procurement processes, covering the process steps and configuration involved in each.

When the configuration is common across processes, we'll simply direct you to Chapter 8, Key Configuration in Materials Management.

4.2 Procure to Pay

In this section, we'll discuss the basic concepts of P2P, including different documents involved in the P2P cycle.

P2P is used widely across different industry verticals, and is the most common and important procurement process. Figure 4.3 shows the complete P2P cycle. It starts with the generation of a purchase requisition, which is converted into a PO and sent to the supplier. The supplier then dispatches the goods based on the quantity and delivery date specified in that PO. Upon receiving the supplied materials, the goods receipt is posted, and the supplier invoice is verified and posted. After that, the invoice posting payment is processed. This last step completes the P2P cycle (Figure 4.3).

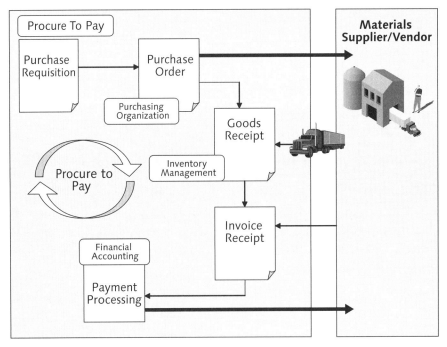

Figure 4.3 Procure to Pay Business Scenario

4.2.1 Business Scenario

To explain the P2P process in more detail, let's use a specific business scenario as an example. An enterprise engaged in the manufacturing of mountain bicycles requires many components (such as tires and suspension systems) that are procured externally and then assembled to form a complete bicycle. To manage the external procurement process, the planning department uses sales forecasts to generate purchase requirements. Once decided, these requirements—including the quantity and delivery date of materials—are passed on to the purchasing department. The purchasing department then identifies the supplier and issues the PO. The store's department ensures that the goods are received on arrival, and that the goods receipt note is issued. Finally, the finance department verifies the invoice and processes payment to the supplier.

Now that we've discussed the general steps involved in the P2P process, let's look at each element of the process in detail.

4.2.2 P2P Documents

In P2P process various documents are used such as purchase requisitions, request for quotations, quotations, POs, goods receipts and invoice receipts. Some of these documents are internal documents and some are external documents. Documents that are required to capture information for the internal use of an enterprise are called *internal documents*. For example, purchase requisitions are internal documents and they're used by various department of an enterprise to request the purchasing department to procure materials or services. External documents are the documents used to send information to external business partners such as vendors. For example, a PO is an external document. POs are sent outside the enterprise to vendors.

We'll now discuss the various documents involved in the P2P cycle.

Purchase Requisition

A *purchase requisition* is an internal document used to request procurement of a material or service. As shown in Figure 4.4, it can be created either manually via Transaction code ME51N or automatically in materials requirement planning (MRP). To create purchase requisitions automatically from MRP, the option to cre-

ate auto purchase requisitions needs to be selected. The purchase requisition contains many fields—such as material or service, quantity, delivery date, and source
of supply—but these fields vary depending on the type of procurement. SAP has
provided predefined document types for various procurement types. For example,
document type NB is used for standard procurement, and UB is used for stock
transfer procurement.

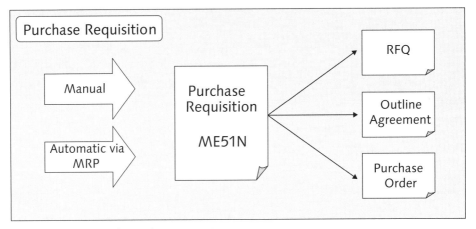

Figure 4.4 Creation of a Purchase Requisition

Preceding documents such as a request for quotation (RFQ), outline agreement, or
PO can be created with reference to a specific purchase requisition.

RFQ/Quotation

An RFQ is an external document used by a purchasing department to identify a
supplier. It can be created automatically with reference to a purchase requisition,
or manually, as shown in Figure 4.5. SAP provides an RFQ predefined document
type called AN, which can be customized to suit customer requirements. An RFQ
typically consists of many fields such as material or service description, quantity, and required-by date. Once received, supplier responses are updated on the
respective RFQ, and the purchasing department can send the POs to the selected
vendors. If vendor prices or conditions aren't acceptable to the purchasing department, it can also send rejection letters to vendors.

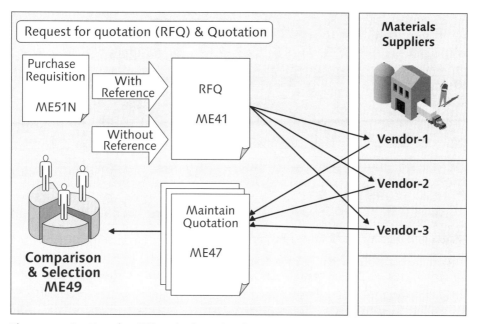

Figure 4.5 Creation of an RFQ and a Quotation Comparison

Preceding documents such as POs or contracts can be created with reference to quotations.

If the Info Update indicator is set in quotations, all of the conditions of the RFQ are copied into the purchasing info record. This info record data is then populated each time you create a PO for the same supplier and material combination.

Purchase Order

A *PO* is a request to a supplier to supply certain goods or services under stated conditions. POs are external documents, sent outside your company to the supplier (Figure 4.6). They can be created with or without reference to purchase requisitions, RFQs, and contracts. SAP offers different ways of automatically converting purchase requisitions into POs; one example of this is Transaction ME59.

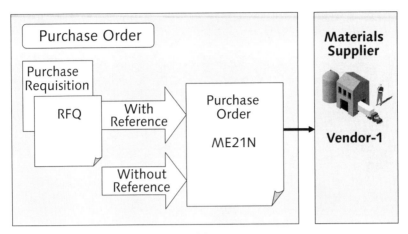

Figure 4.6 Different Ways to Create a PO

When you create a PO, most of the information is default data from master records. This data might include terms of payment, ordering address, and currency from the vendor master record, and material short text, material group, and Unit of Measure (UoM) from the material master record. Similar to purchase requisitions, SAP provides predefined document types for creating POs; for example, FO is provided for the blanket/limit/framework type of procurement.

> **Note**
>
> If an info record exists for the material and vendor combination, all of the conditions such as gross price, discounts, freight, and so on are copied from the info record. A PO created with reference to a contract is called a *contract release order*.

Goods Receipt

A *goods receipt* is an acknowledgement for a receipt of goods (Figure 4.7) and updates both inventory status and PO history. It also generates two documents in the system: a material document and an accounting document. The material document updates the stock in inventory, and the accounting document updates the G/L accounts in Financial Accounting.

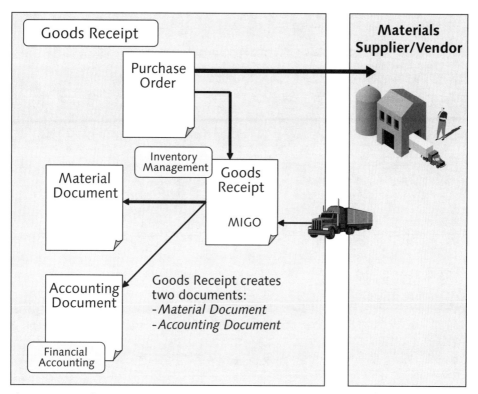

Figure 4.7 Goods Receipt Flow

When a goods receipt is made with reference to a PO, the system supplies the open PO items and quantity. At the time of the goods receipt, the system also checks the under-delivery and over-delivery tolerances from the PO.

Invoice Verification

To process payments to suppliers, you need to post an invoice. The invoice can be posted with or without reference to a PO. A typical invoice verification and posting procedure is illustrated in Figure 4.8.

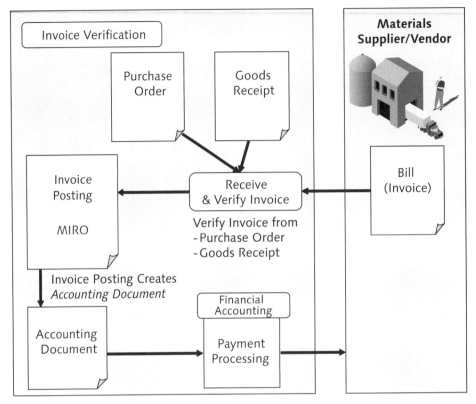

Figure 4.8 Invoice Verification Flow

When you enter an invoice with reference to a PO, the system automatically supplies the information provided in that PO, such as the material, quantity, terms of payment, and amount. After the invoice is posted, it's processed for payment by the finance department. Invoice posting also updates the PO history.

As shown in Figure 4.9, the P2P cycle can be applied in the procurement of stock/direct material or consumable/indirect material. In the next sections, we'll discuss these procurement processes in detail.

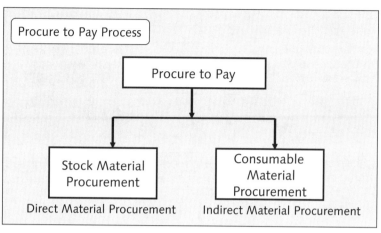

Figure 4.9   The Procure to Pay (P2P) Process

4.3   Direct Material Procurement

The direct material procurement process is used for stock materials. You'll now learn about the business scenario, process steps, and configuration of direct material procurement.

4.3.1   Business Scenario

Consider an enterprise engaged in the manufacturing of mobile handsets. This enterprise needs to procure some of the parts for the handsets—such as batteries and key pads—which are later used during production. These parts are examples of *direct materials*, which are materials required for production (i.e., raw materials). Direct materials are purchased and kept in inventory and issued to the production department on a needs basis. Stock is maintained in inventory levels on a quantity and value basis.

As we've already discussed, a goods receipt transaction creates two documents: a material document and an accounting document (Figure 4.10). The material document updates the stock quantity in the storage location, and the accounting document updates the G/L account in Financial Accounting. Goods receipts for stock materials are relevant for stock valuation.

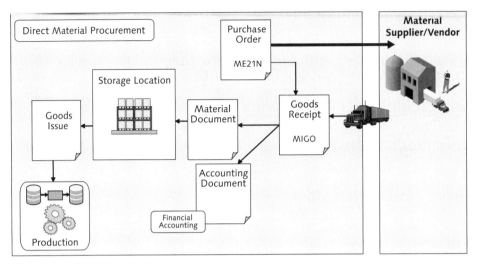

Figure 4.10 Direct Material Procurement

4.3.2 Process Steps

The direct materials procurement process starts with the creation of a purchase requisition and ends with processing payments to the supplier. The steps are as follows:

1. **Create the purchase requisition.**

   Create the purchase requisition via Transaction ME51N, and select document type NB (the document used for standard purchase requisitions). Enter the material, quantity, UOM, delivery date, and plant. Enter "Blank" as the item category, which is the standard item category. You can also assign the source of supply via the source determination process.

2. **Create the PO.**

   Create a PO via Transaction ME21N, with reference to the purchase requisition. Select the NB document type and the Blank item category. If the source isn't assigned in the purchase requisition, enter the vendor and price.

3. **Post the goods receipt.**

   Upon receipt of the material, post the goods receipt via Transaction MIGO, with reference to the PO. All of the details in the goods receipt are copied from the PO.

4. **Post the invoice.**

   Upon receipt of the invoice from the vendor, post the invoice in the system via Transaction MIRO. Enter the document date, posting date, and PO number. The PO will copy the item, quantity, amount, and price. Before saving, you can check the account posting via the Simulate button.

> **Note**
>
> The source determination process can be triggered in the purchase requisition by either checking the source determination checkbox when in create mode or by assigning sources of supply when in change mode.

4.3.3 Configuration Steps

If required, the direct material procurement process can be customized with the help of document types. Document types control many factors such as field selection and number ranges. This is discussed in more detail in Chapter 8, Key Configuration in Materials Management.

Now that you understand direct material procurement, let's move on to the topic of indirect materials procurement.

4.4 Indirect Materials Procurement

Indirect materials are consumable materials such as office supplies and spare parts. Spare parts are parts of a machine that are required whenever the part life is over or it's damaged. We'll now discuss the business scenario, process steps and configuration steps for indirect material procurement.

4.4.1 Business Scenario

An enterprise that manufactures mobile handsets requires indirect materials such as stationery, printers, and computers for their staff to carry out day-to-day business activities. Out of these materials, office supplies are kept in stock, but computers are procured on an as-needed basis. These items are procured directly for a cost center and the costs of the materials are posted into the cost centers consumption G/L accounts as an expense. In this case, these items aren't managed on a value basis in inventory management because the material costs are directly posted into the consumption accounts.

Because indirect materials aren't managed on a value basis, they won't update the stock valuation. The materials are procured for a cost center, and the material value is posted into consumption accounts (Figure 4.11).

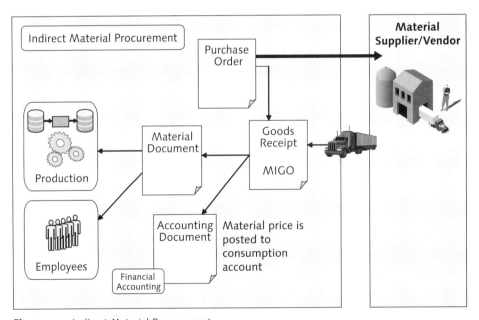

Figure 4.11 Indirect Material Procurement

Because indirect materials are procured for direct consumption, it becomes essential to assign a type of consumption category in the PO. This assignment is facilitated through the account assignment category in the SAP system, which specifies whether accounting for an item is affected via an auxiliary account such as a cost center, project, or sales order. The account assignment category further determines which cost elements are necessary for the particular category. For example, account assignment category C, which represents the sales order, requires the sales order number and the G/L account.

The SAP system includes several predefined account assignment categories such as A (Asset), K (Cost Center), and P (Project), as shown in Figure 4.12.

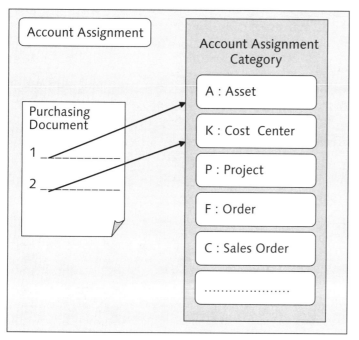

Figure 4.12 Account Assignment Categories

If any customer-specific requirement isn't met through the predefined account assignment categories, you can create your own. This is discussed in Section 4.3.3.

4.4.2 Process Steps

The process steps for indirect material procurement are similar to those in direct material procurement, except for the addition of the account assignment category.

1. **Create the purchase requisition.**
   Create the purchase requisition via Transaction code ME51N and select document type NB (standard purchase requisition). Enter the material, quantity, UOM, delivery date, plant, and any one of the account assignment categories such as cost center, asset, sales order, and so on.

2. **Create the PO.**
   Create the PO via Transaction code ME21N with reference to the purchase requisition. Based on the account assignment category selected, you need to enter the cost elements such as the G/L account number for consumption posting.

3. **Post the goods receipt.**
   On receipt of the material, post the goods receipt via Transaction code MIGO with reference to the PO. All of the details in the goods receipt are copied from the PO such as open PO quantity, plant, and so on. The storage location field isn't required as materils are directly consumed.

4. **Post the invoice.**
   On receipt of the invoice from the vendor, post the invoice in the system via Transaction code MIRO. Enter the document date, posting date, and PO number. The PO will copy the item, quantity, amount, and price. Before saving, you can check the account posting via the Simulate button.

> **Note**
>
> A scenario may exist where you need to procure direct materials for a project or a sales order. This is made possible by designating the account assignment category in the purchasing documents. In this case, materials aren't subject to stock valuation.

4.4.3 Configuration Steps

The indirect material process can also be customized via the account assignment category and material type, as discussed in the following sections.

Account Assignment Category

To create new account assignment categories, go to SAP IMG • MATERIALS MANAGEMENT • PURCHASING • ACCOUNT ASSIGNMENT • MAINTAIN ACCOUNT ASSIGNMENT CATEGORIES and click on New Entries, or copy the SAP-provided account assignment category, as shown in Figure 4.13.

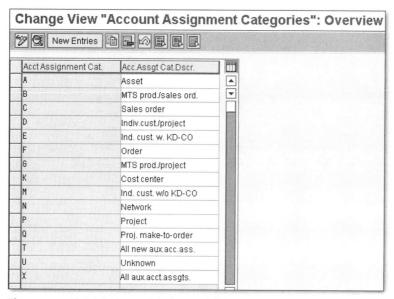

Figure 4.13 Maintain Account Assignment Category

You can define various controlling options for the account assignment category. For example, the Goods Receipt indicator defines whether a goods receipt is required, the GR Non Valuated indicator defines whether the goods receipt should be nonvaluated, and the Invoice Receipt indicator defines whether an invoice is required (Figure 4.14). You can also define different fields to be mandatory, optional, displayed, or hidden.

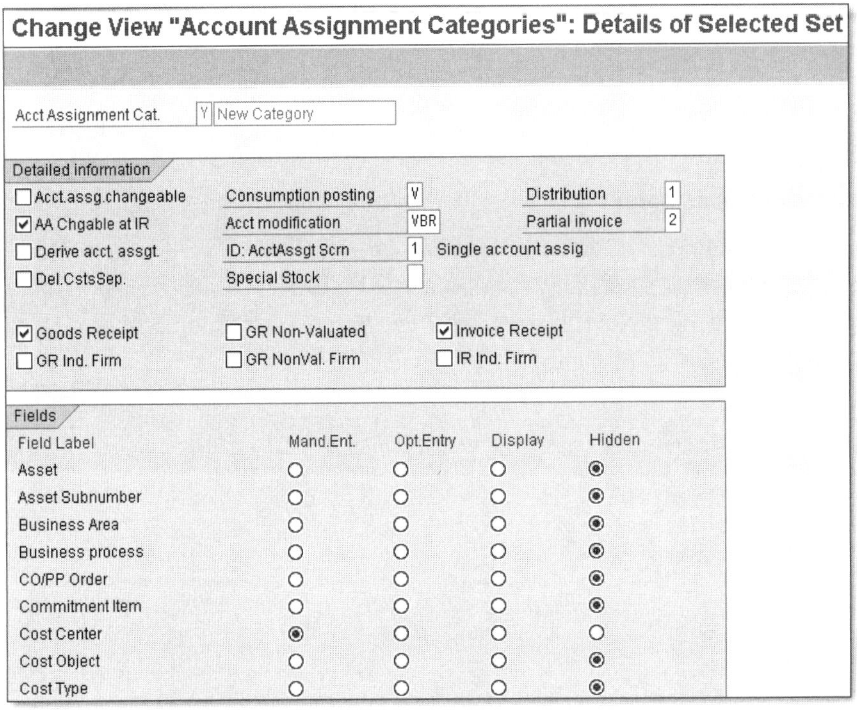

Figure 4.14 Maintain Account Assignment Category: Details

Material Type

Indirect materials may or may not have material master records. Indirect material master records are created with material type UNBW (non-valuated materials) or NLAG (non-stock materials) because these materials aren't valuated. The material type plays an important role in deciding whether materials will be maintained in inventory on a quantity basis, value basis, or both, as follows:

▸ **ROH:** Raw material is maintained on both a quantity and value basis.

▸ **NLAG:** Non-stock material is material that isn't stored and isn't maintained on a quantity or value basis (Figure 4.15).

▸ **UNBW:** Non-valuated material is material that's stored in a storage location, but not valuated (Figure 4.16).

To check the configuration for standard material types provided by SAP, go to SAP IMG • Logistics General • Basic Settings • Material Type • Define Attributes of Material Types.

If you have customer-specific requirements, you can create your own material type for consumable materials. (See the configuration steps necessary to create a new material type in Section 3.2.2.)

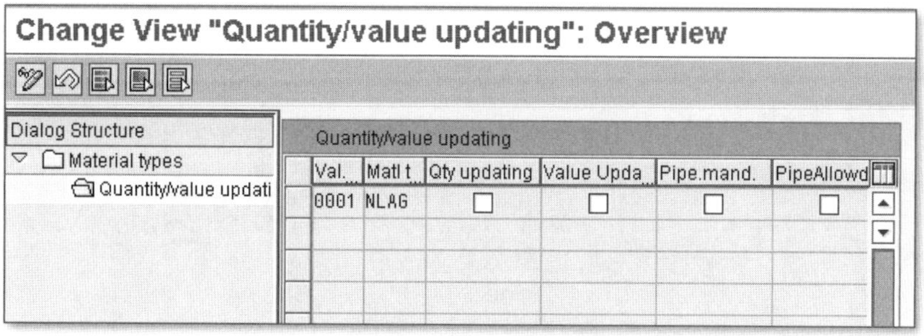

Figure 4.15 Material Type NLAG – Configuration Settings

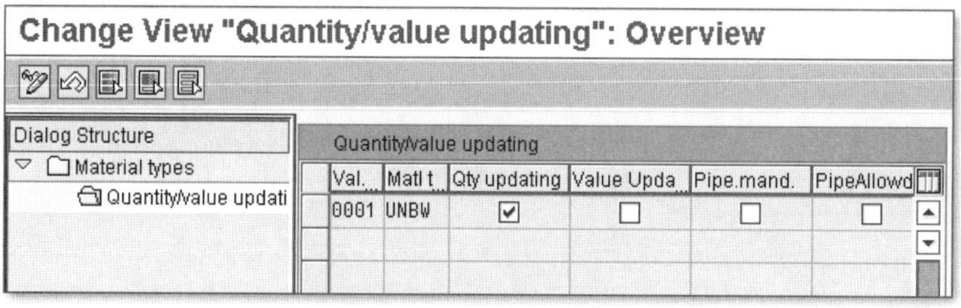

Figure 4.16 Material Type UNBW – Configuration Settings

4.5 Blanket Purchase Orders for Consumable Materials

Blanket POs are often appropriate for low value materials and are used to procure consumable materials and services that are frequently ordered from the same supplier. Blanket POs are valid for a longer term—such as for a year or two—and with a value limit.

4.5.1 Business Scenario

Consider, for example, a business that supplies their offices with general cleaning and janitorial supplies, ordered on a bi-weekly or monthly basis. This company should use a blanket PO rather than creating a separate PO each time they need supplies. When the material is consumed or services are performed, an invoice is posted in the system with reference to the PO, and no goods receipts are posted in the system. You can directly post invoices for the materials procured, as shown in Figure 4.17.

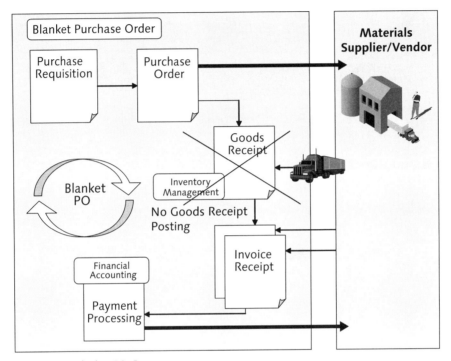

Figure 4.17 Blanket PO: Process

The blanket PO process has several business advantages that result in lower transaction costs, as follows:

▶ Blanket POs are valid for the long term; therefore, you don't need to create them every time you reorder supplies.

▶ A goods receipt isn't required.

▶ Material master records aren't required.

4.5.2 Process Steps

The process steps in a blanket PO are similar to those in the indirect material procurement process, but there is no goods receipt posting. Proceed as follows:

1. **Create the purchase requisition.**

   Create the purchase requisition via Transaction code ME51N and select document type FO (framework order). Enter item category "B – Limit", quantity, UOM, plant, material group, overall limit, and any one of the account assignment categories such as cost center.

2. **Create the PO.**

   Create the PO via Transaction code ME21N with reference to the purchase requisition. Enter the vendor, validity start date, and end date.

3. **Post the invoice.**

   On receipt of the invoice from the vendor, post the invoice in the system via Transaction code MIRO. Enter the document date, posting date, and PO number. The PO will copy the item and quantity. Enter the amount, and save. Before saving, you can check the account posting via the Simulate button.

4.5.3 Configuration Steps

The FO document type provided by SAP is used to create blanket POs. This document type enables you to enter a validity period at the PO header level, and use item category B (limit item) for POs, as shown in Figure 4.18.

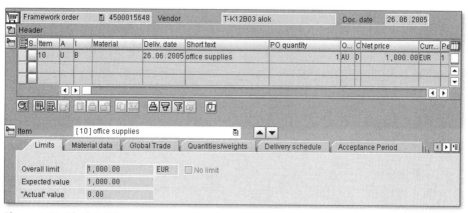

Figure 4.18 Blanket PO

If required, you can create new document types for blanket POs. Document type configuration is discussed in Chapter 8, Key Configuration in Materials Management.

4.6   Service Procurement

Service procurement takes place when a company hires a vendor for external services, which are tasks carried out by an external contractor. Let's go through the business scenario, process steps, and configuration steps.

4.6.1   Business Scenario

Consider, for example, a business that needs to hire a company to perform the painting of an office building or the repair of electric fittings. These are external services. External service procurement is similar to consumable materials procurement because services are also procured for consumption. First, you create and send a service PO to the vendor, and then the vendor performs the services for you. There are no goods receipts in service procurement; instead, you need to maintain a service entry sheet for the work completed by the vendor, as shown in Figure 4.19.

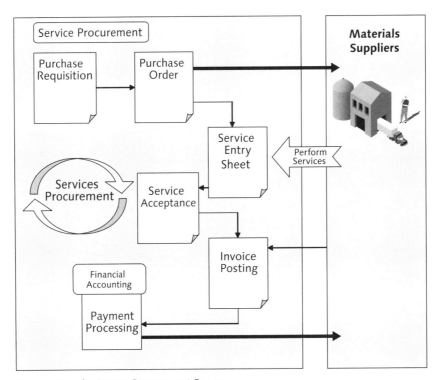

Figure 4.19 The Service Procurement Process

You can create a service master record for service procurement. In the next sections, we'll discuss the service master record and the various documents involved in service procurement.

4.6.2 Service Master Record

For service procurement, a service master record can be created via Transaction AC03. A service master record contains a service description and a unit of measure, as shown in Figure 4.20. Via the conditions, you can assign a price to each service master record. In the next sections, we'll discuss the different documents involved in service procurement.

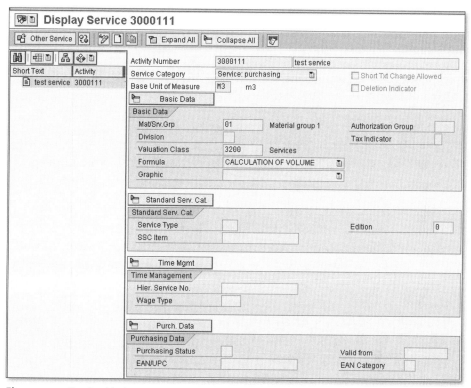

Figure 4.20 Service Master

4.6.3 Documents and Price Conditions in Service Procurement

Services procurement is slightly different than material procurement, because in services procurement, the service entry sheet is used instead of a goods receipt. Performed services are entered in service entry sheets and once it is signed off, the system will allow you to post the invoice. Let's discuss the service entry sheet and invoice verification in detail.

Service Entry Sheet

All of the performed services need to be entered into service entry sheets. After the service entry sheet is signed off, account postings are made. The service entry sheet can be entered and signed off in one transaction, or in two steps.

Invoice Verification for Services

Invoice verification is carried out with reference to POs. All services that are signed off for a particular PO are suggested for invoice verification.

Defining Prices via Master Conditions

There are several ways of storing long term prices for services in the form of service conditions. Prices stored in service conditions will automatically be proposed at the time of the PO creation.

1. **Maintain master conditions at the service level.**
   Prices can be maintained for services, as shown in Figure 4.21. Use Transaction ML45 to add, Transaction ML46 to change, and Transaction ML47 to display service conditions at the service level.

Create Total Price Condition (PRS) : Fast Entry											

Service Conditions (Own Estimate)											
Service	Description	Amount	Unit	per	U...	C..	S..	Valid on	Valid to	Tax..	Wt..
T-LM211	Delivering of new fluores..	100.00	EUR	1	PC	C		26.06.2005	31.12.9999		
☑											

Figure 4.21 Condition for Services at the Service Level

2. **Maintain master conditions at the service and vendor level.**

Select the vendor and enter prices for the different services for the vendor, as shown in Figure 4.22. Use Transaction ML39 to add, Transaction ML40 to change, and Transaction ML41 to display master conditions.

Figure 4.22 Condition for Services at the Service and Vendor Level

3. **Maintain master conditions at the service, vendor, and plant level.**

Select the vendor and plant combination and maintain the prices for services, as shown in Figure 4.23. Use Transaction ML33 to add, Transaction ML34 to change, and Transaction ML35 to display the master conditions.

Figure 4.23 Condition for Services at the Purchasing Organization and Plant Level

4.6.4 Process Steps

Follow the process steps below for services procurement.

1. **Create the PO.**

Create the PO via Transaction ME21N. Use item category D (services), and account assignment category K (cost center) or U (unknown). In the item details, enter the service master number. The quantity and prices will be picked up from condition records (providing they have been maintained), as shown in Figure 4.24.

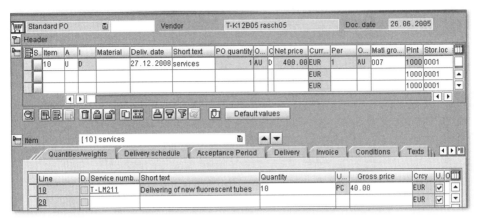

Figure 4.24 A Service PO

2. **Maintain and accept the service entry sheet.**

In service procurement, instead of a goods receipt a service entry sheet is maintained for the work performed. You maintain and accept the service entry sheet via Transaction ML81N. If account assignment category U was selected in the PO, while entering the service entry sheet, you need to change this to any other account assignment category such as cost center or project, as shown in Figure 4.25.

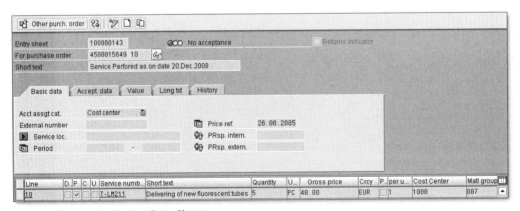

Figure 4.25 Service Entry Sheet

After you accept the service entry sheet by clicking Accept—or via Ctrl+F1— and Save, the system will automatically generate the material and accounting documents.

3. **Verify the invoice.**

You can post the invoice via Transaction MIRO, with reference to the service PO. The system will propose the accepted services quantity that hasn't yet been invoiced.

4.6.5 Configuration Steps

In the following sections, we'll discuss the various configuration steps for service procurement.

Defining the Organizational Status for Service Categories

The SAP system enables you to assign service master records administered in your company to different groups, according to their usage. These groups are called *service categories*. In this step, you maintain the organizational status of the service categories.

To characterize service categories in more detail, they're assigned an organizational status. The *organizational status* indicates the areas in which service master records are used. Examples include basic data, controlling or cost accounting data, purchasing data, and sales data. SAP recommends working with the standard SAP-supplied organizational status for service categories, as shown in Figure 4.26.

To define the organizational status for service categories, go to SAP IMG • MATERIALS MANAGEMENT • EXTERNAL SERVICES MANAGEMENT • SERVICE MASTER • DEFINE ORGANIZATIONAL STATUS FOR SERVICE CATEGORIES. Transactions AS01, AS02, and AS03 are defined by SAP, as shown in Figure 4.26.

OrgSrvCat.	BDS	CnSt	PuSt	SDSt	Org. st. descr. srv. cat.
AS01	✔	☐	☐	☐	Status Basic Data
AS02	✔	✔	☐	☐	Status Basic Data + CO
AS03	✔	☐	✔	☐	Status Basic Data + MM

Figure 4.26 Organizational Service Category

The following organizational statuses can be maintained for service categories.

▶ **BDS: Basic Data Status**
The basic data status indicates that you can store basic data in a service master record.

▶ **CnSt: Controlling Status**
The controlling status indicates that you can store controlling/cost accounting data in a service master record.

▶ **PuSt: Purchasing Data Status**
The purchasing data status indicates that you can store purchasing data in a service master record.

▶ **SDSt: Sales and Distribution Status**
The sales and distribution status indicates that you can store SD data in a service master record.

Defining the Service Category

In this step, you define the service category. The *service category* is most important for structuring service master records, and providing a default value for the valuation classes. Service master records can be assigned to number ranges on the basis of the service category. To define a new service category, go to SAP IMG • MATERIALS MANAGEMENT • EXTERNAL SERVICES MANAGEMENT • SERVICE MASTER • DEFINE SERVICE CATEGORIES.

To define a new service category, select New Entries and enter the service category code. Next, select the organization status service category and account category reference, as shown in Figure 4.27. Account category reference is used for valuation classes, and each account category reference has a set of valuation classes assigned to it.

Assigning a Number Range to the Service Category

In this step, you assign an internal or external number range to the service categories. To do so, go to SAP IMG • MATERIALS MANAGEMENT • EXTERNAL SERVICES MANAGEMENT • SERVICE MASTER • ASSIGN NUMBER RANGE. Create the number range for the number range groups and assign the service category to the number range groups, as shown in Figure 4.28.

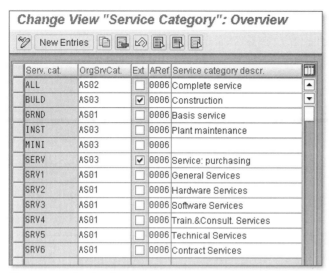

Figure 4.27 Service Category

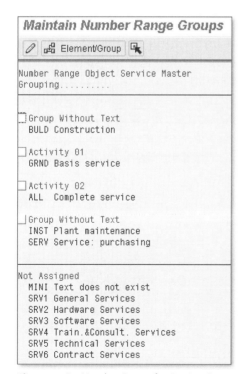

Figure 4.28 Number Range for Service Categories

Defining and Assigning the Number Range for the Service Entry Sheet

Next, define the number range for the service entry sheet and for the service specification. To do so, go to SAP IMG • Materials Management • External Services Management • Number Range (Figure 4.29).

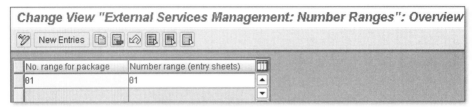

Figure 4.29 Number Range Interval for the Service Entry Sheet

Source Determination and Default Values

In this step, you set up the source determination and various default values at the client or purchasing organization level. If you have created settings at the purchasing organization level, these settings get priority over the client level. If the settings aren't created at the purchasing organization level, the system uses the general settings created at the client level. To define various default values, go to SAP IMG • Materials Management • External Services Management • Source Determination and Default Values. As shown in Figure 4.30, you can define default settings such as Line Number (No) Increment in Service (Serv.) Specifications, Default Material Group at Item Level, and Default Unit of Measure at Item Level.

You can also specify whether the conditions you have maintained for services in the master record should be updated by the data in purchasing documents. To configure this, check the Set condition update indicator as default in purchase order checkbox, as shown in Figure 4.30. Users can deactivate the default indicator for individual service lines in the relevant purchasing document, and the conditions in the master records of these services will remain unchanged.

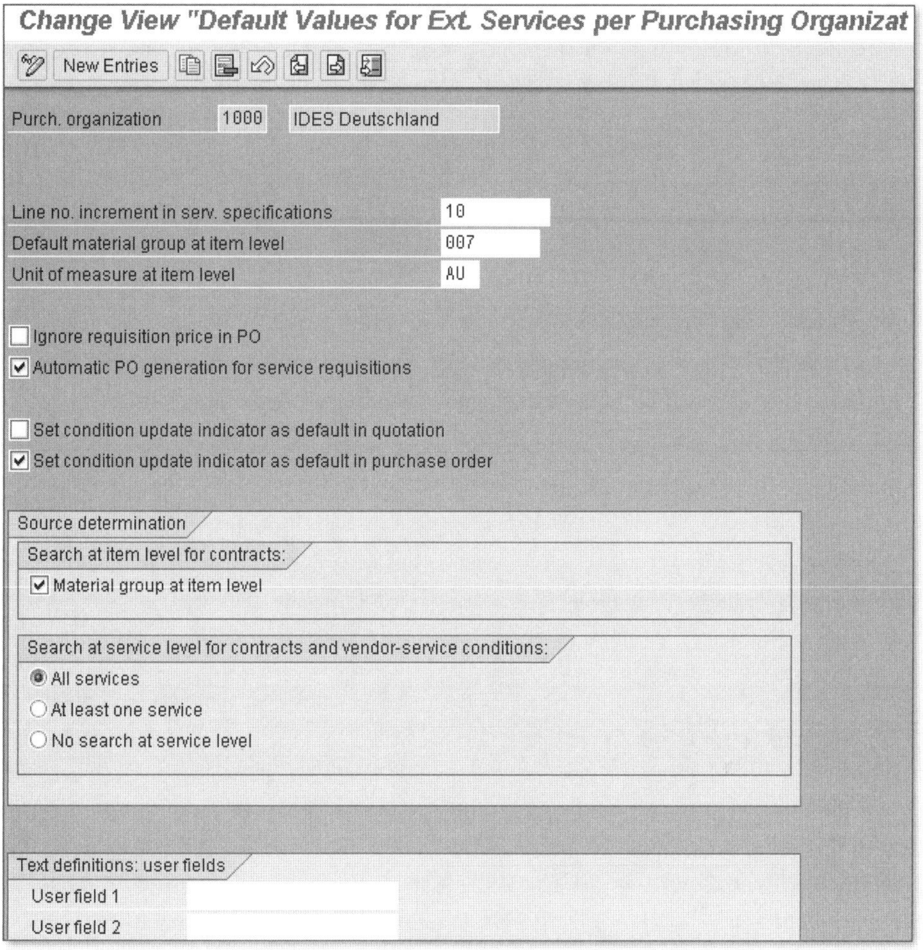

Figure 4.30 Source Determination and Default Values Configuration

Source Determination

For the system to suggest a source when services are procured, you must create a setting in the Source Determination area. If you don't create a setting, no search for suitable sources will take place.

You have two options for having sources suggested. You can make use of either one or both of them:

► **Search at Item Level For Contracts**
For services belonging to a material group, the source determination process is set at the item level. This means that contract items with the same material group are suggested as sources for a requisition item. (It's immaterial whether or not the specific individual service requested is included in the contract in question.)

► **Search at Service Level for Contracts and Vendor-Service Conditions**
The following options are available:

  ► **All Services**
  In the process of determining suitable sources, the system suggests the contracts that contain all services requested in the purchase requisition.

  ► **At Least One Service**
  In the process of determining suitable sources, the system suggests the contracts that contain at least one of the services requested in the purchase requisition.

  ► **No Search at Service Level**
  Source determination isn't carried out at the service line level.

4.7   Consignment Procurement

Consignment procurement takes place when you have an arrangement with a vendor that the vendor keeps his materials on your premises. When the material is issued to your production or stock, you must pay the vendor. In the SAP system, you can settle your consignment liabilities with the vendor on a monthly basis.

4.7.1   Business Scenario

Consider a car manufacturing enterprise that procures tires from a supplier but keeps the stock of tires at the car manufacturing plant. In this case, the car manufacturing enterprise is liable for payment only when the tires are issued to production. Until then, the stock is owned by the supplier. The vendor is informed of material withdrawals on a regular basis, and the quantity withdrawn is invoiced at certain time intervals. The consignment procurement process is illustrated in Figure 4.31.

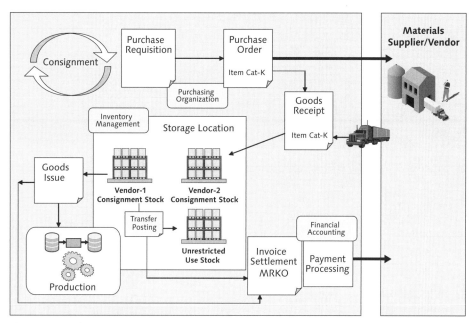

Figure 4.31 The Consignment Process

For consignment procurement, you need to define consignment info records to pick the consignment material price and conditions during invoice settlement. In a consignment PO, prices aren't maintained. At the time of consignment settlement, the prices and conditions are picked up from the consignment info records. This is because invoices are settled periodically, and not posted with reference to a PO.

Consignment Info Record

Info records for consignments are different from info records for stock material procurement. While creating a consignment info record, you need to select the info record category Consignment, as shown in Figure 4.32.

The consignment price, which can be defined periodically, is stored in the consignment info record. You can manage consignment prices in foreign currencies; the PO currency of the vendor is used for consignment withdrawals. You can also use conditions in purchasing, as well as definitions of discounts and price/quantity scales. A vendor consignment price for a material is valid plant-wide.

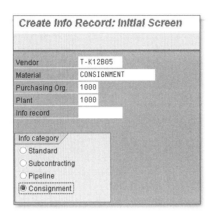

Figure 4.32 Consignment Info Record

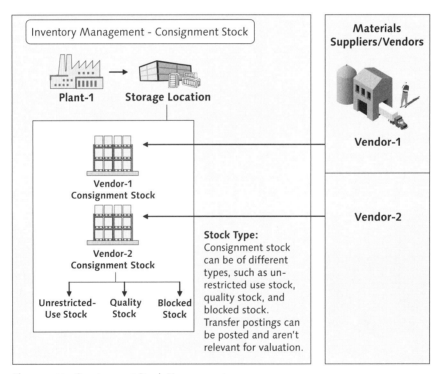

Figure 4.33 Consignment Stock Management

Consignment stocks from a vendor are managed at the storage location level, as shown in Figure 4.33. Consignment stock can be stored with different stock types, such as Unrestricted Use Stock, Quality Stock, and Blocked Stock. Transfer postings are possible to change the stock type. If your company has both its own stock and consignment stock of the same material, the two are managed separately.

4.7.2 Process Steps

Follow these process steps for consignment procurement:

1. **Create a consignment PO.**

   Create a consignment PO via Transaction ME21N. Select item category K (consignment), and enter the material, quantity, plant, and storage location, as shown in Figure 4.34.

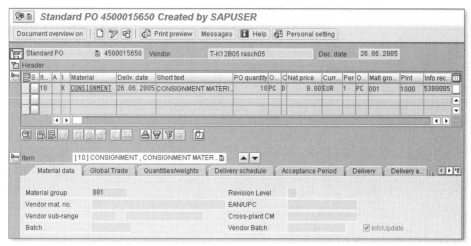

Figure 4.34 Consignment PO

In consignment POs, price and conditions aren't maintained. The consignment PO history isn't updated with the invoice.

2. **Post the goods receipt.**

   You can post the goods receipt via Transaction MIGO. When you post a goods receipt for a consignment PO, it will create only a material document, and the movement type will be 101 K, as shown in Figure 4.35. K is a special stock indicator for consignment material.

> **Note**
>
> An accounting document won't be created at the time of the goods receipt because the received material is still owned by the vendor, and no payment is due.

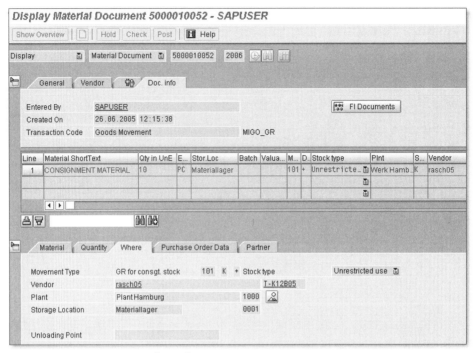

Figure 4.35 Consignment Stock Goods Receipt

You can check the vendor's consignment stock overview via Transaction code MMBE, as shown in Figure 4.36.

Stock Overview: Company Code/Plant/Storage Location/Batch

Material   CONSIGNMENT   CONSIGNMENT MATERIAL
Material type ROH   Raw material
Unit of measurePC   Base unit of measurePC

Cl/CC/Plant/SLoc/Batch D	Unrestricted use	Qual. inspection	Reserved
Total	175.000	0.000	0.000
1000 IDES AG	175.000	0.000	0.000
1000 Plant Hamburg	175.000	0.000	0.000
0001 Materiallager	175.000	0.000	0.000
Vendor consignment	10.000	0.000	

Figure 4.36 Stock Overview Report

Consignment stocks can be managed as the following stock types: unrestricted use stock, quality inspection stock, and blocked stock. Any of the stock types are irrelevant for valuation because the stock is owned by the vendor.

3. **Post goods issue from consignment stock.**

   In this step, you issue the goods to production, or transfer the goods from a consignment stock to your own stock. These processes work as follows:

   ▶ **Transfer material from consignment stock to your own stock**

   You can transfer goods from consignment stock to your own unrestricted use stock via Transaction MIGO_TR. To do so, you must select movement type 411 K, and the vendor code, quantity, and storage location. This transfer posting will create material and accounting documents. When transferring goods from consignment stock into your own stock, liability is generated. Accounts payable will be credited, and the stock account will be debited.

   ▶ **Goods issue from consignment stock to production**

   You can issue goods to production from consignment stock via Transaction MIGO_GI. Select movement type 201 K, and the vendor code, quantity, storage location, cost center, and G/L account for consumption posting. This transaction will create material and accounting documents. When issuing goods to production from consignment stock, liability is generated. Accounts payable will be credited, and the consumption account will be debited.

4. **Settlement of consignment liabilities.**

   You can settle consignment withdrawals online, as well as on a batch basis. Enter the invoices for consignment liabilities without reference to a PO.

   Transaction Code MRKO is used to settle consignment liabilities. Select the company code, vendor, and plant combination for invoice settlement, and select the processing option as Settle. Figure 4.37 illustrates the list of material documents pending for settlement. Figure 4.38 illustrates the list of material documents and invoice documents after the consignment liability has been processed. The vendor account will be credited, and accounts payable will be debited.

Consignment and Pipeline Settlement

CoCd	Vendor	Mat.Doc.	MatYr	Item	Doc..Date	Plant	Material	Qty Withdr	Un	Amount	Crcy	DocumentNo	Year	Item	Info
1000	T-K12B05	4900030281	2006	1	26.11.2006	1000	CONSIGNMENT	2	PC	20.00	EUR				Not settled
1000	T-K12B05	4900030282	2006	1	26.11.2006	1000	CONSIGNMENT	2	PC	20.00	EUR				Not settled

Figure 4.37 Consignment Settlement: Before Invoice Processing

Figure 4.38 Consignment Settlement: After Invoice Processing

> **Note**
>
> The price and conditions are picked up from the consignment info records.

Now that you have a good understanding of the consignment process steps, let's move on to configuration steps.

4.7.3 Configuration Steps

If your client requires it, you can configure the automatic settlement of consignment liabilities. In this case, the system will automatically settle the consignment liability by executing Transaction MRKO.

You can also settle consignment liabilities via a batch job. To do so, you need to create a batch job via Transaction SM36 and Program RMVKON00, with the required variant.

4.8 Subcontract Procurement

The subcontract procurement process is different from the other material procurement processes we've discussed so far. It involves an agreement where you issue raw materials to a vendor, and the vendor makes finished or semi-finished products from the raw materials. These finished or semi-finished products are then supplied back to you, as shown in Figure 4.39. Let's discuss a business scenario and the process steps.

4.8.1   Business Scenario

Consider, for example, an enterprise engaged in car manufacturing that procures components such as ring gears, pinions, and axle shafts from a supplier. With subcontract procurement, the car manufacturing enterprise issues the raw materials (such as steel sheets) to the supplier, who then manufactures the components. The supplier produces components per the design and quality standards given by the car manufacturing company, and the supplier is paid for the labor.

The subcontract scenario process flow is shown in Figure 4.39, where the purchase requisition is converted to a PO and sent to the vendor, and then the raw materials are issued via a goods issue. Upon arrival of the semi-finished or finished components, a goods receipt is posted in the system. The vendor invoice is then posted, and payment is processed by the finance department.

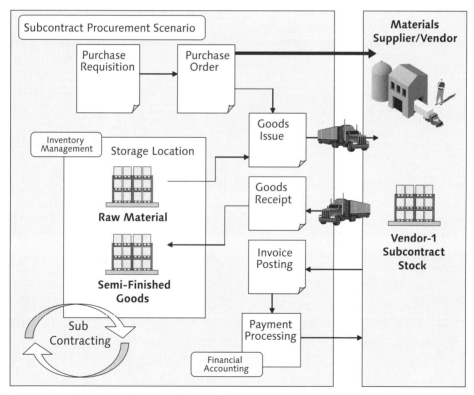

Figure 4.39   Subcontract Scenario: Process Flow

When you issue goods to subcontractors, there is no G/L account posting because the stock is still owned by you (Figure 4.40). Stock issued to the subcontractor is valuated in stock valuation, and is also shown in stock overview reports until you post the goods receipt of the ordered material. When you post the goods receipt, the system creates the material and accounting documents.

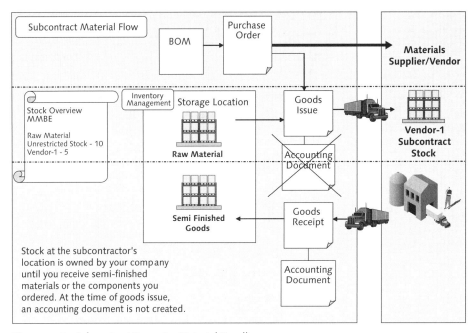

Figure 4.40 Subcontract Scenario: Material Handling

After the goods receipt is posted, the vendor's invoice is entered with reference to the PO, and a subsequent adjustment for excess consumption or under-consumption of the components can be made at the same time.

For the subcontract process, the bill of material (BOM) and subcontract info records can be defined. The BOM is a list of materials—quantity included—required to manufacture a component. You must create a BOM for the material you want a subcontract vendor to produce or assemble for you (Figure 4.41). Use Transaction CS01 and select BOM Usage 1 (Production BOM). Then define all of the materials, with their quantities, that are required to make one unit of subcontract material.

You may have a scenario where co-products are produced while manufacturing the end product. (Co-products are the products that are produced along with the production of the main product.) You can define these products in the BOM with a minus (-), as shown in Item 0040, Component T-T401, in Figure 4.41.

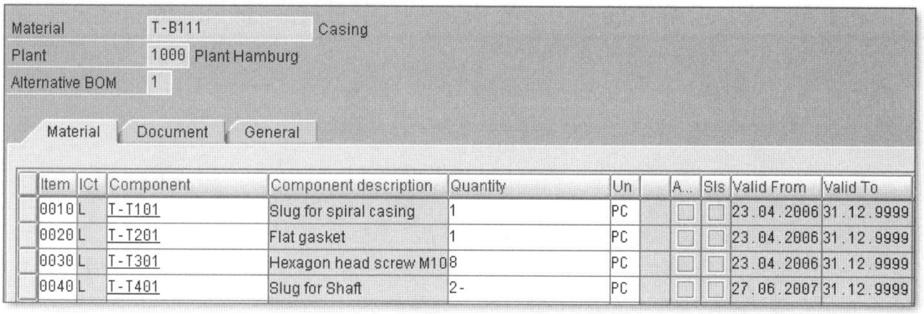

	Item	ICt	Component	Component description	Quantity		Un	A..	Sls	Valid From	Valid To
	0010	L	T-T101	Slug for spiral casing	1		PC			23.04.2006	31.12.9999
	0020	L	T-T201	Flat gasket	1		PC			23.04.2006	31.12.9999
	0030	L	T-T301	Hexagon head screw M10	8		PC			23.04.2006	31.12.9999
	0040	L	T-T401	Slug for Shaft	2 -		PC			27.06.2007	31.12.9999

Material T-B111 Casing
Plant 1000 Plant Hamburg
Alternative BOM 1

Material | Document | General

Figure 4.41 Bill of Material

Subcontract info records for subcontract procurement are different from info records for stock material procurement. When creating an info record, select the info records category Subcontracting, as shown in Figure 4.42. The conditions defined in the info records are then copied into the subcontract PO.

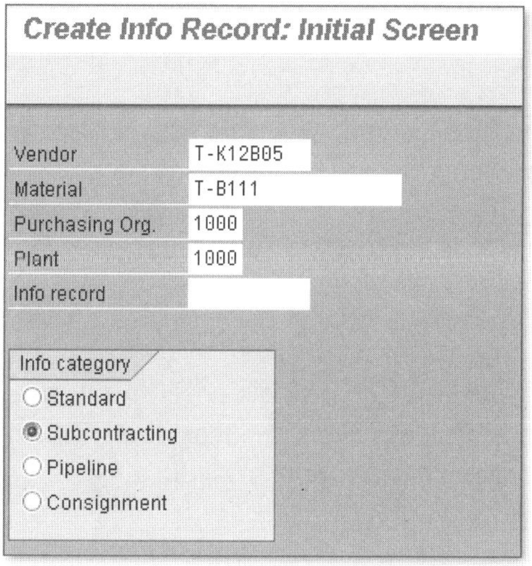

Create Info Record: Initial Screen

Vendor T-K12B05
Material T-B111
Purchasing Org. 1000
Plant 1000
Info record

Info category
○ Standard
◉ Subcontracting
○ Pipeline
○ Consignment

Figure 4.42 Subcontracting Info Records

4.8.2 Process Steps

The following are the process steps for subcontracting procurement:

1. **Create a subcontract PO.**

   The subcontract PO is created with item category L, as shown in Figure 4.43. Each item contains the components that should be provided to the vendor, and these components can be entered manually or can be determined using BOM explosion. The PO price is the vendor's service price for the labor. Conditions for subcontract orders can be stored in subcontract info records.

   Create a subcontract PO via Transaction ME21N, and select item category L. Enter the material, quantity, delivery date, plant, and supplier.

Figure 4.43 Subcontract PO

2. **Post the goods issue.**

   After the subcontract PO is issued, you need to issue materials to the subcontractor. You can check this component requirement via Transaction ME2O, which provides the SC Stock Monitoring for Vendor report (Figure 4.44).

Figure 4.44 Subcontract Stock Overview Report

You can post a goods issue from the report by selecting the item and clicking on the Post Goods Issue button. This will issue goods to the subcontractor. You can also issue goods via Transaction MIGO_TR, with movement type 541. Enter the PO number, and the system will use the PO to determine the materials and quantity that should be issued to the vendor.

When you issue goods to a subcontractor, the SAP system will create only a material document. An accounting document isn't necessary because this material is still owned by your company.

3. **Post the goods receipt.**

Based on your subcontract PO, the subcontractor produces the material and supplies it to you. When you receive the goods, you need to post a goods receipt transaction with reference to the appropriate PO. This will update your stock quantity and will also post the consumption of components you have issued to the subcontractor. Post the goods receipt via Transaction MIGO, enter the PO number, and the system will supply the open PO quantity (Figure 4.45).

When you post a goods receipt, the system will receive the final material with Movement Type 101. All of the components required to manufacture the final material are posted with Movement Type 543, and co-products are posted with Movement Type 545. The Direction column in the goods receipt screen shows plus and minus (+/-) signs based on receipt and consumption, as shown in Figure 4.45.

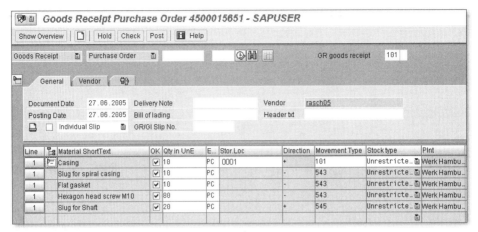

Figure 4.45 Goods Receipt: Subcontract Material

The subcontracting goods receipt will create an accounting document, and a minimum of six G/L accounts will be posted (Figure 4.46). These accounts are as follows:

▶ **Raw materials price**
When you receive semi-finished goods from a subcontractor, the raw materials have been consumed. Therefore, the SAP system will post the raw material price to the following accounts:

  ▶ Raw material stock account: credit

  ▶ Consumption account: debit

▶ **Semi-finished materials price**
When you receive semi-finished materials, their valuation price will be a total of the raw material price and labor charges. Therefore, the SAP system will post to the following accounts:

  ▶ Semi-finished material stock account: debit

  ▶ Cost of goods manufactured: credit

▶ **External labor price**
Labor charges will be posted into intermediate accounts (that is, GR/IR accounts) because vendor liability will be created only when you post an invoice.

  ▶ GR/IR account: credit

  ▶ External labor account expense: debit

Example

You have a BOM for a semi-finished product, and you issue a PO to your vendor for one piece. One piece each of material RM-1 and RM-2 is required to manufacture semi-finished good SM-1. RM-1's valuation price is $10, RM-2's valuation price is $20, and the labor charge is $5. Figure 4.46 shows the G/L accounts that will be posted at the time of the goods receipt.

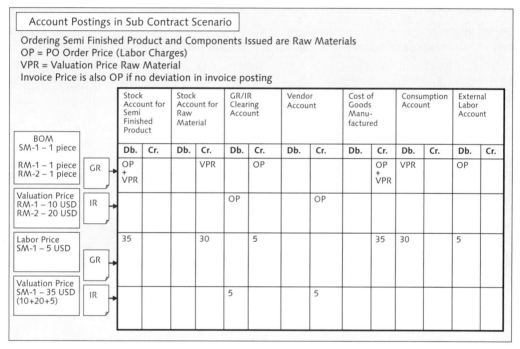

Account Postings in Sub Contract Scenario

Ordering Semi Finished Product and Components Issued are Raw Materials
OP = PO Order Price (Labor Charges)
VPR = Valuation Price Raw Material
Invoice Price is also OP if no deviation in invoice posting

		Stock Account for Semi Finished Product		Stock Account for Raw Material		GR/IR Clearing Account		Vendor Account		Cost of Goods Manu-factured		Consumption Account		External Labor Account	
BOM SM-1 – 1 piece		Db.	Cr.	Db.	Cr.	Db.	Cr.	Db.	Cr.	Db.	Cr.	Db.	Cr.	Db.	Cr.
RM-1 – 1 piece RM-2 – 1 piece	GR	OP + VPR			VPR	OP					OP + VPR	VPR		OP	
Valuation Price RM-1 – 10 USD RM-2 – 20 USD	IR					OP		OP							
Labor Price SM-1 – 5 USD	GR	35			30	5					35	30		5	
Valuation Price SM-1 – 35 USD (10+20+5)	IR					5		5							

Figure 4.46 Account Postings in a Subcontracting Procurement Example

4. **Post the invoice.**

   Upon receipt of the invoice from the vendor, post the invoice in the SAP system via Transaction MIRO. Enter the document date, posting date, and PO number. The PO will supply the item, quantity, amount, and price. Before saving, you can check the account posting via the Simulate button.

5. **Post the settlement.**

   If the vendor informs you of over- or under-consumption after the goods receipt has been posted, you must make an adjustment. In this case, settlement is entered with reference to the PO. Transaction MIGO_GS is used for under- and over-consumption adjustments. After you post an under-consumption, this material will be listed in the stock to be received from the subcontractor, and the vendor should return the material to you.

The movement type for under-consumption is 544, which will increase the stock quantity in the available subcontractor stock. The movement type for over-consumption is 543, which will decrease the stock quantity from the available subcontractor stock. You can also use Transaction MB04 for over-consumption.

4.8.3 Configuration Steps

If required, you can use document types to customize the subcontract procurement process. Document types control many factors, such as field selection and number ranges. This is discussed in more detail in Chapter 8, Key Configuration in Materials Management.

4.9 Third-Party Procurement

Third-party procurement takes place when you order goods from a vendor, and the vendor ships the goods to a third party (usually your customer or subcontract vendor). In this case, the vendor sends you an invoice, and you make the payment, as shown in Figure 4.47. This process is advantageous because it reduces transportation, loading, and unloading costs, as well as delivery time.

4.9.1 Business Scenario

As an example, consider an enterprise selling and distributing cement to a customer constructing a bridge. This enterprise procures cement from a cement manufacturing company, and then asks this company to ship the cement to the customer involved in the bridge construction.

When you place an order to your vendor in the third-party procurement scenario, the delivery address will be the address of the business partner to whom you want to ship the goods. In this case, you post a statistical goods receipt in your system for the confirmation of the goods shipped to the third party. The invoice is posted and paid using the normal procurement process.

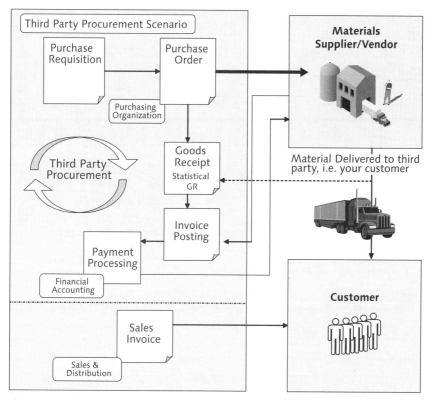

Figure 4.47 The Third-Party Procurement Process

4.9.2 Process Steps

The following steps are for the third-party procurement process with respect to two separate scenarios: third-party procurement for a subcontract vendor and third-party procurement for a customer.

Scenario 1: Third-Party Procurement for a Subcontract Vendor

1. **Create the PO.**

   Create a PO for the vendor from whom you want to purchase goods via Transaction ME21N. In the item details, go to the Delivery Address tab and enter the subcontracting vendor code. Select the checkbox SC Vendor, as shown in Figure 4.48.

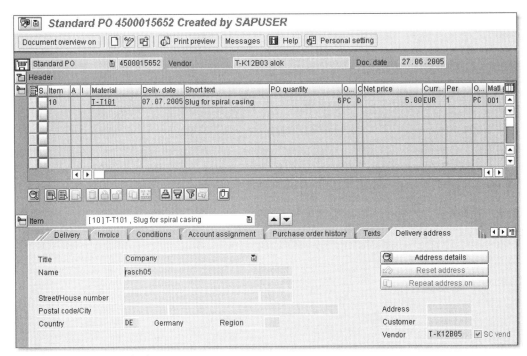

Figure 4.48 Third-Party PO

After you enter your subcontracting vendor, the system will supply the delivery address from the vendor master record.

2. **Post the goods receipt.**
Post the goods receipt with reference to the PO. The SAP system will create material and accounting documents. Because goods are shipped directly to subcontracting vendors, you can see this stock via Transaction ME2O. Movement type 101 O is used in the goods receipt.

3. **Post the invoice.**
Upon receipt of the invoice from the vendor, post the invoice in the system via Transaction MIRO. Enter the document date, posting date, and PO number. The PO will supply the item, quantity, amount, and price. Before saving, you can check the account posting via the Simulate button.

Scenario 2: Third-Party Procurement for a Customer

This scenario is used when you're involved in trading, and you want the vendor to ship the goods to your customer directly. Use the steps we listed in the previous scenario with a few amendments, as described in the next paragraph.

Settle your invoice with the vendor, and issue sales billing documents to your customer. When creating the PO, select item category S (third party) and account assignment category 1 (third party). After you select item category S, you can see the Customer field on the PO Item Details Delivery Address tab. Enter the customer number to whom the vendor should send the materials. After the PO is sent, you can post a goods receipt for it. This goods receipt will generate material and accounting documents.

In this scenario, the consumption raw material account will be debited, and the GR/IR account will be credited.

4.9.3 Configuration Steps

If required, document types can be used to customize the third-party procurement process. Document types control many factors, such as field selection and number ranges. This is discussed in more detail in Chapter 8, Key Configuration in Materials Management.

4.10 Outline Agreements

An outline agreement is a longer-term purchase arrangement with a vendor. It concerns the supply of materials or the performance of services according to predetermined conditions. These conditions are valid for a certain period of time and cover a predefined total purchase quantity or value. Delivery dates aren't specific in outline agreements. Instead, this information is provided separately in release orders or rolling delivery schedules, depending on the type of agreement. As shown in Figure 4.49, there are two types of outline agreements: contract and scheduling agreements.

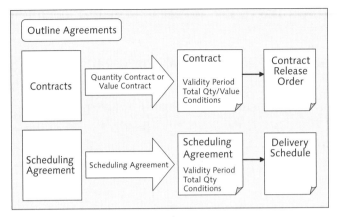

Figure 4.49 Outline Agreement Flow

4.10.1 Contract Agreements

Contract agreements are outline agreements with a vendor concerning the supply of material or performance of services. They don't contain details of the delivery dates for each of the items. Rather, delivery dates are imposed on the vendor via release orders. Contract agreements are created for long periods—for example, one year—and POs, with reference to the contract, are created on a needs basis release (Figure 4.50). The prices and conditions are copied from the contract to the PO, goods are received against the PO, and the invoice is posted with reference to the PO.

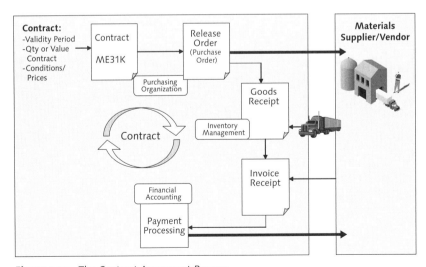

Figure 4.50 The Contract Agreement Process

Business Scenario

As an example, consider an enterprise engaged in paper manufacturing that has a one-year contract (including negotiated rates, terms, and conditions) with a chemical supplier. Each time this enterprise requires chemicals, the paper manufacturing company issues a PO with reference to the contract.

There are two types of contracts: quantity contracts and value contracts (Figure 4.51).

▶ **Quantity contract**
This contract is based on quantity and is fulfilled when the total agreed-upon quantity is supplied by the vendor.

▶ **Value contract**
This contract is based on total value and is fulfilled when the total agreed-upon value is supplied by the vendor.

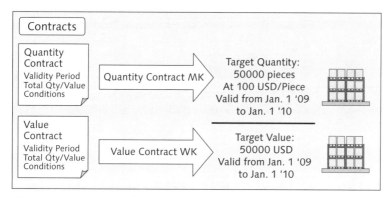

Figure 4.51 Quantity and Value Contracts

You can create contracts manually, with reference to other contracts, purchase requisitions, and RFQs or quotations. The validity period is mandatory in the contract header. For each item in a quantity contract, you need to define the target quantity and item conditions.

Item categories M (material unknown) and W (material group) are used for contracts (Figure 4.52). Item category M is recommended for materials that have the same price but different material numbers. In the contract, enter the material group, quantity, and unit of measure, but no material number. The material number is entered at the time of release orders. Item category W is recommended for materials that belong to the same material group but have different prices. In the contract, enter the material group, but not a price. Item category W can only be used for value contracts.

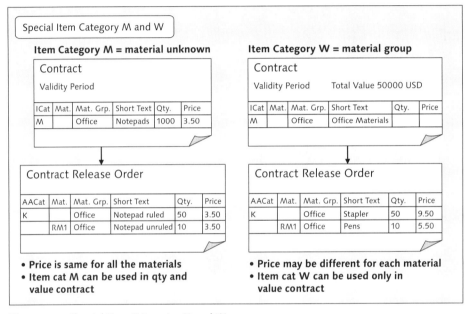

Figure 4.52 Special Item Categories M and W

Contracts can be created for a plant or for multiple plants belonging to the same purchasing organization. This is known as a *centrally-agreed* contract. All of the plants that are assigned to a purchasing organization can order against a centrally-agreed contract (Figure 4.53). A centrally-agreed contract gives more negotiation power to an enterprise. Using the plant conditions function, the centrally-agreed contract allows you to stipulate separate prices and conditions for each receiving plant.

In the following sections, we'll discuss the process steps and configuration involved in contract agreements.

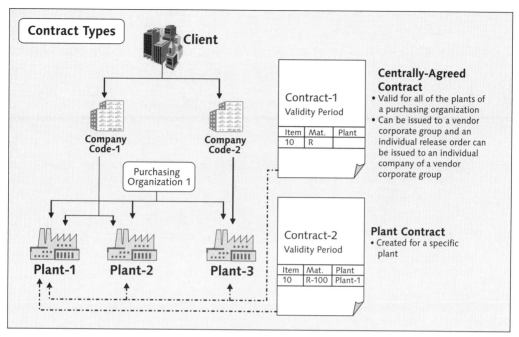

Figure 4.53 Contract Types: Centrally-Agreed Contract

Process Steps

Follow these steps for contract processing:

1. **Create the contract.**

   The following transaction codes are used to create, change, and display contracts:

   ▶ ME31K: Create contract

   ▶ ME32K: Change contract

   ▶ ME33K: Display contract

   During the creation of a contract, select agreement type MK for a quantity contract, and WK for a value contract. When you create a contract for a purchasing organization, the prices (i.e., conditions) are valid for all of the plants within this purchasing organization. However, you can also define plant-specific conditions in contracts.

To enter a plant-specific condition, select the appropriate line and from the top menu, select EDIT • PLANT CONDITIONS • OVERVIEW. Enter the plant and press [Enter], which will bring up a price screen where you can define plant-specific prices. In Figure 4.54, you can see that plant-specific conditions are defined for Conditions Plant 1000.

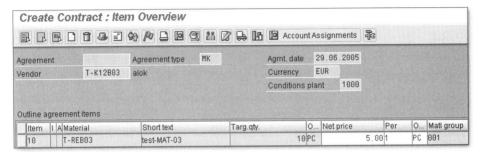

Figure 4.54 Contract: Plant-Specific Conditions

2. **Create the release orders.**

Release orders are POs you create with reference to the contract. This is done via Transaction ME21N. Select the contract, and choose Adopt. You then need to enter the quantity, plant, and delivery date. The plant prices will be picked up from the contract.

The goods receipt and invoice receipt steps are the same as those in the direct material procurement process.

Configuration Steps

You can define number ranges and document types in contracts. To define a number range, go to SAP IMG • MATERIALS MANAGEMENT • PURCHASING • CONTRACT • DEFINE NUMBER RANGE. Click on Change Intervals, and then on Insert Interval. You need to enter the From Number and To Number (Figure 4.55). Then, click Save.

To create new document types, go to SAP IMG • MATERIALS MANAGEMENT • PURCHASING • CONTRACT • DEFINE DOCUMENT TYPE. In this screen, you must assign different characteristics such as Item Interval, Allowed Item Categories, Field Selection Reference Key, Allowed Follow-on Document Types, and Number Range (Figure 4.56).

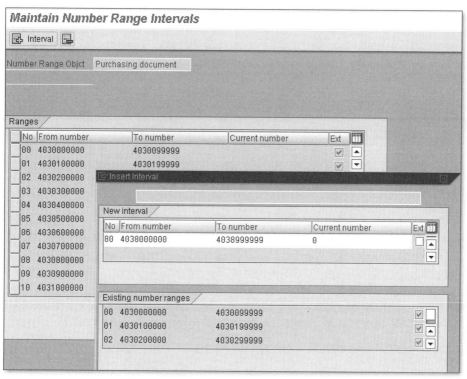

Figure 4.55 Define the Number Range

	Type	Doc. type descri...	Item...	NR int.as	No.rng.ext	No.rng.ALE	Updat...	Field sel.	Slint	Share...	
	DC	Distribtd contracts	10	47		70	SAP	WKK		☐	
	MK	Quantity contract	10	46	44		SAP	MKK		☐	
	WK	Value contract	10	46	44		SAP	WKK		☐	

Document Types Contract Change

New Entries

Dialog Structure
- Document types
  - Allowed item categor
    - Link purchase re

Figure 4.56 Document Type for Contracts

Now that we've discussed contract agreements, let's move on to scheduling agreements.

4.10.2 Scheduling Agreements

A scheduling agreement is an outline agreement where a vendor supplies the materials according to predetermined conditions.

Business Scenario

As an example, consider a car manufacturing business. They plan their production on a monthly and on a daily basis. Based on the daily production schedule, the supplier needs to deliver specific components (for example, material required for horn assembly).

In this case, delivery dates and quantities are communicated to the vendor in the form of schedule lines. Schedule lines can also be generated manually or using MRP. Schedule lines don't constitute separate documents; rather, they are part of the scheduling agreement.

Schedule lines are generated automatically based on the release type selected in the scheduling agreement. There are two types of scheduling agreement releases:

▶ Forecast (FRC) delivery schedules are used to give the vendor a medium term overview of your requirement. They're based on the forecast demand.

▶ Just-in-time (JIT) delivery schedules are used to inform your vendor of a near-future requirement. Such schedules may comprise a daily or hourly breakdown of your requirements over the next few days or weeks.

Process Steps

Follow these process steps for scheduling agreements:

1. **Create the scheduling agreement.**
   The following transaction codes are used to create, change, and display scheduling agreements:

   ▶ ME31L: Create scheduling agreements

   ▶ ME32L: Change scheduling agreements

   ▶ ME33L: Display scheduling agreements

Create a scheduling agreement with Document Type LPA, and enter the validity date and target quantity. In the additional data screen, you can check to make sure that the release creation profile has copied from the vendor master record.

To generate FRC and JIT delivery schedules under a scheduling agreement, you must first define the necessary prerequisite in the material master and vendor master records, as follows:

▶ **Prerequisite in the material master.**
On the Purchasing tab of the material master record set the JIT Delivery Schedule Indicator to 1 (Figure 4.57).

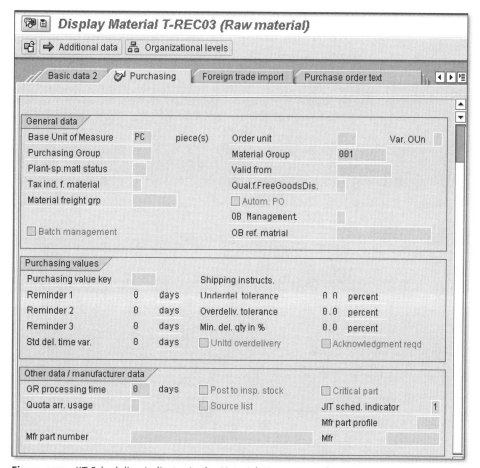

Figure 4.57 JIT Scheduling Indicator in the Material Master Record

▶ **Prerequisite in the vendor master.**

Assign a Creation Profile in the vendor master in the plant-specific purchasing data, as shown in Figure 4.58. To do so, use Transaction XK02.

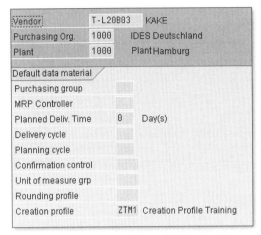

Figure 4.58 Creation Profile in the Vendor Master

2. **Maintain the delivery schedule.**

Maintain the delivery schedule via Transaction ME38. Select the appropriate line item and go to ITEM • DELIVERY SCHEDULE (Figure 4.59).

	Maintain Sch. Agmt. Schedule : Delivery Schedule for Item 00010								

Agreement	5500000124		Quantity			830	PC		
Material	T-REC03		test-MAT-03						
Cum. rec. qty.		0	Old qty.			0	○○○		

C	Delivery date	Scheduled quantity	Time	F	C	Stat.d.dte	Purch.req.	Item	Cum. schd. qty.	Prev. cum. qty.	Sc...
D	29.06.2005	50	10:00	R		29.06.2005			50		1
D	29.06.2005	60	14:00	R		29.06.2005			110		2
D	30.06.2005	80	10:00	R		30.06.2005			190		3
D	30.06.2005	40	14:00	R		30.06.2005			230		4
D	02.07.2005	60	10:00	R		02.07.2005			290		5
D	02.07.2005	80	14:00	R		02.07.2005			370		6
D	06.07.2005	50	10:00	R		06.07.2005			420		7
D	06.07.2005	60	14:00	R		06.07.2005			480		8
D	13.07.2005	150		R		13.07.2005			630		9
D	20.07.2005	200		R		20.07.2005			830		10

Figure 4.59 Scheduling Agreement: Delivery Schedule

The goods receipt and invoice receipt steps are the same as those in the direct material procurement process.

Configuration Steps

You can configure the number range and document types for scheduling agreements. To define the number range, go to SAP IMG • MATERIALS MANAGEMENT • PURCHASING • SCHEDULING AGREEMENT • DEFINE NUMBER RANGE. Click on Change Intervals and then on Insert Interval. Enter the From Number and To Number (Figure 4.60). Then click Save.

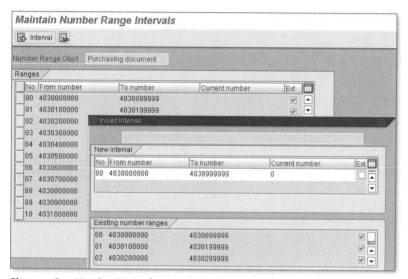

Figure 4.60 Number Range for Scheduling Agreement

The SAP system includes preconfigured document types, such as LP and LPA. However, you can also create new document types by going to SAP IMG • MATERIALS MANAGEMENT • PURCHASING • SCHEDULING AGREEMENT • DEFINE DOCUMENT TYPE. In this screen, define characteristics such as Item Interval, Allowed Item Categories, Field Selection Reference Key, Allowed Follow-on Document Types, and Number Range (Figure 4.61).

Document Types Scheduling agreement Change

New Entries

Dialog Structure	Type	Doc. type descript.	Item...	NR int.as.	No.rng.ext	Updat.	Field sel.	Cont..	Slint
▽ Document types	LP	Scheduling agreement	10	55	56	SAP	LPL		
▽ Allowed item categor	LPA	Scheduling agreement	10	55	56	SAP	LPL		
Link purchase re	LU	Transp. sched. agmt.	10	55	56	SAP	LUL	T	
	Z1	TDSA		ZA	00	SAP	LPL		

Figure 4.61 Document Type for Scheduling Agreements

4.11 Stock Transfer

You can transfer the stock from one storage location to another, from one plant to another, or from company code to another. Figure 4.62 shows the different stock transfer scenarios.

Stock transfers can be carried out at three different levels:

▶ Stock transfer from one company code to another

▶ Stock transfer from one plant to another

▶ Stock transfer from one storage location to another

4.11.1 Business Scenario

A business engaged in car manufacturing has two manufacturing plants, and during production, the company transfers many of the components from one plant to the other plant, based on the requirement and available quantity, to reduce the inventory carrying cost.

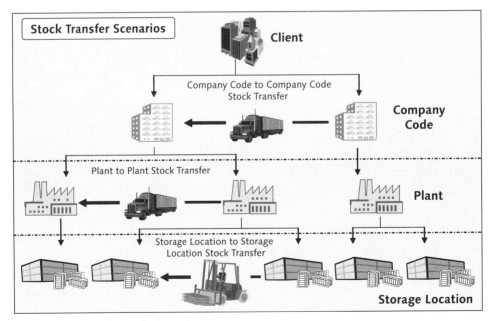

Figure 4.62 Stock Transfer Scenarios

There are two different ways to transfer stock:

▸ One step stock transfer

▸ Two step stock transfer

We'll discuss both of these processes in the following sections.

4.11.2 One Step Stock Transfer

The one step stock transfer process transfers the stock from one location to another in single step; therefore, a single transaction posts results in goods issue (from the issuing location) and goods receipt (into the receiving location).

The one step stock transfer is used to transfer stock from one storage location to another storage location within one plant. Because materials are transferred within the same plant, the stock valuation won't be changed. Therefore, no accounting document is created.

The one step stock transfer can also be used to transfer stock from one plant to another plant. This procedure doesn't involve stock in transit and materials are posted directly to unrestricted use stock in the receiving plant. If the valuation area is at the plant level, the stock transfer from one plant to another will create an accounting document.

Stock transfer takes place in one transaction, as shown in Figure 4.63.

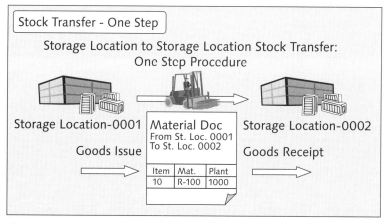

Figure 4.63 One Step Stock Transfer Process

Process Steps

To carry out a stock transfer from one storage location to another within the same plant, you can transfer stock from one storage location to another via Transaction MIGO_TR. Enter the material and "from" and "to" storage locations. Movement type 311 is used to transfer goods from one storage location to another in the same plant, as shown in Figure 4.64.

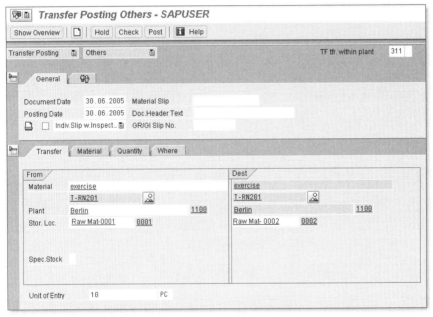

Figure 4.64 Transfer Posting – One Step

When you post the transaction, the stock is transferred. You can check the stock quantities via Transaction MMBE (stock overview report).

The stock transfer transaction won't create any accounting documents because the valuation area (i.e., plant) is the same.

On the other hand, you may want to transfer stock from one plant to another. You can do so using the one step stock transfer procedure. Go to Transaction MIGO_TR and enter the material, from plant and storage location, and to plant and storage location. Specify movement type 301 and save the transaction. The system will transfer the stock quantities to the destination storage location/plant. You can check this via Transaction MMBE.

A stock transfer between two different plants will create an accounting document if the valuation area is at the plant level.

4.11.3 Two Step Stock Transfer

In a two step stock transfer, goods are issued from one issuing point. The stock will remain in transit until the goods are received at the receiving point.

The two step procedure is used for transferring stock between two different plants in different locations. Stock valuation takes place if the valuation area is at the plant level.

> **Note**
>
> The goods receiving plant will be responsible for any damage of goods during transit.

As shown in Figure 4.65, Plant 1000 located in Los Angeles posts the goods issue transaction. The stock is then transported to Plant 2000 located in Atlanta. The goods will remain in transit for several days. When they arrive at the Atlanta plant, this plant needs to post a goods receipt transaction in the system. This will update the stock quantity in the storage location.

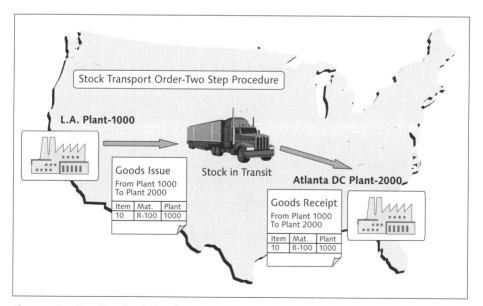

Figure 4.65 Two Step Stock Transfer Scenario

Process Steps

To transfer stock via the two-step procedure, use Transaction MIGO_TR and fill in the fields for Material, Quantity, From Plant, and To Plant and enter movement type 303 (plant to plant transfer stock removal). After you post this transaction, stock is removed from the issuing plant and will show as stock in transit. If the valuation area is at the plant level, the SAP system will create an accounting document.

After the material is received in the receiving storage location/plant, you need to post the transaction with movement type 305 (transfer posting plant to plant – place in storage location).

4.11.4 Stock Transport Orders

You can use stock transport orders to transfer goods from one plant to another. Stock transport orders are used to define delivery costs and they're created via Transaction ME21N (create PO).

You can use the one step or two step procedures with stock transport orders.

Process Steps

1. **Create the stock transport order.**
   Create the stock transport order via Transaction code ME21N and select document type UB (stock transport order). Enter the supplying plant, material, quantity, and receiving plant. You can also maintain conditions such as delivery cost. Item category "U" should be used for stock transport orders, as shown in Figure 4.66.

2. **Post the goods issue from the issuing plant.**
   To post the goods issue from the issuing plant, use Transaction MIGO_GI. Enter movement type 351 and the stock transport order number. After you save this transaction, the stock will be removed from the issuing plant and it will remain in transit until the receiving plant makes a goods receipt entry. The SAP system will create the accounting document.

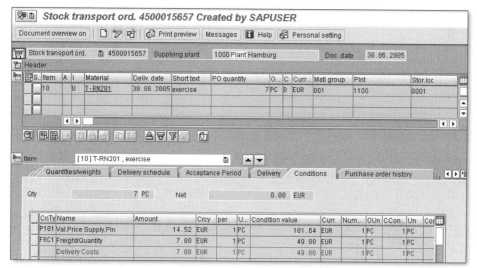

Figure 4.66 A Stock Transport Order

3. **Post the goods receipt into the receiving plant.**

To post the goods receipt into the receiving plant, use Transaction MIGO_GR. Enter the stock transport order number and movement type 101; then save. The system will update the stock into the receiving plant and storage location. The system won't create an accounting document because account postings are already made at the time of goods issue.

4.11.5 Stock Transfer from One Company Code Plant to Another Company Code Plant

You can transfer stock from one company code to another via stock transport orders without the involvement of the sales and distribution department.

This process is similar to a stock transfer between two plants of the same company code.

Process Steps

1. **Create the stock transport order.**

Create the stock transport order via Transaction ME21N. Select document type UB and item category U. Enter the supplying plant, receiving plant, material, quantity, delivery dates, and condition for transportation cost.

In the next few steps, we'll use an example where the supplying plant is plant 1000 of company code 1000, and the receiving plant is plant 1001 of company code 1001.

2. **Post the goods issue.**
   Post the goods issue from supplying plant 1000 via Transaction MIGO_GI and enter movement type 351.

3. **Post the goods receipt.**
   Post the goods receipt into receiving plant 1001 via Transaction code MIGO_GI and enter movement type 101.

4.12 Inter-Company Purchases

A corporate group may have multiple company codes within an SAP system. In this case, one company in the corporate group can procure goods from another company in the group.

4.12.1 Business Scenario

For example, you might need to purchase goods from one company code to another. This can be done via normal sales and purchasing processes because both company codes are independent legal accounting entities. In these cases, you need to post all of the sales transactions for the issuing company code and all of the purchase transactions for the receiving company code.

However, SAP provides inter-company stock transfer via the SD component, which is simpler and more user-friendly than using the normal sales and purchasing cycle. Inter-company stock transfers via the SD process is shown in Figure 4.67.

There are two ways to set up inter-company stock transfers via the SD component:

▶ Stock transport order with delivery via shipping.

▶ Stock transport order with delivery and billing document.

We'll discuss both of these options in the following sections.

4.12.2   Stock Transport Order with Delivery via Shipping

Stock transport orders with delivery via shipping uses purchasing, shipping, and inventory functions. The stock transport order is created by the plant of the receiving company code, and the issuing company code creates a delivery document and issues goods. After the material is received, the receiving plant posts a goods receipt (Figure 4.67).

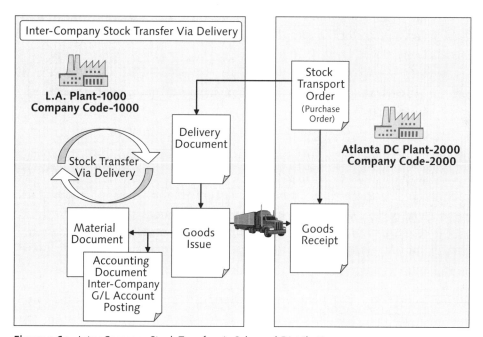

Figure 4.67   Inter-Company Stock Transfer via Sales and Distribution

Delivery costs can be entered in the stock transport order. In this case, the system creates two accounting documents when the goods issue is posted. The stock posting is offset against a company code clearing account.

Follow these process steps for inter-company stock transfers via the delivery process:

1. **Create a stock transport order at the receiving plant.**
   As an example, let's say that plant A would like to order materials from plant B.

Plant A enters a stock transfer order via Transaction ME21N. The stock transfer is then used to plan the movement.

2. **Post a delivery at the issuing plant.**
   Plant B supplies the goods to plant A. Plant B enters a replenishment delivery in shipping. The goods are then posted to the stock in transit of the receiving plant. Post the goods issue with movement type 641.

3. **Post the goods receipt at the receiving plant.**
   After the goods arrive at the receiving plant, the plant posts a goods receipt for the delivery. The stock in transit is therefore reduced, and the unrestricted-use stock is increased.

4.12.3 Stock Transport Order with Delivery and Billing Document/ Invoice

Stock transport orders with delivery and billing uses the purchasing, shipping, sales billing, inventory management, and invoice verification functions. The stock transport order is created by the plant of the receiving company code. Issuing company code creates a delivery document and issues the goods. After the material is received, the receiving plant posts a goods receipt (Figure 4.68). Issuing company code generates the billing document via the SD billing transaction, and the receiving company code posts the invoice via the MM invoice posting transaction.

With this type of stock transfer, the transfer posting isn't valuated at the valuation price of the material in the issuing plant. Instead, it's defined—using conditions—in both the issuing and receiving plants. The price determination is carried out in both purchasing and SD. In purchasing, the price of the material is determined in the usual manner (for example from the info record). In SD, the pricing is also carried out as it normally is during the billing process. The goods movements are valuated at the price determined in each case. Accounting documents are created for the goods issue, the goods receipt, billing, and the invoice receipt.

Follow these process steps for inter-company stock transfers via the delivery and billing process:

1. **Create the stock transport order at the receiving plant.**

   Create the stock transfer order via Transaction ME21N. Select document type NB, and enter the vendor (which must have the supplying plant assigned in the vendor master record), material, quantity, and delivery dates. Save the document.

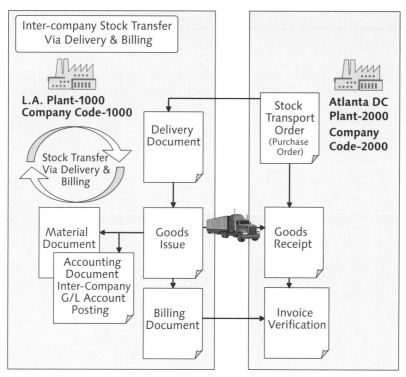

Figure 4.68 Inter-company Stock Transfer via Delivery and Billing

2. **Post the delivery at the issuing plant.**

   The issuing plant enters a replenishment delivery in SD. Unlike a stock transfer without a billing document, no stock in transit is created. Post the goods issue with movement type 643.

3. **Create the billing document at the issuing plant.**

   The issuing plant creates the billing document for the delivery.

4. **Post the goods receipt at the receiving plant.**

The receiving plant posts the goods receipt for the delivery. The goods are posted to unrestricted-use stock. For proper document flow, we recommend posting the goods receipt with reference to the delivery document.

5. **Post the invoice at the receiving plant.**

The invoice referring to the billing document is entered at the receiving plant.

4.12.4 Configuration Steps

Follow the configuration steps to define cross-company stock transport with delivery via shipping, with or without billing.

Defining Shipping Data for Plants

To define shipping data, go to SAP IMG • Materials Management • Purchasing • Purchase Order • Setup Stock Transport Order • Define Shipping Data for Plants. In this step, you maintain the shipping data for plants for stock transfer processing, as shown in Figure 4.69.

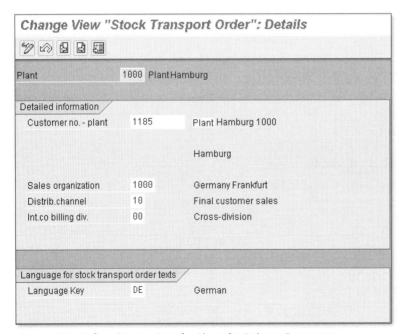

Figure 4.69 Define Shipping Data for Plants for Delivery Document

You also maintain the customer number of the receiving plant. If a custom provision has been made for a stock transfer to be carried out with an SD delivery, this customer number is used in the SD shipping process to identify the goods recipient (ship-to party).

You can also define the sales organization, distribution channel, and division for the supplying plant. With this data, the system determines the shipping data for the material to be transferred (e.g., the shipping point).

Creating Checking Rules

In this step, you create rules for the availability check for stock transport orders, as shown in Figure 4.70. This check lets you find out whether the quantity requested is available in the supplying plant; for example, in the case of materials that will be transferred over longer distances from one site to another. To create a checking rule, go to SAP IMG • Materials Management • Purchasing • Purchase Order • Setup Stock Transport Order • Create Checking Rule.

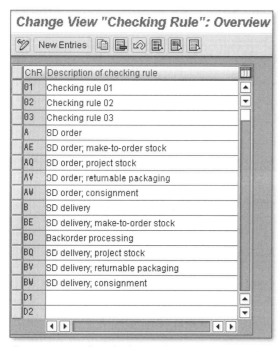

Figure 4.70 Define Checking Rule

Defining Checking Rules

To define a checking rule, go to SAP IMG • Materials Management • Purchasing • Purchase Order • Setup Stock Transport Order • Define Checking Rule. In this step, you specify which requirements and stocks should be taken into account before the stock transfer takes place (Figure 4.71). For materials that should be transferred from one site to another, you can carry out an availability check to find out whether the requested quantity is actually available at the supplying plant.

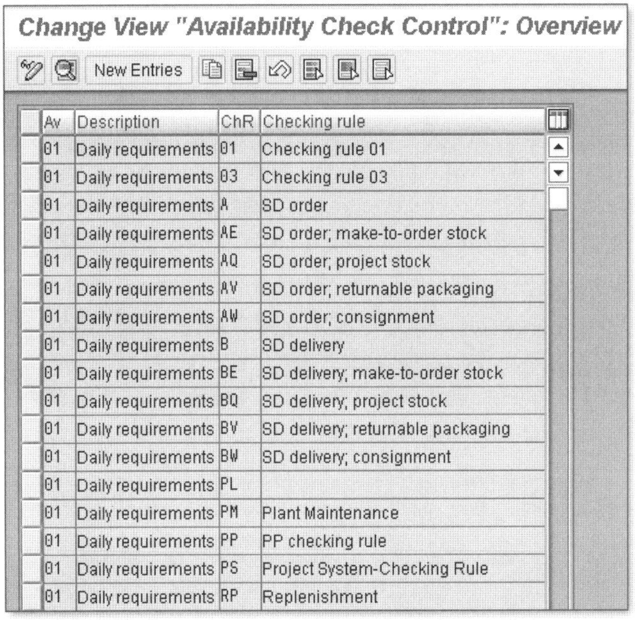
Change View "Availability Check Control": Overview

New Entries

Av	Description	ChR	Checking rule
01	Daily requirements	01	Checking rule 01
01	Daily requirements	03	Checking rule 03
01	Daily requirements	A	SD order
01	Daily requirements	AE	SD order; make-to-order stock
01	Daily requirements	AQ	SD order; project stock
01	Daily requirements	AV	SD order; returnable packaging
01	Daily requirements	AW	SD order; consignment
01	Daily requirements	B	SD delivery
01	Daily requirements	BE	SD delivery; make-to-order stock
01	Daily requirements	BQ	SD delivery; project stock
01	Daily requirements	BV	SD delivery; returnable packaging
01	Daily requirements	BW	SD delivery; consignment
01	Daily requirements	PL	
01	Daily requirements	PM	Plant Maintenance
01	Daily requirements	PP	PP checking rule
01	Daily requirements	PS	Project System-Checking Rule
01	Daily requirements	RP	Replenishment

Figure 4.71 Define Checking Rule for Availability Check

Assigning Delivery Types and Checking Rules

To assign a delivery type and checking rule, go to SAP IMG • Materials Management • Purchasing • Purchase Order • Setup Stock Transport Order • Assign Delivery Type and Checking Rule. In this step, you specify whether an SD delivery should be created for a certain combination of supplying plant and document type. You can also specify which delivery type should be used, as shown in Figure 4.72. The delivery type in SD determines how a delivery is handled.

Change View "Stock Transfer Data": Overview

New Entries

	Type	OTyp.descr	SPlt	Name 1	DlvTy	Description	C...	Description o...	S...	R...	Del...	Del...	DT ...
	NB	Standard PO	1000	Werk Hamburg	NL	Replenishme...	B	SD delivery	☐	☐			
	NB	Standard PO	1111	Werk Hamburg	NL	Replenishme...	B	SD delivery	☐	☐			
	NB	Standard PO	1200	Dresden	NLCC	Replen.Cross...	B	SD delivery	☑	☐			
	NB	Standard PO	1400	Stuttgart	NLCC	Replen.Cross...	B	SD delivery	☑	☐			
	NB	Standard PO	2000	Heathrow / Ha...	NLCC	Replen.Cross...	B	SD delivery	☑	☐			
	NB	Standard PO	2010	DC London	NLCC	Replen.Cross...	B	SD delivery	☑	☐			
	NB	Standard PO	2200	Paris	NLCC	Replen.Cross...	B	SD delivery	☑	☐			
	NB	Standard PO	2300	Barcelona	NL	Replenishme...	B	SD delivery	☐	☐			
	NB	Standard PO	2400	Milano Distrib...					☐	☐			
	NB	Standard PO	2500	Rotterdam Dis...					☐	☐			
	NB	Standard PO	3000	New York					☐	☐			
	NB	Standard PO	3100	Chicago	NLCC	Replen.Cross...	B	SD delivery	☐	☐			
	NB	Standard PO	3200	Atlanta					☐	☐			
	NB	Standard PO	3800	Denver Distrib...					☐	☐			
	NB	Standard PO	4000	Toronto	NLCC	Replen.Cross...	B	SD delivery	☑	☐			

Figure 4.72 Assign a Delivery Type to a Document Type and Supplying Plant

Assigning Document Types, One-Step Procedures, and Underdelivery Tolerances

To assign a document type for the supplying plant and issuing plant combination, go to SAP IMG • MATERIALS MANAGEMENT • PURCHASING • PURCHASE ORDER • SETUP STOCK TRANSPORT ORDER • ASSIGN DOCUMENT TYPE, ONE STEP PROCEDURE, UNDERDELIVERY TOLERANCE. In this step, you define which document type should be used for a certain combination of supplying and receiving plants (Figure 4.73).

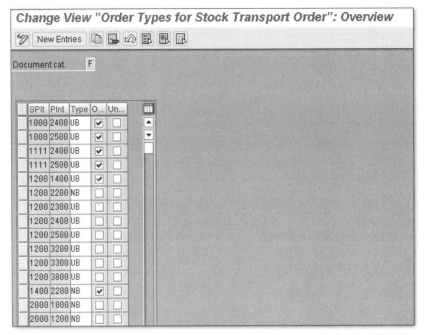

Figure 4.73 Assign a Document Type to a Supplying and Receiving Plant Combination

Aside from the previously mentioned configuration, you also need to ensure that the vendor master record is created for the supplying plant. To do so, use Transaction XK01, and create the supplying plant as a vendor at the receiving plant. Then, in the Purchasing view, assign the supplying plant to this vendor master record by going to EXTRAS • ADDL PURCHASING DATA.

4.13 Summary

You should now have a good understanding of the various transactions and documents involved in procurement processes. This will enable you to suggest the business process that will best meet the requirements of your customer and configure the required procurement processes.

In the next chapter, we'll discuss various inventory management processes.

The concept of inventory management consists of the procedures and techniques used to manage stock materials on a quantity and value basis.

5   Inventory Management Processes

Companies store and manage materials (such as raw materials, semi-finished goods, and finished goods) in storage locations. Frequently, for various reasons, materials must be moved in and out of these storage locations. If a storage location *receives* goods, the stock quantity is updated with a goods receipt entry (in this case, the quantity will have increased). If a storage location *issues* goods, the quantity is updated with a goods issue entry (in this case, the quantity will have decreased). For every goods movement transaction, whether it's a goods issue or a goods receipt, the SAP system creates a material document. If materials and transactions are subjected to stock valuation, the SAP system also creates an accounting document. The process of overseeing the movement of materials between storage locations is known as *inventory management*. See Figure 5.1 for an illustration of the inventory management process.

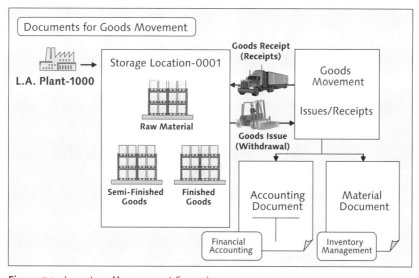

Figure 5.1   Inventory Management Scenario

As shown in Figure 5.2, you can view the stock quantity available for each material at the storage location, plant, company code, and client (also known as the corporate group) level. Stock overview reports can be generated via Transaction MMBE.

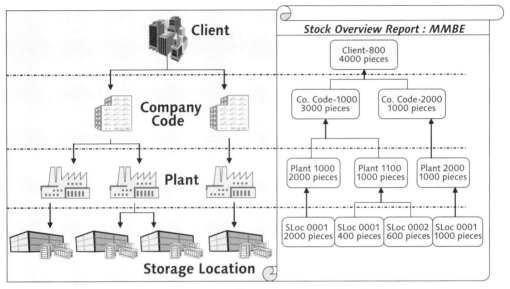

Figure 5.2 Stock Overview Report at Different Organizational Levels

In this chapter, we'll discuss the five different areas of inventory management:

▸ Inbound processes

▸ Outbound processes

▸ Internal inventory management processes

▸ Physical inventory management processes

▸ Vendor returns processes

We'll also discuss the different types of stock that can be involved in these processes. However, before we get into specifics, we must cover an essential concept involved in all of these processes: movement types.

5.1   Movement Types

One of the key concepts in inventory management is the idea of a *movement type*. The SAP system uses movement type numbers to distinguish between various types of goods movement, such as a goods receipt against a PO, vendor return, or cost center return; or, alternatively, a goods issue against a cost center issue, customer issue, and so on.

The movement type is a three-digit number (also known as a movement type key). As illustrated in Figure 5.3, different receipts and different issues are differentiated by movement type. As such, movement types have important control functions in inventory management, and play a central role in automatic account determination. Together with other influencing factors, the movement type determines which stock or consumption accounts are updated in Financial Accounting.

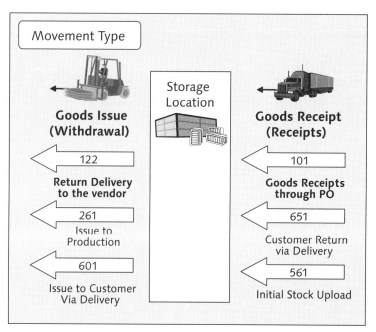

Figure 5.3 Movement Types

There are SAP-defined movement types, but you can also create your own to meet specific client requirements. Let's discuss the configuration steps used to create movement types:

1. **Record the reason for the goods movement.**

   In this step, you record the reason for the goods movement. For example, consider a scenario where you're required to define a reason whenever you're returning materials to a vendor. You can define the reason keys, with the descriptions as follows:

   ▶ 0001: Poor quality

   ▶ 0002: Damaged materials

   When returning goods to the vendor, select the appropriate reason key, and the reason for the movement will be stored in the material document. In inventory management, you can use a report to evaluate the material documents in which a reason for movement was specified. Display a list of material documents that have been posted for a particular reason via Transaction MBGR.

   To define the reason for the goods movement, follow the menu path SAP IMG • Materials Management • Inventory Management and Physical Inventory • Movement Types • Record Reason for Goods Movement. Next, click on the Control Reason button, and specify whether the Reason entry is optional, mandatory, or suppressed for each movement (Figure 5.4). For example, for movement type 101, the Reason field is suppressed. This means that during goods receipt entry for movement type 101, the Reason field won't be displayed in the document.

Change View "Control: Reason for Movement": Overview

MvT	Movement Type Text	Reas.	Control reason
101	GR goods receipt	-	Field is suppressed.
102	Reversal of GR	.	Entry in this field is optional.
103	GR into blocked stck	.	Entry in this field is optional.
104	Rev. GR to blocked	-	Field is suppressed.
105	GR from blocked stck	-	Field is suppressed.
106	Rev.GR from blocked	-	Field is suppressed.
121	GR subseq. adjustm.	-	Entry in this field is optional.
122	RE return to vendor	+	Entry in this field is required.
123	RE rtrn vendor rev.	-	Field is suppressed.
124	GR rtrn blocked stck	+	Entry in this field is required.
125	GR rtn blkd stck rev	-	Field is suppressed.
131	Goods receipt	-	Field is suppressed.
132	Goods receipt	-	Field is suppressed.
141	GR G subseq. adjustm	-	Field is suppressed.
142	GR G subseq. adjustm	-	Field is suppressed.
161	GR returns	-	Entry in this field is optional.

Figure 5.4 Control: Reason for Movement Types

Now, click on the Reason for Movement button, and you will get a list of SAP-defined reasons for different movement types (Figure 5.5). Click on the New Entries button and enter the reason key and description of the reason for movement. The reason code you define in this step can be selected during materials movement.

MvT	Movement Type Text	Reason	Reason for movement
103	GR into blocked stck	103	Spoiled
122	RE return to vendor	1	Poor quality
122	RE return to vendor	2	Incomplete
122	RE return to vendor	3	Damaged
261	GI for order	261	Unplanned use
262	RE for order	262	Reversal Reason
543	GI issue sls.ord.st.	543	Damage in transport
544	GI receipt sls.or.st	544	Damage in ret.transp
551	GI scrapping	1	Shrinkage
551	GI scrapping	2	Spoiled
552	RE scrapping	1	Shrinkage
552	RE scrapping	2	Spoiled
922	RE return to vendor	1	Poor quality
922	RE return to vendor	2	Incomplete
922	RE return to vendor	3	Damaged
943	GI issue sls.ord.st.	543	Damage in transport

Figure 5.5   Reasons for Goods Movements

2. **Copy or change the movement type.**
   In this step, you can define a new movement type, or change the setting of an existing movement type. To define or change existing movement types, go to SAP IMG • Materials Management • Inventory Management and Physical Inventory • Movement Types • Copy, Change Movement Types.

A pop-up window for field selection will appear. Check the Client and Movement Type checkbox, and enter the client number and movement type in the From and To fields. This will result in a list of movement types, as shown in Figure 5.6. To change an existing movement type, select the movement type, and use the tree menu in the left side of the screen to make the required changes. To create a new movement type, click on Copy, enter the new movement type key, and press Enter. The system will then ask you whether you want to copy everything or only copy a specific entry. If you select Copy All, the system will copy all of the dependent settings also.

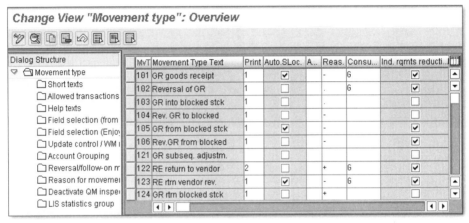

Figure 5.6 Movement Type: Change View

As shown in Figure 5.7, you can set many controlling parameters for a movement type. For example, under Entry Control, you can define whether printing the material document is allowed, whether the G/L account field is displayed, and more. You can also define Updating Control for movement type, for example, whether Automatic Storage Location Creation and Automatic PO is allowed at the time of goods receipt.

From the tree menu on the left side of the screen, you can also define other control fields; for example: Short Texts, Allowed Transactions, Field Selection, Reason for Movement, Deactivate QM Inspection, and Account Grouping.

> **Note**
>
> Account Grouping is required for automatic account determination.

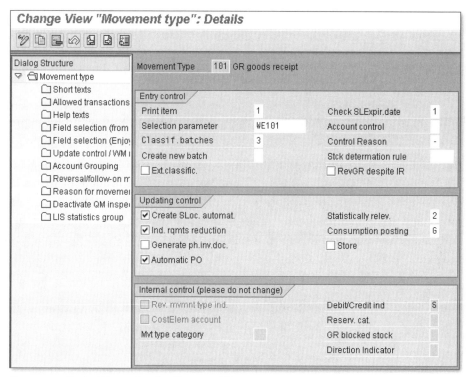

Figure 5.7 Control Parameters for Movement Type

Now that we've explained the concept and configuration of movement types, let's move on to the topic of inbound and outbound processes in inventory management.

5.2 Inbound and Outbound Processes

Materials issue and receipt are the two major business processes in inventory management. As previously discussed, materials are received via goods receipts, and issued via goods issues. The *inbound process* comprises all of the steps that must occur when goods are received into a storage location. The *outbound process* comprises all of the steps that must occur when goods are shipped out of a storage location.

In the following sections, we'll discuss the major aspects of inbound and outbound processes, including their definitions and configuration options.

5.2.1 Inbound/Outbound Process Definitions

In the SAP system, the inbound process pertains to all incoming goods. This can include receiving materials from a vendor against a PO, or receiving return materials from a customer due to quality issues. Whenever goods arrive at the goods receiving area, the store keeper posts the goods receipt transaction in the system via Transaction MIGO (Figure 5.8). This creates a material document, which is proof of goods movement in a storage location. If required, the goods receipt slips can be printed. If incoming materials are subjected to quality inspection, materials will be received and kept as quality inspection stock.

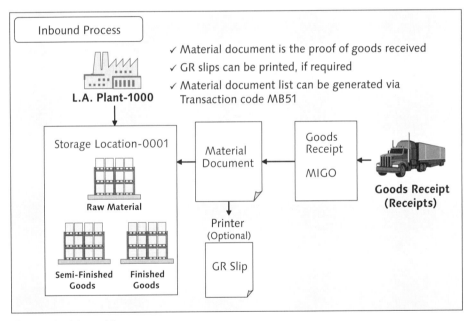

Figure 5.8 Inbound Process

The outbound process, on the other hand, pertains to all outgoing goods. This can include issuing goods to a customer against a sales order, or returning materials to a vendor because of quality issues. Whenever goods are issued from storage locations, the store keeper posts the goods issue transaction in the system via Transaction MIGO_GI (Figure 5.9). This creates a material document, which is proof of goods movement in a storage location.

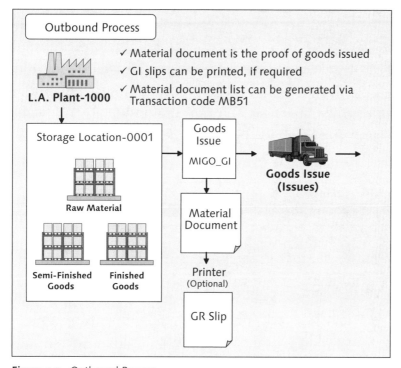

Figure 5.9 Outbound Process

In the outbound process, when post goods issue (PGI) is done, the system issues goods to the customer and posts a material document and an accounting document.

> **Note**
>
> You can set up outbound delivery for stock transport orders. For more information about this, see Chapter 4, Section 4.12.2, Stock Transport Order with Delivery via Shipping.

5.2.2 Inventory Management Configurations

In the following sections, we'll discuss the two ways you can configure inbound and outbound processes: by setting plant parameters, and by defining number ranges for material documents. We'll also discuss the default parameters set in the system.

Setting Plant Parameters

In inventory management, you can define control parameters for each plant via menu path SAP IMG • MATERIALS MANAGEMENT • INVENTORY MANAGEMENT AND PHYSICAL INVENTORY • PLANT PARAMETERS. This allows you to define control parameters for categories such as Goods Movements, Physical Inventory, and Negative Stocks (Figure 5.10).

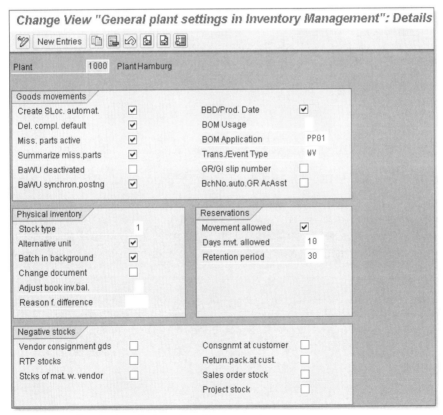

Figure 5.10 Plant Settings for Inventory Management

If you want to allow negative stock for a plant, go to menu path SAP IMG • MATERIALS MANAGEMENT • INVENTORY MANAGEMENT AND PHYSICAL INVENTORY • GOODS ISSUE/TRANSFER PROCESS • ALLOW NEGATIVE STOCK. In this step, you specify whether negative stocks are allowed for unrestricted-use stock in the valuation area, in the plant, and in the storage location (Figure 5.11).

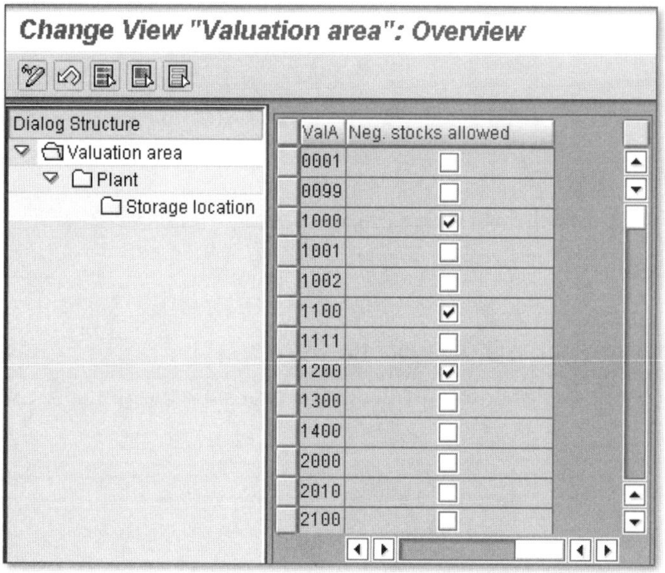

Figure 5.11 Allow Negative Stock for Valuation Area, Plant, and Storage Location

Negative stocks are necessary, for example, when goods issues are entered prior to the corresponding goods receipts, and the material is already physically located in the warehouse. After the goods receipts have been posted, the book inventory balance must again correspond to the physical stock; that is, the book inventory balance can no longer be negative.

For example, consider a scenario where 1,000 pieces of material are physically available in a storage location. However, due to time limitations, the goods receipt document isn't posted in the system. In this case, the system stock will show up as zero:

▶ Physical Stock: 1,000 pieces

▶ Book Inventory Stock: 0 pieces

Suddenly, 100 pieces of material must urgently be issued, and the goods issue is posted in the system. Because the book inventory balance was zero before, it will now be negative.

► Physical stock: 900 pieces
► Book inventory stock: (-)100 pieces

At a later time, the goods receipt is posted in the system, which updates the book inventory balance:

► Physical stock: 900 pieces
► Book inventory stock: 900 pieces

After the goods receipt is posted, the stock number in the system matches the actual physical stock. Now, there is no more negative stock.

Defining Number Ranges for Material Documents

In the standard SAP system, the following document types are predefined for inventory management:

► WA: Goods issues, transfer postings, and other goods receipts
► WE: Goods receipts with reference to POs
► WF: Goods receipts with reference to production orders
► WI: Inventory differences
► WL: Goods issues with reference to deliveries (SD)
► WN: Net posting of goods receipts
► PR: Revaluation documents

Each document type is already assigned a number range. In company code 0001, number intervals are defined for each number range, both for the current and the previous fiscal year. Number range 49, with the year-related interval 4900000000 to 4999999999, is assigned to the document types for all goods movements, except goods movements with reference to purchase/production orders.

Document type WE is used for goods receipts with reference to POs and production orders. This document type is assigned number range 50, with the year-related interval 5000000000 to 5099999999. Note that net postings of goods receipts (document type WN) aren't active in the standard SAP system. If you want to post net goods receipts, you have to assign document type WN instead of WE to Transaction MB01.

Document type WI is used for posting inventory differences. This document type is assigned the number range 01, with the year-related interval 0100000000 to 019999999999.

To define your own number range, go to SAP IMG • MATERIALS MANAGEMENT • INVENTORY MANAGEMENT AND PHYSICAL INVENTORY • NUMBER ASSIGNMENT • DEFINE NUMBER ASSIGNMENT FOR MATERIAL AND PHYS. INV. DOC.

Number ranges for material documents are year-specific. Click on Insert Year from the top menu and enter the Year, From Number, and To Number, as shown in Figure 5.12.

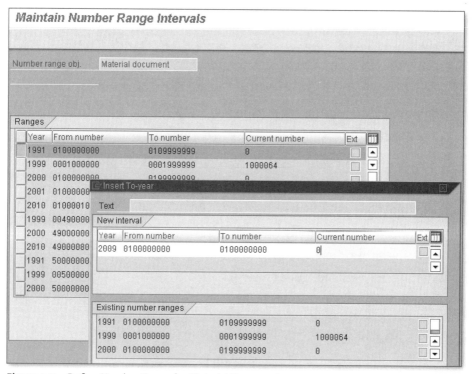

Figure 5.12 Define Number Range for Material Documents

Default Settings

In the standard system, transaction/event types and number range intervals are preset as follows:

▶ **Physical inventory documents**
These have a number range interval from 0100000000 to 0199999999 and contain the following transaction/event types:

- ▶ IB: Physical inventory documents

- ▶ ID: Physical inventory documents for counts and difference without reference

- ▶ IN: Physical inventory documents for recounts

- ▶ IZ: Physical inventory documents for count without reference

- ▶ WV: Physical inventory documents for difference postings in the WM system

▶ **Material documents for goods movements and inventory differences**
These have a number range interval from 4900000000 to 4999999999 and contain the following transaction/event types:

- ▶ WA: Goods issues, transfer postings, and other goods receipts

- ▶ WH: Goods movements for handling units (HU)

- ▶ WI: Material documents for inventory adjustment postings

- ▶ WL: Goods issues for delivery documents (SD)

- ▶ WQ: Goods movements for usage decisions (QM)

- ▶ WR: Goods movements for completion confirmations (PP)

- ▶ WS: Goods movements for run schedule headers (PP)

- ▶ WZ: Documents for batch status changes

▶ **Material documents for goods receipts**
These have a number range interval from 5000000000 to 5999999999 and contain the following transaction/event types:

- ▶ WE: Goods receipts for POs

- ▶ WF: Goods receipts for production orders

- ▶ WO: Subsequent adjustment of subcontract orders

- ▶ WW: Subsequent adjustment of active ingredient materials

▶ **Inventory sampling numbers**
These have number range intervals from 0200000000 to 0299999999 and contain transaction/event type SI.

Now that we've covered the essential topics in inbound and outbound processes, let's move on to discussing the different stock types in inventory management.

5.3   Stock Types in Inventory Management

In inventory management, stock types vary depending on the business requirement. The stock type of a specific material specifies its usability, whether it's valuated or non-valuated, and its availability for MRP, and more. The various types of stock provided by the SAP system are:

▶ Standard stock (which includes unrestricted-use stock, quality-inspection stock, and blocked stock)

▶ Goods receipt blocked stock

▶ Special stock

We'll discuss each of these in more detail in the following sections. Then, we'll discuss how to change stock from one type to another.

5.3.1   Standard Stock Types

There are three SAP-defined stock types based on material usability:

▶ Unrestricted-use stock

▶ Quality-inspection stock

▶ Blocked stock

When you receive goods into a storage location via Transaction MIGO, you can select the stock type. The system will then update the stock quantity for that stock type (Figure 5.13). (Again, you can see stock overview reports via Transaction MMBE, which will display the stock available for each stock type.)

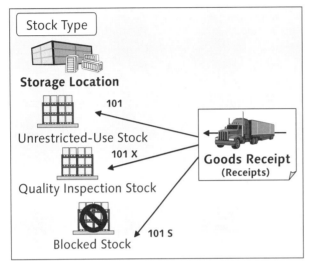

Figure 5.13   Stock Types

We'll now discuss the definition of each stock type.

Unrestricted-Use Stock

Unrestricted-use stock is company stock that's physically located in a storage location. It's valuated, and there's no restriction for usage. Unrestricted-use stock can be issued to production or customers.

Quality-Inspection Stock

Quality-inspection stock is company stock that's physically located in a storage location, but is subjected to quality inspection. Quality-inspection stock is valuated, and cannot be issued to production or to a customer because it's under quality inspection. This means that the quality management functionality has been implemented, and the materials are being inspected by a quality inspector. Based on the results of the inspection, usage decisions are made. Depending on this usage decision, quality-inspection stock can be changed to unrestricted-use stock or blocked stock.

Blocked Stock

Blocked stock is company stock that cannot be used because the status is blocked. The materials that are under dispute, of poor quality, or damaged are kept as blocked stock. If you want to issue these materials to production or to a customer, you need to transfer them to unrestricted-use stock.

As should be apparent from these three definitions, materials for production can be issued only from unrestricted-use stock. You can, however, withdraw a sample and scrap a quantity from blocked stock. Additionally, physical inventory can be carried out for all three types of stock, and differences can be posted.

It's possible to change a material's stock type. This is called a *transfer posting*, and is discussed in the next section.

Transfer Postings

Although their names sound similar, a transfer posting is different from a stock transfer, and is used for changing stock types of a material. For example, if you want to withdraw materials from blocked or quality-inspection stock, you have to first carry out a transfer posting into unrestricted-use stock, and then withdraw the material from unrestricted-use stock. Figure 5.14 illustrates the different movement types used for transfer postings.

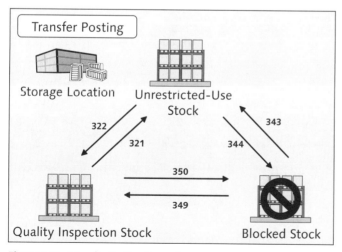

Figure 5.14 Transfer Posting Scenario

Transfer postings change stock type and batch numbers, and may also involve physical stock transfers. Transfer postings always create a material document, and, if a change in valuation is involved, they also create an accounting document.

5.3.2 Goods Receipt Blocked Stock

When you post a goods receipt, the system updates the stock in a storage location. Alternatively, the stock is posted for direct consumption. However, there is another option in addition to these two: you can also manage the stock as goods receipt blocked stock.

Business Scenario

Consider, for example, a car manufacturing business that procures gear box assembly materials from a supplier. During the goods receipt, the company finds that some of the materials are damaged. They need to discuss the situation with the vendor, and decide whether to use this material or send it back. Until this decision is made, this material needs to be kept in stock; however, the enterprise doesn't want to own it because it's under dispute.

The SAP system includes goods receipt blocked stock functionality that allows the materials to be received, but not valuated (Figure 5.15). Goods receipt blocked stock materials are subject to conditional acceptance due to either damaged or unexpected deliveries. The transaction is updated in the PO history.

Goods receipt blocked stock can be sent back to the vendor or transferred to the company's own stock. If it's sent back to the vendor, the system will create a material document and update the PO history. If it's transferred to the company's own stock, it becomes valuated and creates a material document and an accounting document. You can release goods receipt blocked stock to any other type of stock, such as unrestricted-use, quality-inspection, or blocked stock.

The following process steps are provided for when dealing with goods receipt blocked stock.

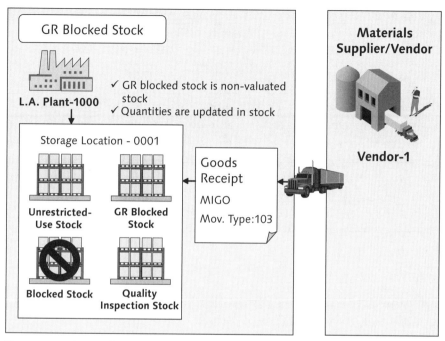

Figure 5.15 The Goods Receipt Blocked Stock Scenario

Process Steps

1. **Post the goods receipt.**
   Post the goods receipt with reference to a PO via Transaction MIGO and movement type 103. This will create a material document, and the stock quantity of goods receipt blocked stock will be updated in the plant stock.

2. **Release the goods receipt blocked stock, or return it.**
   To release goods receipt blocked stock to your own company, post a goods receipt with reference to a PO, using movement type 105. The system will release the goods receipt blocked stock to the company's own stock. A material document and an accounting document will be created.

To return goods receipt blocked stock to the vendor, post a goods return via Transaction MIGO with reference to the PO. Use movement type 124. The system will return the goods receipt blocked stock to the vendor.

In addition to the standard stock types and goods receipt blocked stock, special stock types also exist. We'll discuss these in the following section.

5.3.3 Special Stock Types

Special stocks are managed separately because they're either owned by a business partner (such as a vendor or customer), or stored in some other location (such as customer or vendor premises). These special stock types are split up into two groups: company-owned special stock and externally-owned special stock. The list that follows shows which special stocks belong in each group; the letter in parentheses is the indicator in the SAP system:

- **Company-owned special stock**
  - Subcontract stock (O)
  - Customer consignment stock (W)
  - Returnable transport packaging stock to customer (V)
- **Externally-owned special stock**
  - Vendor consignment stock (K)
  - Returnable transport packaging stock to vendor (M)
  - Sales order stock (E)
  - Project stock (Q)
  - Pipeline material (P)

Company-Owned Special Stock

Company-owned special stock is stock that's stored with the vendor or the customer. For example, material issued to a subcontractor is a company's stock that's stored on vendor premises.

The following are definitions of the company-owned special stocks available in the SAP system:

- **Subcontract stock**
  This is stock provided to the vendor for further processing.

▶ **Customer consignment stock**
This is stock stored on customer premises. It's still owned by the company until it's consumed by the customer or transferred to the customer's own stock.

▶ **Returnable transport packaging stock to customer**
This is packaging materials or means of transport (for example, pallets or crates) that are supplied by your company to a customer and must be returned.

> **Note**
>
> Because these special stocks aren't located at your own company, they're managed at the plant level and not at the storage location level.
>
> Two stock types are possible: unrestricted-use stock and quality-inspection stock.

Externally-Owned Special Stock

Externally-owned special stock is stock that your customer or vendor stores at your company. The owner of the materials is still the customer or vendor, so it's not valuated in your stock valuation.

The following are definitions of the externally-owned special stocks available in the SAP system:

▶ **Vendor consignment stock**
This is stock provided by a vendor and kept at your company's storage location. The vendor remains the owner of the materials until they're consumed or transferred to the company's own stock.

▶ **Returnable transport packaging stock to vendor**
This is packaging materials or means of transport (for example, pallets or crates) that are supplied to your company by the vendor and must be returned.

▶ **Sales order stock**
This is material that's procured directly for a sales order. Sales order stock can only be used to produce material ordered by the customer. Furthermore, the finished product can only be delivered to the customer via a sales order.

▶ **Project stock**
This is material that's procured directly for a project. The project stock is allocated to a work breakdown structure (WBS) element. Components can only be withdrawn for the WBS element.

> **Note**
>
> Because these special stocks are located at your company, they're managed at the storage location level.
>
> All three standard stock types are possible with this type of special stock.

5.4 Physical Inventory Management Processes

Physical inventory management is the process of physically verifying stock quantities in storage locations. If there are any differences in the system stock and physical stock, these differences are posted in the system. This is required to keep system stock up to date; otherwise, stock quantity discrepancies may impact materials requirement planning.

You can check the stock of material in the storage locations by counting the quantities in unrestricted-use stock, blocked stock, and quality-inspection stock. You can also carry out physical inventory for special stock and your own stock separately, using different physical inventory documents.

The physical inventory management process can be divided into three phases:

1. **Physical inventory preparation.**
   This phase includes creating physical inventory documents, blocking material for posting, and printing and distributing physical inventory documents.

2. **Physical inventory count.**
   This phase includes physically counting stock and entering the inventory count in the system.

3. **Physical inventory check.**
   In this phase, the physical count result is checked. If required, a recount can be initiated; otherwise, differences are accepted and posted. System stock is corrected after posting the differences.

Figure 5.16 illustrates the physical inventory process. The process starts with the creation of a physical inventory document. After physical counting, the inventory count and differences are posted in the system. Posting difference transactions will create a material document and an accounting document.

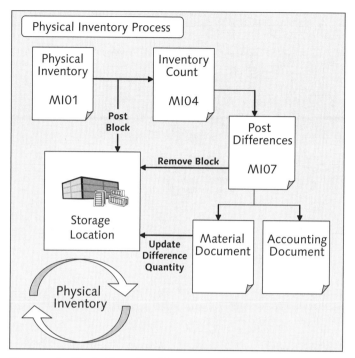

Figure 5.16 Physical Inventory Management Process

In the following sections, we'll discuss different types of physical inventory methods, as well as the process and configuration steps involved in physical inventory management.

5.4.1 Process Steps

Follow these steps for the physical inventory process:

1. **Create a physical inventory document.**
   The first step is to create a physical inventory document via Transaction MI01. Enter the Document Date, Planned Count Date, Plant, and Storage Location. You can block the posting by checking the Posting Block checkbox, as shown in Figure 5.17. If it's special stock, select the Special Stock indicator. Press Enter. In the next screen, enter the material number for which you want to do a physical inventory, and then save. This will generate a physical inventory document, which can be printed via Transaction MI21.

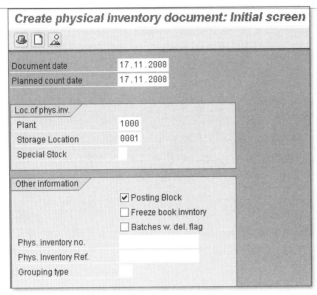

Figure 5.17 Creating a Physical Inventory Document

If you've selected Posting Block in a physical inventory document, you cannot post any materials movement until you complete the inventory count.

2. **Enter the physical inventory count.**

Enter the count result for the material via Transaction MI04, as shown in Figure 5.18.

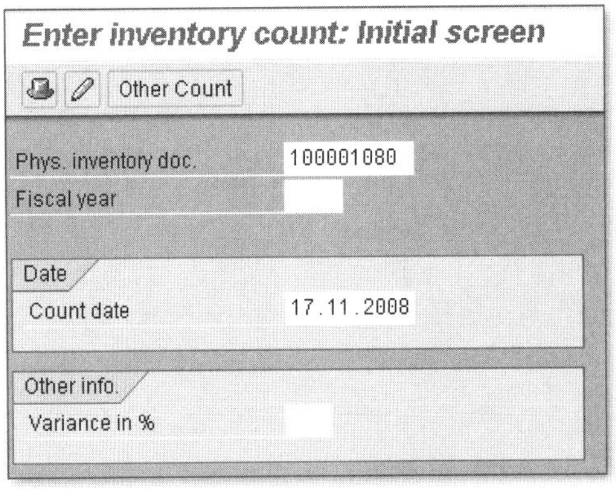

Figure 5.18 Entering the Inventory Count

3. **Post the difference.**

   You can post the difference with Transaction MI07, as shown in Figure 5.19. The system will create a material document for the difference quantity. It will also post an accounting document because discrepancies in stock quantity impact stock valuation.

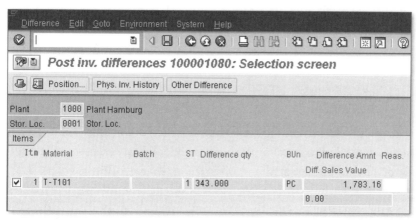

Figure 5.19   Posting Differences

With respect to account postings, if the physical inventory count is more than the system stock, the stock G/L account will be debited. If the physical inventory count is less than the system stock, the stock G/L account will be credited. For a gain in stock due to physical inventory, movement type 701 is used; for a loss in stock due to physical inventory, movement type 702 is used.

Now that you've learned about the basics of the physical inventory process, let's discuss the different types of physical inventory methods.

5.4.2   Cycle Counting Method

There are a number of physical inventory methods that can be used. The following are provided by the SAP system:

▶ **Periodic inventory**

   All company stocks are physically counted on the balance sheet key date. Every material has to be counted, and the entire storage location must be blocked for materials movement.

▶ **Continuous inventory**
Stocks are counted throughout the fiscal year. Every material is counted at least once during the fiscal year.

▶ **Cycle counting**
Materials are counted at regular intervals within a fiscal year. These intervals depend on the cycle counting indicator set for each material.

▶ **Inventory sampling**
Randomly-selected company stocks are physically counted on the balance sheet key date. If the variances between the result of the count and the book inventory balances are small, it's presumed that the book inventory balances for other stocks are correct.

For our purposes, we'll focus on the cycle counting method, because it's the most preferred method in the industry. With this method, all materials to be included in the inventory count are classified into different cycle categories such as A, B, C, and D (Figure 5.20). Each cycle category has a different time interval assigned to it. You can set these parameters via the cycle counting indicator.

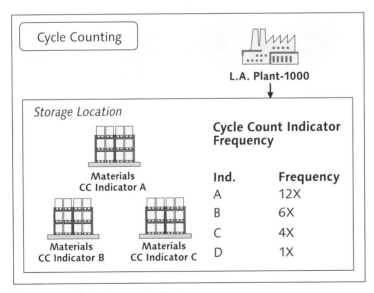

Figure 5.20 Cycle Counting Indicator

To configure the cycle counting indicator and its frequency, go to SAP IMG • Materials Management • Inventory Management and Physical Inventory • Physical Inventory • Cycle Counting. In this step, you configure the system settings
for the physical inventory method of cycle counting by defining the individual
cycle counting indicators for a given plant (Figure 5.21). The cycle counting indicators are used to group the materials together into individual categories.

For each plant, define the CC (cycle counting) Physical Inventory Indicator. This
indicates that a given material is subject to the cycle counting method of inventory.
The indicator also defines at which time intervals a physical inventory should be
carried out for the material.

Change View "Settings for Cycle Counting": Overview

New Entries

Plnt	CC phys. inv. ind.	No.of phys.inv.	Interval	Float time	Percentage
0001	A	12	20	5	56
0001	B	6	41	10	28
0001	C	3	82	20	14
0001	D	1	247		2
1000	A	12	20	5	55
1000	B	6	41	10	28
1000	C	3	83	20	14
1000	D	1	249		2
1000	X	1	248	5	1
1001	A	12	20	5	56
1001	B	6	41	10	28
1001	C	3	82	20	14
1001	D	1	247		2
1002	A	12	20	5	56
1002	B	6	41	10	28
1002	C	3	82	20	14
1002	D	1	247		2

Figure 5.21 Defining the Cycle Counting Indicator

For materials that should be verified by the cycle counting method, you must
assign the cycle count indicator in the material master record. This can be done
either manually or automatically.

To set the physical inventory indicator manually, use Transaction MM02. Select the Plant Storage View in the material master record, and select the CC Phys. Inv. Ind. indicator (Figure 5.22).

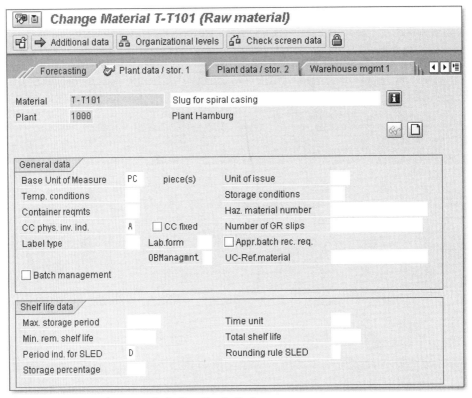

Figure 5.22 Material Master: Cycle Counting Indicator

To set the indicator automatically, you need to execute program RMCBIN00 via Transaction SE38 or use Transaction MIBC. This carries out ABC analysis (Figure 5.23). You can analyze based on requirements or consumption.

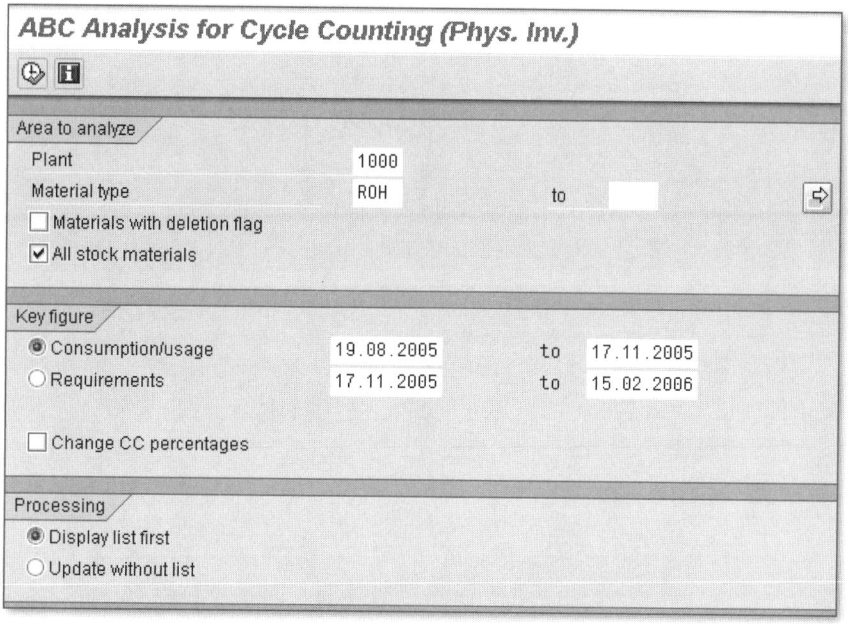

ABC Analysis for Cycle Counting (Phys. Inv.)

Area to analyze

Plant	1000		
Material type	ROH	to	
☐ Materials with deletion flag			
☑ All stock materials			

Key figure

◉ Consumption/usage	19.08.2005	to	17.11.2005
○ Requirements	17.11.2005	to	15.02.2006

☐ Change CC percentages

Processing

◉ Display list first
○ Update without list

Figure 5.23 ABC Analysis for Cycle Counting

Performing an ABC analysis based on requirements means that you're analyzing the requirement values (planned independent requirements, sales orders, dependent requirements, and requirements from stock transport orders) for a specified period. Performing an ABC analysis based on consumption means you're analyzing consumption values for a specified period.

In either case, select the plant and material type, and then select the appropriate ABC analysis indicator. Under Processing, select Display List First, as shown in Figure 5.23. The system will display the material list with the new and old cycle counting indicator. If you want to update all of the material master records for the proposed cycle counting indicator, and execute the report by selecting the checkbox Update Without List in the Processing section.

To create a physical inventory document automatically, use program RM07ICN1 or Transaction MICN (Figure 5.24). This program automatically checks the due date for inventories for all cycle counting materials.

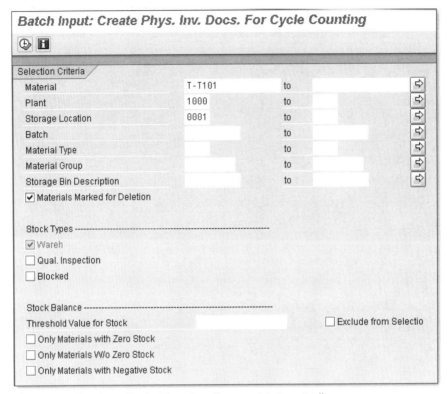

Figure 5.24 Creating a Physical Inventory Document Automatically

5.5 Vendor Return Process

There may be a scenario where you need to return materials to a vendor due to poor quality, damaged goods, or excess delivery. Vendor material can be returned through the following processes:

▶ Return without return PO

▶ Return with return PO

▶ Return with return PO and outbound delivery

We'll now discuss each of these scenarios in detail.

5.5.1 Return without Return Purchase Order

The return without return PO process is used when you don't want to process return POs. Materials are directly returned (i.e., issued) to the vendor with reference to the PO against which materials were received (Figure 5.25). In this case, material prices are picked up from the PO, and the returned quantity becomes the open quantity (the quantity to be delivered) in the PO.

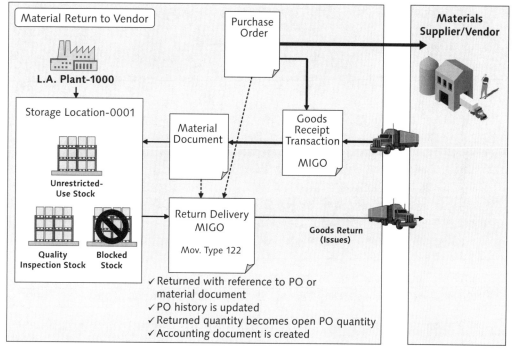

Figure 5.25 Vendor Return Without Return PO

Materials can be returned to a vendor via Transaction MIGO. Select the goods receipt with reference to PO, and then enter the PO number (that is, the PO number against which the material was received) and Movement Type 122 (Figure 5.26).

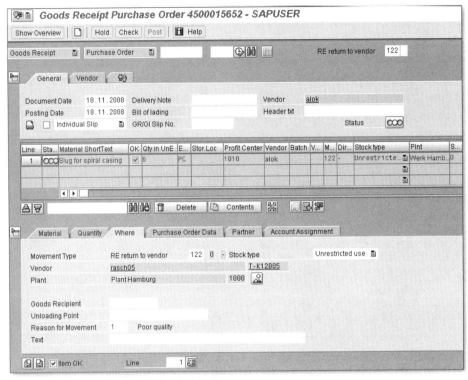

Figure 5.26 Goods Receipt: Return to Vendor

This transaction will issue the material to the vendor, and update the PO history. The returned quantity will become the open quantity in the PO.

You can also return material via return delivery. Select the material document number (i.e., the material document number through which the material was received) and Movement Type 122. This transaction will be updated in the PO history.

Regarding account postings, an accounting document will be created. The GR/IR (goods receipt/invoice receipt) account will be debited, and the stock G/L account will be credited.

5.5.2 Return with Return Purchase Order

The return with return PO scenario is used when you want to return material via a return PO. This scenario is required when you don't have a record of the PO or goods receipt number against which the material was received. This may happen when you have multiple POs and goods receipts from the same vendor. In this case, a return PO is created and materials are issued to the vendor via return delivery with reference to the return PO (Figure 5.27). A credit memo is issued to the vendor with reference to the return PO.

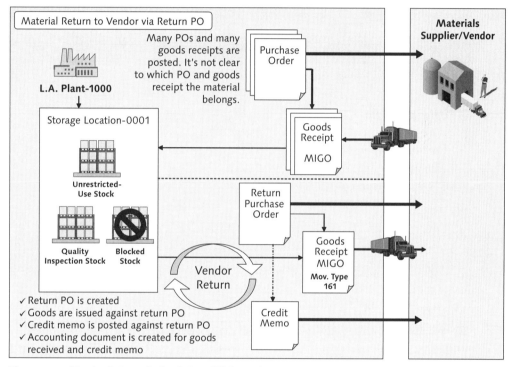

Figure 5.27 Vendor Return via the Return PO Scenario

Follow the process steps that follow for this type of return:

1. **Create a return PO.**

   Create a return PO via Transaction ME21N. Select the vendor, material, quantity, plant, and other identifying information. Then select the Returns Item checkbox, located in the PO item line (Figure 5.28). Use document type NB.

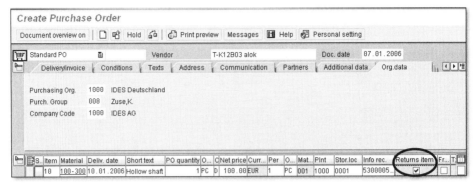

Figure 5.28 Purchase Order: Returns Item Indicator

2. **Post a goods issue.**

   Post a goods issue with reference to the return PO, via Transaction MIGO. Select movement type 161. A material document and an accounting document will be created in the system, the GR/IR account will be debited, and the stock G/L account will be credited.

3. **Post a credit memo.**

   Post a credit memo with reference to the return PO, via Transaction MIRO. The system will create an accounting document, the GR/IR account will be credited, and the vendor account will be debited.

5.5.3 Return with Return Purchase Order and Outbound Delivery

The return with return PO and outbound delivery scenario is similar to the return with PO scenario except that the goods are issued via outbound delivery. The outbound delivery is created with reference to the return PO. Goods are issued, followed by the pick and pack process (Figure 5.29).

Process Steps

Follow these process steps for a vendor return via return order and outbound delivery:

1. **Create a return PO.**

   Create a return PO via Transaction ME21N. Select the vendor, material, quantity, plant, and other identifying information. Then select the Returns Item checkbox, located in the PO item line. Use document type NB.

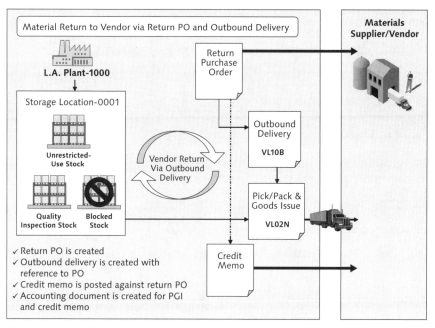

Figure 5.29 Vendor Return via Return PO and Outbound Delivery Scenario

2. **Create an outbound delivery.**
   Create an outbound delivery with reference to the return PO via Transaction VL10B.

3. **Post a goods issue.**
   Perform the pick and pack activities and post the PGI via Transaction VL02N. Movement type 161 is used for a goods issue. The material document and accounting document are posted in the system.

4. **Post the credit memo.**
   Post the credit memo with reference to the return PO via Transaction MIRO. The system will create an accounting document, the GR/IR account will be credited, and the vendor account will be debited.

Configuration Steps

You can define the delivery type and supplying plant for a return PO. To do so, go to SAP IMG • MATERIALS MANAGEMENT • PURCHASING • PURCHASE ORDER • RETURNS ORDER • RETURNS TO VENDOR (Figure 5.30). In the standard system, return delivery type RL is used for vendor returns.

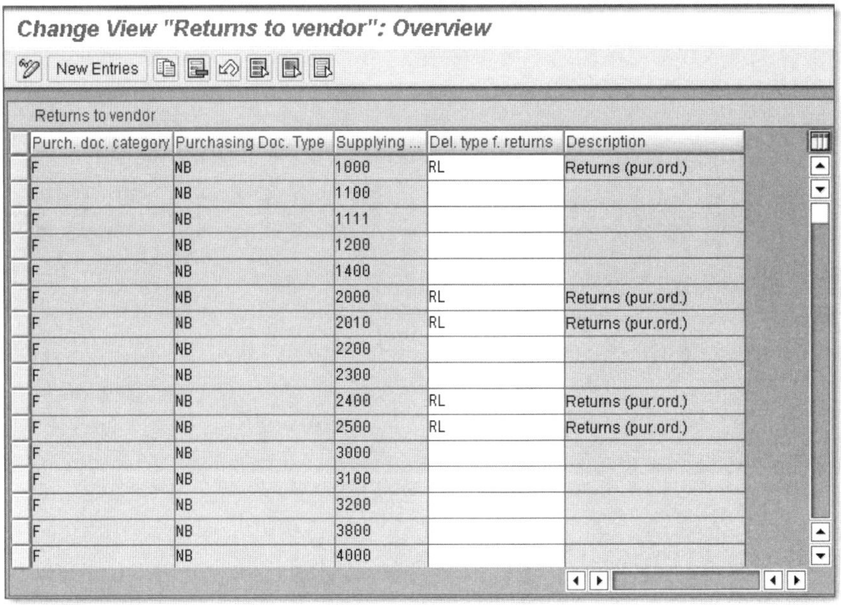

Change View "Returns to vendor": Overview

New Entries

Returns to vendor

Purch. doc. category	Purchasing Doc. Type	Supplying ...	Del. type f. returns	Description
F	NB	1000	RL	Returns (pur.ord.)
F	NB	1100		
F	NB	1111		
F	NB	1200		
F	NB	1400		
F	NB	2000	RL	Returns (pur.ord.)
F	NB	2010	RL	Returns (pur.ord.)
F	NB	2200		
F	NB	2300		
F	NB	2400	RL	Returns (pur.ord.)
F	NB	2500	RL	Returns (pur.ord.)
F	NB	3000		
F	NB	3100		
F	NB	3200		
F	NB	3800		
F	NB	4000		

Figure 5.30 Defining a Delivery Type for Vendor Returns

When processing returns in this manner, you must also edit the vendor master record. In the purchasing data screen under Control Data, select the Returns Vendor checkbox (Figure 5.31). This indicator enables vendor returns to be carried out via the shipping process.

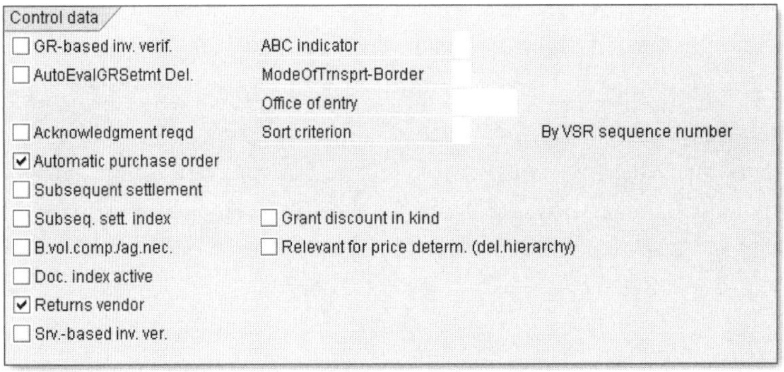

Figure 5.31 Vendor Master: Returns Vendor Setting

5.6 Summary

In this chapter, we've discussed the processes involved in inventory management including movement types, stock types, and types of returns. We've also covered some more technical topics, such as SAP system configuration for various processes. With the skills you've acquired in this chapter, you can now configure your customers' inventory management procedures so that they're perfectly tailored to the customers' requirements.

In the next chapter, we'll discuss another important process in MM: invoice verification.

This chapter explains the invoice verification process and the various business requirements involved in invoice verification such as invoice reduction, double invoice check, and subsequent debit/credit.

6   Invoice Verification

From a materials management perspective, the procurement process ends with invoice verification, which results in payments being issued to vendors by the finance and accounting department. An *invoice* is a legal document that vendors send as a record of goods supplied or services performed; it contains details including item price, taxes, freight charges, discounts, and terms of payment. Purchasing departments verify the invoice using the PO and goods receipt, and then post it. Finally, the finance and accounting department process the payment to the vendor.

Invoice verification creates an MM invoice document and a Financial Accounting invoice document (Figure 6.1). Invoice posting updates the PO history and, if materials are subjected to stock valuation, the valuation price in the material master record.

As shown in Figure 6.2, invoices can be posted in several different ways. With *manual entry*, invoices are received by mail or via a courier, and employees manually verify and enter the invoices into the system. In *EDI/XML*, invoices can be transmitted electronically in the form of intermediate documents (IDocs) via EDI or in XML format.

The system creates invoices using settlement programs that run at regular intervals for consignment, invoicing plans, and evaluated receipt settlement (ERS).

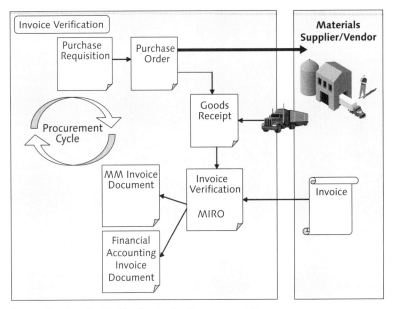

Figure 6.1   Invoice Verification in the Procurement Process

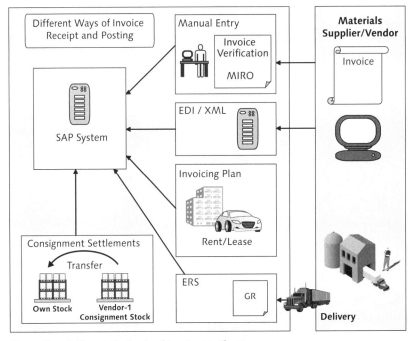

Figure 6.2   Different Methods of Invoice Verification

In this chapter, we'll be discussing various scenarios in invoice verification, including the following:

▶ PO-based invoice

▶ Goods receipt-based invoice

▶ Subsequent debit/credit

▶ Invoices for account-assigned POs (blanket PO)

▶ ERS

▶ Invoicing plans

▶ Subsequent debit/credit

▶ Credit memo and reversals

▶ Invoice verification in background

▶ Invoices with reduction

Before we proceed to discussing each of these scenarios, we'll cover the basic concepts of the invoice verification process in the SAP system.

6.1 Basics of Invoice Verification

In general, an invoice from a vendor contains a number of fields, as illustrated in Figure 6.3. Important fields are invoice number, item description, item quantity, item amount, and taxes.

```
ABC Materials Inc.        12/1, Sea Rock Road, CA
                          VAT - 99119900

Invoice Number - 100-1201     Date - 02/09/2009
Reference PO 4500000045

Item              Qty        Amount
Valve            2 pcs       50
Seal             2 pcs       20
Basic Cost                   70
Discount                     10
                             60
Tax @ 10%                    06
Fright                       05
Total                        71

Terms & Conditions:
Payment is due within 30 days.
```

Figure 6.3 Sample Invoice

As shown in Figure 6.4, invoice verification in the SAP system is carried out via Transaction MIRO. This transaction allows you to post invoices pertaining to different scenarios by simply selecting the required option from a dropdown list. In addition, incoming invoices can be directly posted with reference to a material or a G/L account. Transaction MIRO also provides various layouts that ease the invoice verification process.

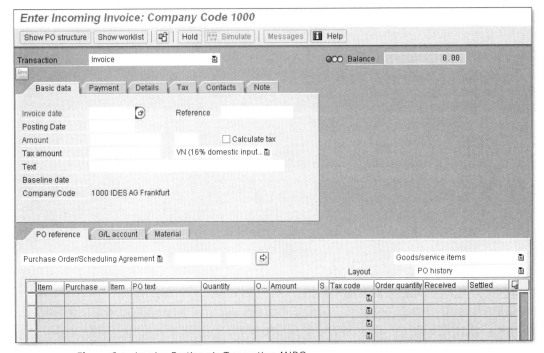

Figure 6.4 Invoice Posting via Transaction MIRO

Figure 6.4 shows a typical screen layout in Transaction MIRO. The following list is an explanation of the most important fields in this transaction:

▶ **Transaction**
In this field, you can select any one of the four options available from the dropdown list: Invoice, Credit Memo, Subsequent Debit, and Subsequent Credit. Based on the selected option, the screen layout will change.

▶ **Basic Data**
This tab contains several fields such as Invoice Date, Posting Date, and Amount. Invoice Date is the date printed on the invoice, Posting Date is the date on

which you wish to post the invoice, and Amount is the amount mentioned in the vendor invoice (this is a mandatory field). You can also enter references and tax amount in their respective fields. If you select the Calculate Tax checkbox, the system calculates tax based on the selected tax code.

▶ **PO Reference**
On this tab, from the leftmost dropdown list, you can select any option with reference to which you wish to post an incoming invoice. The options include Purchase Order/Scheduling Agreement, Delivery Note, Bill of Lading, and Service Entry Sheet.

▶ **Layout**
Also located on the PO Reference tab, you can select a layout from the Layout dropdown list. The layout plays a vital role for invoice reduction because the system will display the fields based on the layout.

▶ **Simulate**
Before posting an invoice, it's possible to check the different G/L account postings using the Simulate button.

▶ **Hold**
You select this option when you've insufficient information to post the invoice but want to save the partially-entered data. Held invoices can be posted later when entering the missing information.

▶ **Balance**
This shows the balance between the PO value and the invoice value. It's for display only.

▶ **Messages**
You click on this button to see the messages issued by the system.

After all of the required information has been supplied, an invoice can be posted. Invoice posting has the following effects:

▶ MM and Financial Accounting invoice documents are generated.

▶ Various G/L accounts are debited or credited.

▶ The PO history is updated to reflect the invoice posting.

▶ Payment can be processed to the vendor.

Now that you've learned about the basic concepts involved in invoice verification, let's move on to discussing the different types of invoice verification, starting with PO-based.

6.2 Purchase Order-Based Invoice Verification

In the PO-based invoice verification scenario, the system allows invoice posting with reference to a PO, even though goods haven't yet been delivered. The line items of the PO are copied into the invoice posting screen at the time of invoice verification. As shown in Figure 6.5, the invoice can be posted both before and after the delivery of goods.

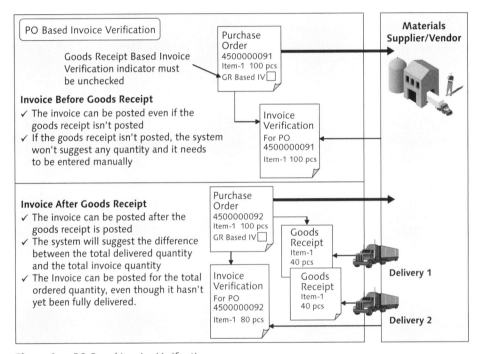

Figure 6.5 PO Based Invoice Verification

Note

The PO line item details what you can see on the Invoice tab. This includes the GR-Based Invoice Verification indicator, which should be unchecked for PO-based invoice verification

6.3   Goods Receipt-Based Invoice Verification

In this scenario, the SAP system allows you to post invoices only after the goods receipt has been posted in the system (Figure 6.6) and invoices are matched with the received quantity of a PO. For multiple deliveries, the system supplies each delivery on a separate line.

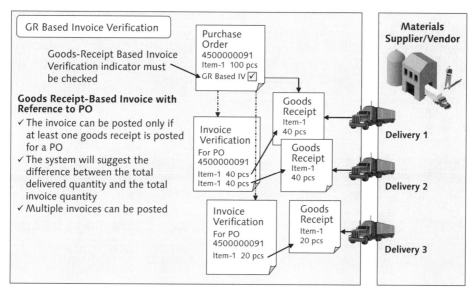

Figure 6.6   Goods Receipt-Based Invoice Verification

Note

The GR Based Invoice Verification indicator can be set in the info record. The info record setting is copied at the time of the PO creation; however, you can edit it for a particular document.

6.4   Invoices for Account-Assigned Purchase Orders

As you learned in Chapter 4, POs for materials procured for consumption are account-assigned POs. We'll now explain how to post an invoice for an account-assigned PO.

The account assignment category is used to define account assignment and can be configured via SAP IMG • MATERIALS MANAGEMENT • PURCHASING • ACCOUNT ASSIGNMENT • MAINTAIN ACCOUNT ASSIGNMENT CATEGORIES. As shown in Figure 6.7, the account assignment category controls the following.

▶ Goods receipt posting is allowed

▶ Invoice receipt posting is allowed

▶ Account assignment is changeable at the time of invoice receipt

If the Account Assignment Changeable checkbox is selected and a valuated goods receipt isn't allowed, the account assignment category defined in the PO can be changed at the time of invoice posting.

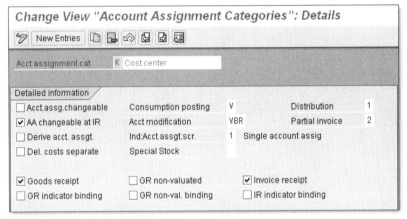

Figure 6.7 Account Assignment Category Configuration

In the following sections, we'll discuss account postings and the process steps for posting an invoice for an account-assigned PO.

6.4.1 Account Postings

As shown in Figure 6.8, if a valuated goods receipt is defined for a PO with account assignment, the consumption G/L account is debited during goods receipt. The offsetting entry is posted into the GR/IR account. Furthermore, during the invoice posting, the GR/IR account is debited and the vendor account is credited. If a price variance exists in the invoice, the difference is posted to the consumption account.

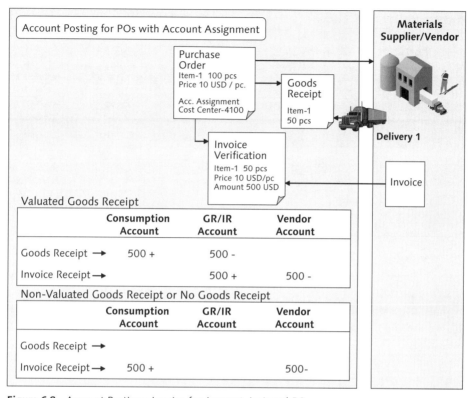

Figure 6.8 Account Postings: Invoice for Account-Assigned PO

For a non-valuated goods receipt, there isn't an account posting. The invoice posting debits the consumption account and credits the vendor account.

6.4.2 Process Steps

You can post invoices via Transaction MIRO. Enter the PO number and press Enter . As shown in Figure 6.9, two line items are supplied from the PO. The first line item is defined as a valuated goods receipt in the PO; therefore, the account assignment is in display mode only and cannot be changed. The second line item is defined as a non-valuated goods receipt in the PO and has account assignment category K (cost center, changeable). This means that the account assignment can be changed and that multiple account assignments are possible.

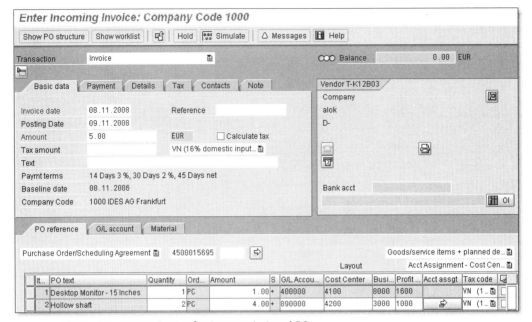

Figure 6.9 Invoice Posting for Account-Assigned PO

6.5 Invoices for Blanket Purchase Orders

Blanket POs are used to procure consumable materials or services when you don't want to create a PO each time. Blanket POs are valid for a longer period, and invoices can be directly posted for the materials and services procured. When posting an invoice for a blanket PO, the system checks for the validity date and limits that are defined in the PO. Tolerances for value limits and validity periods can also be configured in the system; if the invoice exceeds these tolerance limits, it's blocked.

To configure the tolerance limits for a blanket PO, go to SAP IMG • MATERIALS MANAGEMENT • LOGISTICS INVOICE VERIFICATION • INVOICE BLOCK • SET TOLERANCE LIMITS. In the standard system, Tolerance Key LA is defined for blanket PO value limits, and Tolerance Key LD is defined for blanket PO time limits (Figure 6.10).

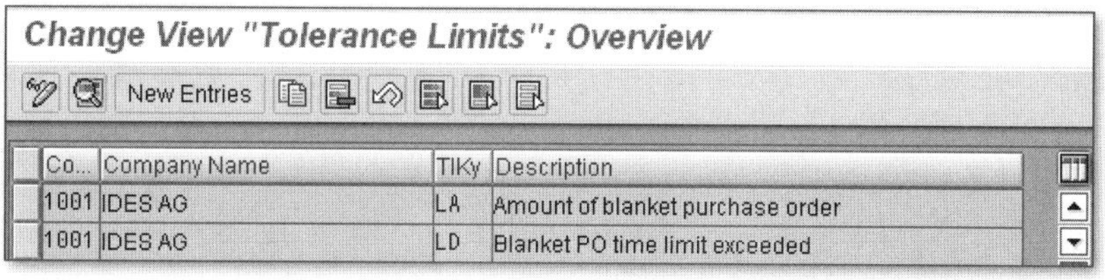

Figure 6.10 Tolerance Limits

Figure 6.11 shows an example of how you might define tolerance limits.

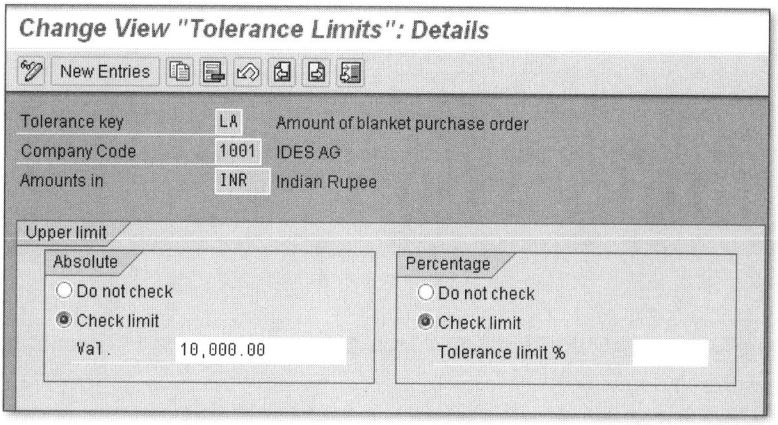

Figure 6.11 Tolerance Limits: Details

6.6   Evaluated Receipt Settlements

With the ERS scenario, the system automatically posts invoices after the goods receipt is posted in the system. This effectively reduces paperwork and data entry errors.

6.6.1   Business Scenario

Consider, for example, a car manufacturer with a vendor that delivers goods based on PO quantities and delivery schedules. The company posts the invoices based on the goods receipts, and subsequently, the vendor is paid. In this scenario, the vendor doesn't send invoices (Figure 6.12). The system uses the prices and discount conditions from the PO, and settlement information is sent to the vendor via messages generated at the time of settlement.

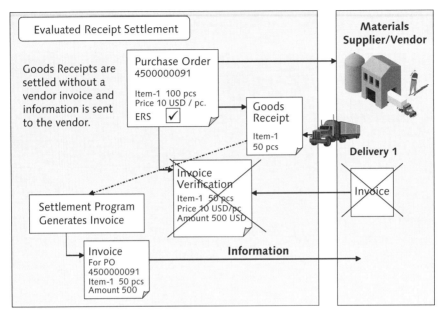

Figure 6.12 ERS Scenario

In the following sections, we'll discuss the prerequisites in the master data and process steps as they relate to ERS.

6.6.2 Prerequisites in Master Data

For the ERS functionality, you must configure certain settings in the vendor master data and in the info record. In the vendor master data, activate the ERS indicator and the GR Based Invoice Verification indicator. If the vendor is already defined, use Transaction XK02 (change vendor). If you're creating a new vendor, use Transaction XK01 (create vendor). Under Control Data in the Purchasing view, select the checkbox for GR-Based Inv. Verif. and AutoEvalGRSetmt Del., as shown in Figure 6.13.

In the info record, set the ERS indicator for a material and vendor combination and define the tax code so that it's copied at the time of PO creation. Use Transaction ME11 (create info record) and enter the material, vendor, and purchase organization. Then go to the Purchase Organization Data view, and select the GR-based IV indicator. Don't select the checkbox NO ERS. Enter the tax code (Figure 6.14).

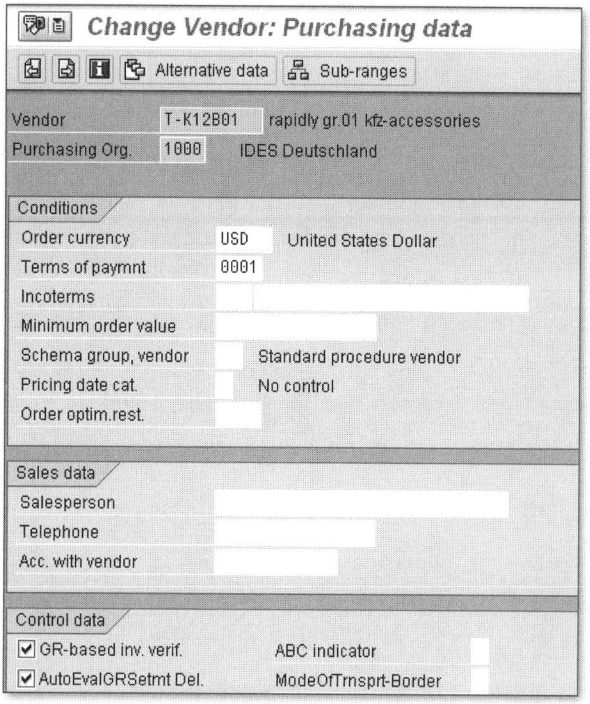

Figure 6.13 Vendor Master Data: ERS Indicator

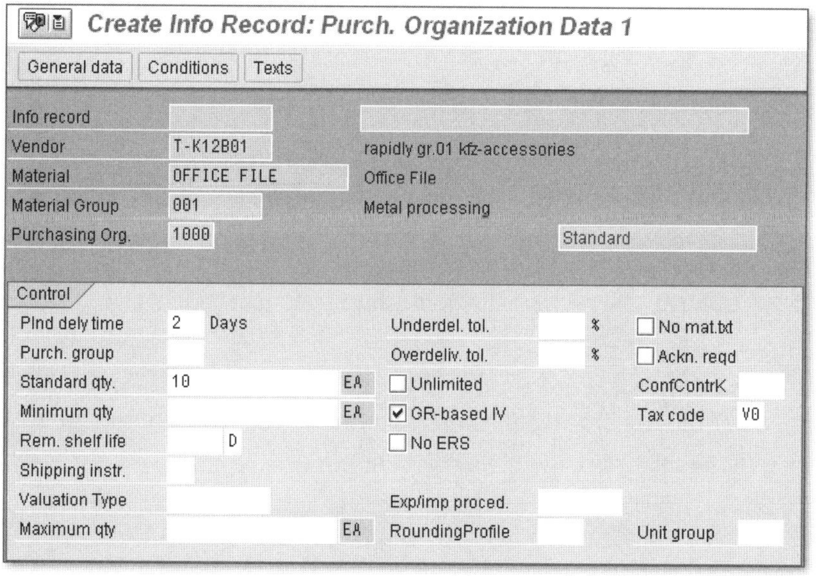

Figure 6.14 Purchasing Info Record: ERS Indicator

6.6.3 Process Steps

For an ERS scenario, follow these process steps:

1. **Create the PO.**
   Go to Transaction ME21N and enter the vendor, company code, purchasing organization, purchase group, material, quantity, and delivery date. Check the GR-Based IV and ERS indicators on the Invoice tab of the item details, as shown in Figure 6.15.

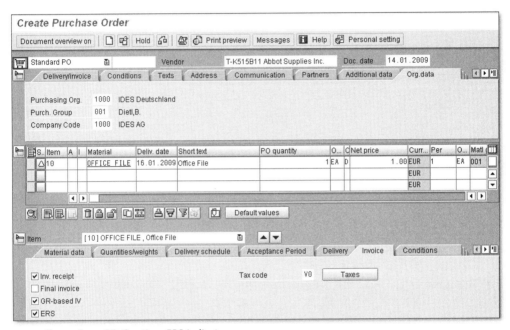

Figure 6.15 PO Creation: ERS Indicator

2. **Post the goods receipt.**
   Go to Transaction MIGO and post the goods receipt for the PO.

3. **Execute the settlement program for ERS.**
   Go to Transaction MRRL and enter the company code, plant, and vendor (Figure 6.16). Select the Document Selection from the Processing Options and execute. The system will create the invoice document.

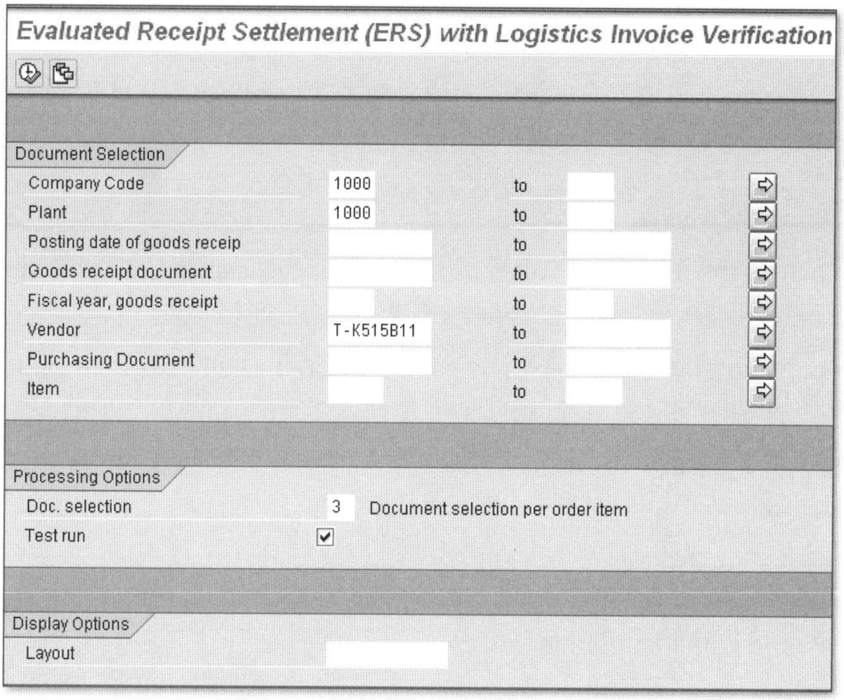

Figure 6.16 ERS Execution via Transaction MRRL

Invoices can be generated with the following options:

▶ One invoice document per vendor

▶ One invoice document per PO

▶ One invoice document per PO item

▶ One invoice document per delivery document/service entry sheet

> **Note**
>
> To create invoices automatically, you can define ERS as a batch job. Schedule the batch job with the program name RMMR1MRS and the required variant. The system will automatically pick up the deliveries due to ERS and post the invoices.

6.7 Invoicing Plans

An *invoicing plan* consists of a series of invoicing dates and values and involves invoices that are automatically posted by the system.

6.7.1 Business Scenario

For example, an enterprise that wants to automatically generate invoices for the monthly office rent might use an invoicing plan.

An invoicing plan is defined in the PO for repetitive procurement transactions such as rental, leasing, or service agreements. There are two types of invoicing plans:

▶ Periodic invoicing plan

▶ Partial invoicing plan

We'll discuss both invoicing plans in detail.

6.7.2 Periodic Invoicing Plan

Periodic invoicing plans are used for repetitive procurement transactions such as building rent (Figure 6.17). In these plans, the total value of the PO is invoiced on each due date.

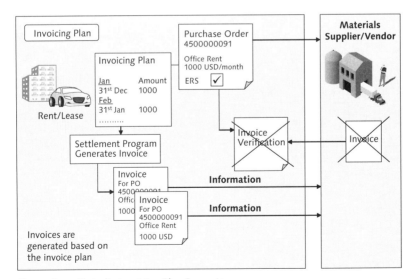

Figure 6.17 Periodic Invoicing Plan Scenario

6.7.3   Partial Invoicing Plan

Partial invoicing plans are used for transactions involving invoicing in stages. For example, construction projects use partial invoicing plans, where the total value of the project is invoiced and paid in partial increments throughout the life of the project. If a model invoicing plan is defined in the system, invoice due dates are automatically supplied. Otherwise, the due dates have to be defined manually in the PO.

The total value of a PO can be split among due dates on either a percentage or absolute value basis. Figure 6.18 shows the construction project example. In the PO, the partial invoicing plan is defined based on the completion of each stage of the project.

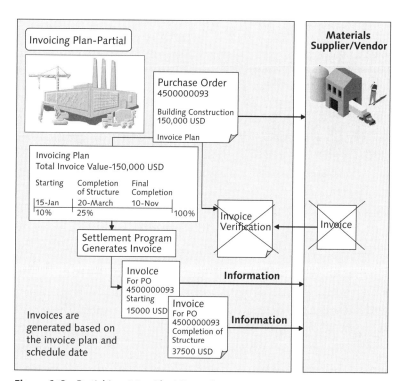

Figure 6.18   Partial Invoicing Plant Scenario

In the following sections, we'll discuss the customization options available and the process steps involved in invoicing plans.

6.7.4 Customization

Invoicing plan types can be customized to control how the system creates the invoicing schedule.

Maintain Periodic Invoicing Plan Types

To maintain partial invoicing plan types, go to SAP IMG • MATERIALS MANAGEMENT • PURCHASING • PURCHASE ORDER • INVOICING PLAN • INVOICING PLAN TYPES • MAINTAIN PERIODIC INVOICING PLAN TYPES. In this step, you define the periodic invoicing plan types by specifying the relevant control data (Figure 6.19). Enter the Starting Date, End Date, and Horizon in the Origin of General Data section. In the Invoice Data: Suggestion for Dates section, select the periodic invoice date to determine the next billing date.

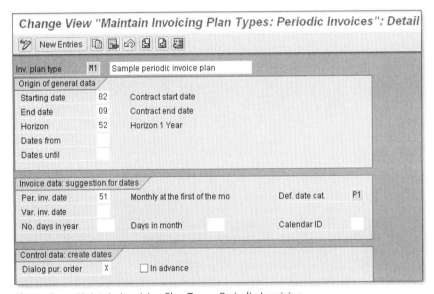

Figure 6.19 Maintain Invoicing Plan Types: Periodic Invoicing

Maintain Partial Invoicing Plan Types

To maintain partial invoicing plan types, go to SAP IMG • MATERIALS MANAGEMENT • PURCHASING • PURCHASE ORDER • INVOICING PLAN • INVOICING PLAN TYPES • MAINTAIN PARTIAL INVOICING PLAN TYPES. In this step, you define the partial invoicing plan types by specifying the relevant control data (Figure 6.20).

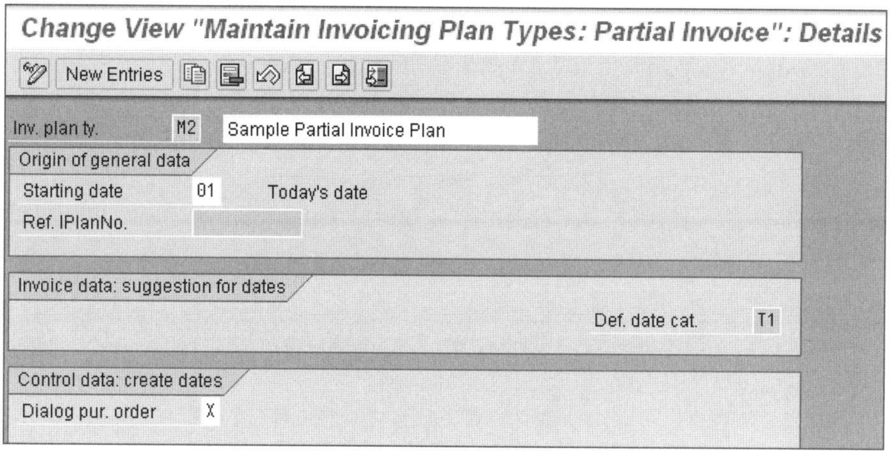

Figure 6.20 Maintain Invoicing Plan Types: Partial Invoices

Maintain Date IDs

To define date IDs, go to SAP IMG • MATERIALS MANAGEMENT • PURCHASING • PURCHASE ORDER • INVOICING PLAN • MAINTAIN DATE IDs. In this step, you can define the Date Description as shown in Figure 6.21.

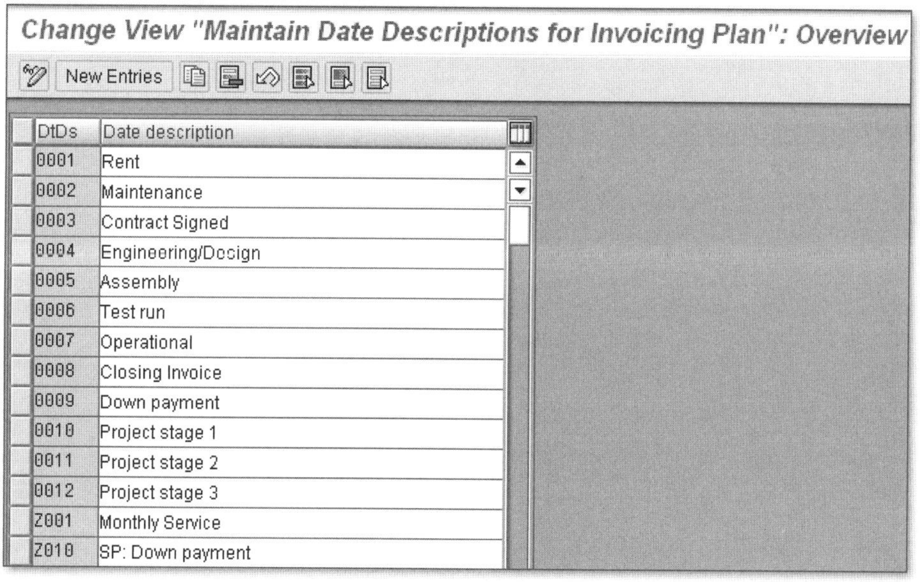

Figure 6.21 Maintain Date IDs

Maintain Date Category for Invoicing Plan Type

To define a date category, go to SAP IMG • Materials Management • Purchasing • Purchase Order • Invoicing Plan • Date Categories • Maintain Date Category for Invoicing Plan Type. In this step, you can assign one or more date categories to each invoicing plan type (Figure 6.22). Enter the Date Category and select the Date Description and Calculation Rule, which defines how the billed value is determined.

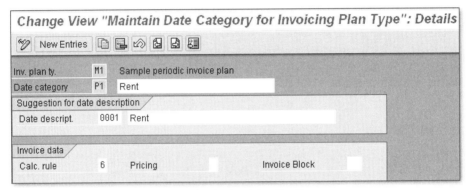

Figure 6.22 Maintain a Date Category for the Invoicing Plan Type

Define Default Date Category for Invoicing Plan Type

To define a default date category, go to SAP IMG • Materials Management • Purchasing • Purchase Order • Invoicing Plan • Date Categories • Define Default Date Category for Invoicing Plan Type. In this step, you can define a Date Category as the default value for each Invoicing Plan Type (Figure 6.23).

Inv. pl. ty.	Invoicing plan type	DD	Date category
M1	Sample periodic invoice plan	P1	Rent
M2	Sample Partial Invoice Plan	T1	Percentage partial invoice
MM		P1	Rent
PR		P1	Rent
TR		T1	Percentage partial invoice

Figure 6.23 Assign a Date Proposal Category to the Invoicing Plan

Maintain Date Proposal for Partial Invoicing Plans

To maintain date proposals for partial invoicing plans, go to SAP IMG • MATERIALS MANAGEMENT • PURCHASING • PURCHASE ORDER • INVOICING PLAN • MAINTAIN DATE PROPOSAL FOR PARTIAL INVOICING PLANS (Figure 6.24).

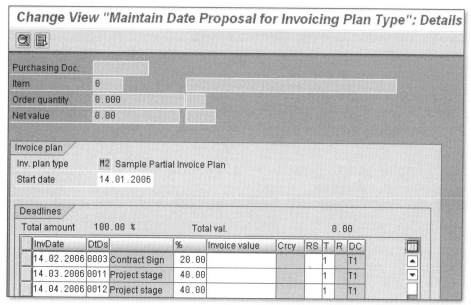

Figure 6.24 Maintain Date Proposals for the Invoicing Plan Type

6.7.5 Process Steps

Follow these process steps to use invoicing plans:

1. **Create a PO.**
   Create a PO via Transaction ME21N. Document type FO (framework order) is used for POs with invoicing plans. Select the account assignment category and the cost object (such as cost center) for account assignment category K (Figure 6.25). If you want to select the GR indicator in the PO, you must select the non-valuated goods receipt indicator as well.

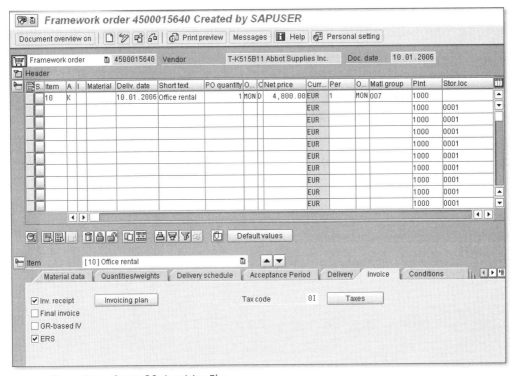

Figure 6.25 Create PO: Invoicing Plan

Invoicing plan functionality doesn't work with valuated goods receipts.

Click on the Invoicing Plan button located on the Invoice tab of the item details, and select the invoicing plan type. The system will propose the invoice schedules from the template created in customizing.

2. **Execute the invoicing plan settlement.**
   Go to Transaction MRIS (invoicing plan settlement), enter the Company Code, Plant, and Vendor, and Execute. The system will generate the invoices. You can check the invoice status on the Invoicing Plan tab of the PO. Billing Status C stands for completely processed.

To create invoices automatically, you can define invoicing plan settlement via a batch job. Schedule the batch job with the program name RMMR1MIS and the required variant. The system will automatically pick up the items due for billing from the PO invoicing plan.

6.8   Subsequent Debit/Credit

Subsequent debit or credit happens when an invoice or credit memo is received from a vendor after the invoice for a particular PO has already been posted.

6.8.1   Business Scenario

Consider, for example, that a business receives invoices or credit memos for a PO that has already been invoiced. Additional invoices are sent by a vendor because the original invoices contained prices that were too low. Similarly, credit memos may be sent by a vendor if the original invoice contained prices that were too high.

The SAP system provides subsequent debit or credit functionality to handle situations where invoices or credit memos are received from a vendor after posting an invoice for a particular PO. Subsequent debits and credits are posted with reference to a PO, which changes the PO value but doesn't affect the total quantity. Subsequent debit or credit may be posted for a PO item only if the invoice has already been posted and the PO history is updated.

In the following sections, we'll discuss the account postings and process steps involved in invoice verification for subsequent debit/credit.

6.8.2   Account Postings

Subsequent debit and credit transactions update the G/L account based on different scenarios.

For stock materials with price control V (moving average price), the subsequent debit/credit amount is posted to the vendor and GR/IR account. Figure 6.26 shows an example of an account posting for a subsequent debit transaction. A PO is issued for 10 pieces of material Mat-1 with a price of $10 per piece. After the goods receipt and invoice receipt are posted for a total quantity of 10 pieces with an amount of $100, the vendor realizes that the amount charged is less by $20 and sends another invoice for $20. A subsequent debit is posted for an amount of $20 for 10 pieces of material. Different transactions involved in the entire process will update the G/L accounts as follows:

▶ Goods receipt: stock account (+) 100, GR/IR account (-) 100

▶ Invoice receipt: GR/IR account (+) 100, vendor account (-) 100

▶ Subsequent debit: stock account (+) 20, vendor account (-) 20

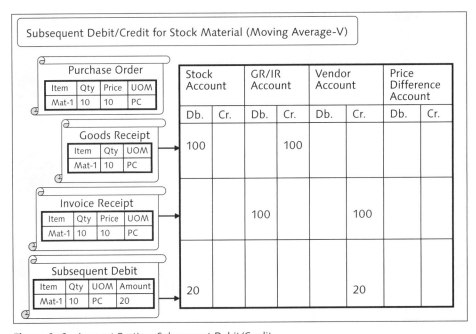

Figure 6.26 Account Posting: Subsequent Debit/Credit

In the following scenarios, the account posting may differ:

▶ **Stock material with price control "S" (standard price)**
For stock material with price control S (standard price), the subsequent debit/credit amount is posted to the vendor account and the price difference account.

▶ **Consumable materials (account-assigned POs)**

For account-assigned POs (which are used for consumable materials), subsequent debit/credit transactions update the vendor account and post the offsetting entry to the cost account.

▶ **Subsequent debit/credit before the goods are delivered**

For situations where there is a subsequent debit/credit transaction before the goods are delivered (i.e., before the goods receipt transaction), the vendor and GR/IR accounts are posted. At the time of the goods receipt, the stock account or price difference account will be posted, depending on the price control of the material master data.

Now that we've gone through the subsequent debit/credit business scenario and various account postings, let's next go through the process steps.

6.8.3   Process Steps

Subsequent debit/credit is posted via Transaction MIRO. Select Subsequent Debit or Subsequent Credit in the Transaction Field, as shown in Figure 6.27. After you enter the PO number, the system will supply the material and quantity. Enter the amount and save. The PO history will be updated.

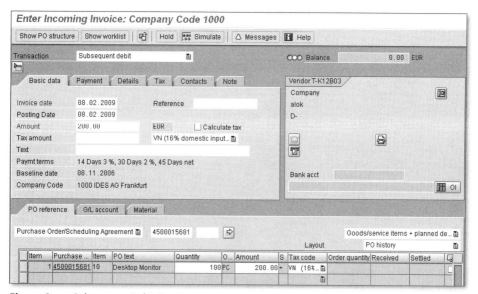

Figure 6.27   Subsequent Debit Posting via Transaction MIRO

6.9 Credit Memos and Reversals

Credit memos are used to adjust amounts owed to a vendor. Credit memos are different from subsequent debits/credits, which don't change the invoiced quantity but only post the amounts. Credit memos, on the other hand, are used when the invoice is posted for more than the received quantity. With a credit memo, the invoiced quantity is updated.

6.9.1 Business Scenario

Consider, for example, a situation where a vendor has sent your company an invoice for more quantity of material than was delivered, and this invoice is posted to the system.

In this scenario, a vendor credit memo is posted with reference to the PO for the excess quantity (Figure 6.28). The credit memo updates the G/L accounts and PO history.

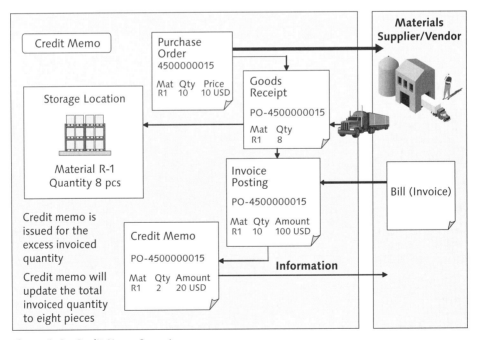

Figure 6.28 Credit Memo Scenario

> **Note**
>
> Subsequent credit/debit is used when a vendor has charged you at a too high or too low price respectively. If a vendor has charged you for a greater quantity, this is settled with a credit memo.

Credit memos are also used in cases of reversal (cancellation) of an invoice. In the SAP system, cancelling an invoice isn't possible but it can be reversed by posting a credit memo. Credit memos will update the same G/L accounts (with opposite debit/credit entries) that were posted with the invoice.

Let's move on to learning how to post a credit memo in the system.

6.9.2 Process Steps

Credit memos are posted via Transaction code MIRO. Select Credit Memo in the Transaction field and enter the PO number and Posting Date (Figure 6.29). The system will propose the total invoiced quantity and amount from the PO. With partial reversals, you can change the quantity and amount.

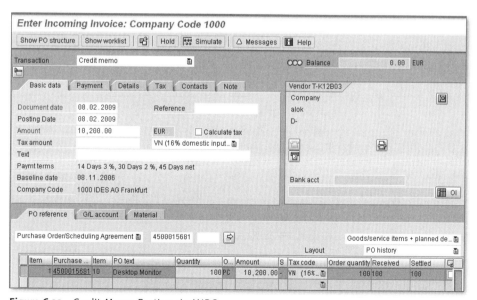

Figure 6.29 Credit Memo Posting via MIRO

6.10 Invoice Verification in Background Processing

When you post an invoice, the system compares the invoice amount with the PO value. For large invoices with hundreds of line items, this process can take a long time. Thus, to save time, large invoices can be processed via *background processing*.

6.10.1 Business Scenario

Consider an example of a business involved in car manufacturing. The business receives an invoice from a vendor and posts it online via Transaction MIRO. However, sometimes the business receives large invoices that contain several line items and due to time limitations and large workloads, it becomes difficult to post the invoices online via Transaction MIRO. These invoices can be posted via invoice verification in the background.

For invoice verification in background processing, enter the general invoice data such as invoice amount, tax information, dates, PO number, and so on. This data is saved in the invoice document. Item data isn't entered manually, but is instead created by the settlement program. The system checks the total quantity and amount that should be invoiced from the PO, with the amount and tax data entered.

If the total balance amount is zero or within tolerance limits, the SAP system posts the invoice document in the background. If the balance exceeds the tolerance limits, the invoice document and the items created are saved and must be processed later. Settlement program RMBABG00 is used for background processing. This program can be scheduled in the batch job.

Next, you'll learn how to post invoices through the invoice verification in background functionality.

6.10.2 Process Steps

1. **Enter the invoice via Transaction MIRA.**
   Enter the invoice via Transaction MIRA, as shown in Figure 6.30. Enter the Invoice Date, Posting Date, Amount, tax details, and PO number. Upon saving, the system will generate an invoice document number.

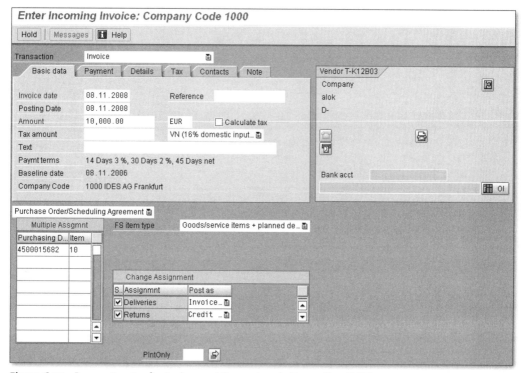

Figure 6.30 Process Invoice for Background Processing via Transaction MIRA

2. **Execute the settlement program to post the invoice in the background.**
   Execute program RMBABG00 via Transaction SA38. Enter the Company Code, as shown in Figure 6.31, and execute the transaction. You will receive a report of results, as shown in Figure 6.32.

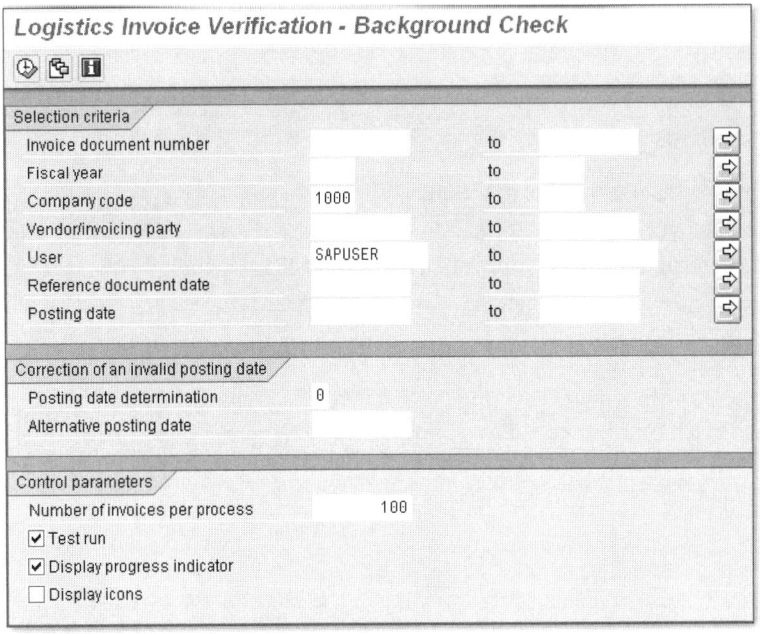

Figure 6.31 Invoice Verification in Background Processing

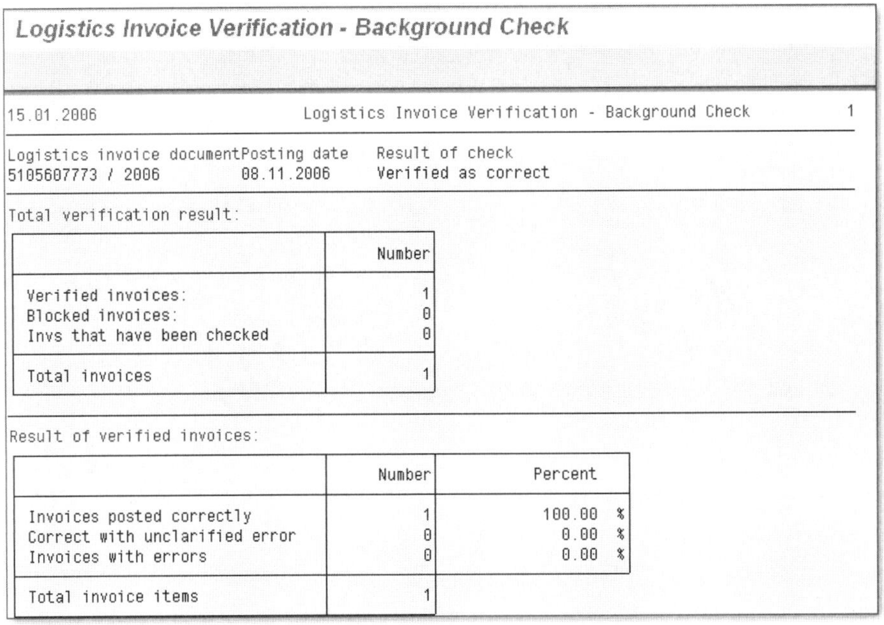

Figure 6.32 Results of Invoice Verification in Background Processing

The results report for background processing will also show the error log for an invoice document that contained errors. Invoices with error statuses need to be changed manually. They can then be posted manually, or marked for another background processing job.

6.11 Invoice Reductions

In cases where the amount of an invoice has been reduced, the invoice can be posted with this reduced amount. The system handles this by generating a credit memo.

6.11.1 Business Scenario

Consider, for example, a manufacturing enterprise that has a procedure to post invoices for delivered materials and their quantities. Sometimes, however, due to a vendor error, the enterprise receives invoices for both delivered quantities and pending delivery quantities. During the invoice posting, the company wants to reduce the invoice amount so that it doesn't include the undelivered quantity.

The SAP system functionality for invoice posting with reduction allows you to post invoices that contain a greater quantity/value due to a vendor error. While posting the invoice, you can reduce the quantity or value. In this case, the system creates two accounting documents: the first document contains the actual quantities and value, and the second document contains a credit memo for the difference between the actual invoiced quantities/values and the system-suggested quantities/values.

Take a look at Figure 6.33. In this example, the PO is issued to the vendor for 100 pieces of material Mat-1 at $10 per piece. The vendor delivers only part of the order, 60 pieces, and the goods receipt is posted in the system. However, you then receive an invoice from the vendor for the entire 100 pieces instead of the delivered 60. Naturally, you don't want to pay for the undelivered quantity; therefore, you post an invoice with the reduction functionality. When posting the invoice, the system will propose a quantity of 60 pieces and a value of $600. You can enter the quantity and amount specified in the vendor invoice in the Vendor Quantity and Vendor Amount fields, respectively.

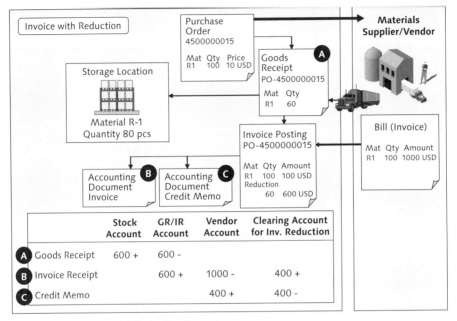

Figure 6.33 Invoice with Reduction Scenario

With the invoice reduction functionality, you don't actually reduce the invoice. Instead, you post an invoice for the actual quantities and values specified in the vendor invoice, and the system posts a credit memo for the amount that needs to be reduced.

The sections that follow discuss the account postings and process steps involved in invoice reductions.

6.11.2 Account Posting

In an invoice reduction, the system creates an invoice and credit memo, which means that two accounting documents will be created. An example of an account posting is shown in Figure 6.33.

6.11.3 Process Steps

1. **Create a PO.**
   Create a PO for the vendor via Transaction ME21N. In our example, you would create a PO for 100 pieces at $10 a piece.

2. **Post the goods receipt.**

   Suppose that the vendor has delivered a partial quantity. Post the goods receipt for the partial quantity via Transaction MIGO. In our example, you would post a goods receipt for 60 pieces.

3. **Post the invoice with reduction.**

   Once again using our example, suppose you've received an invoice for 100 pieces for a total amount of $1,000, instead of for 60 pieces and an amount of $600. Post an invoice with reduction via Transaction MIRO. Then, enter the PO number and select Invoice Reduction in the Layout field. The system will propose the quantity and amount due, as shown in Figure 6.34. In the Invoice Posting screen, you also see two fields called Invoice Qty Acc. to Vendor, and Invoice Amount Acc. to Vendor, respectively. These fields are there to enter the amount and quantity specified in the vendor invoice.

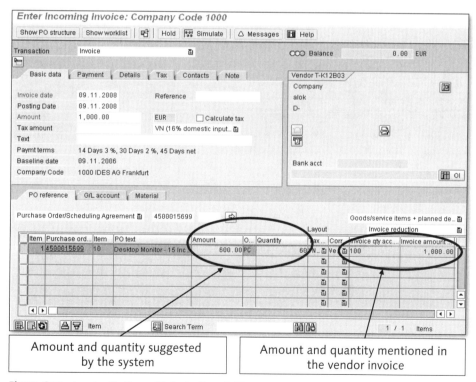

Figure 6.34 Invoice Posting with Reduction via Transaction MIRO

You can view the accounting documents from the Display Invoice Document screen by clicking the Follow-On Documents button. The system has created two accounting documents (as shown in Figure 6.35): one for the invoice and one for the credit memo.

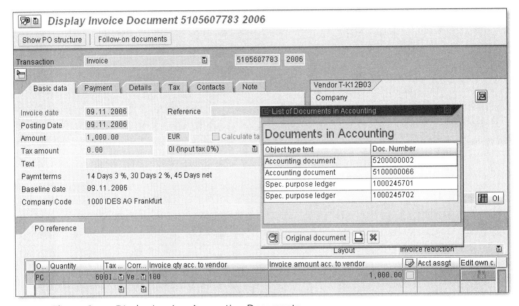

Figure 6.35 Display Invoice: Accounting Documents

6.12 Invoices with Variances

For a particular purchase, the total amount on the vendor invoice and the total amount suggested in the system may have a variance, meaning that their values are different from one another. This may happen due to a price difference in any one or more line items. For invoices with more than 100 line items, it becomes very tedious to find those that are causing the difference. Let's discuss the business scenario and process steps of how the SAP system deals with such scenario.

6.12.1   Business Scenario

Consider a manufacturing business that has a vendor responsible for supplying many of its materials (several components). Most of the time, the POs contain as many as 200 line items, and sometimes, the vendor invoice total amount and the system-suggested total amount don't match. In such a scenario, it becomes cumbersome and time-consuming to identify the line item or items responsible for the variance. Therefore, the enterprise posts an invoice reduction without reference to a specific item. This scenario is called *total-based invoice reduction*. The business also has another requirement, where in the event of a small difference, the system should accept the vendor invoice and post the difference into a small differences account.

There are two ways to do this:

▶ Total-based invoice reduction
▶ Total-based invoice acceptance

We'll now look at the account postings in both scenarios.

6.12.2   Account Posting

The G/L account posting will vary for these scenarios; thus, we'll discuss how the G/L account postings will be carried out in each scenario.

Account Posting in the Total-Based Invoice Reduction Scenario

In total-based invoice reduction, the system creates two accounting documents; the first contains the invoice posting and the second contains a credit memo for the difference amount. Figure 6.36 shows an example of this. In this figure, you can see that the vendor invoice contains 100 line items and has a total amount of $100,480. However, while posting this invoice, the system supplies a total amount of $100,470. This is a variance of $10. Because there are 100 line items on the invoice, it's time-consuming to identify the line item responsible for the difference; therefore, the invoice should be posted using the total-based reduction functionality. Figure 6.36 also shows the account postings for total-based reductions.

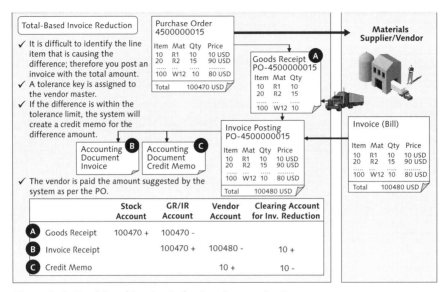

Figure 6.36 Total Based Invoice Reduction: Account Posting

Account Posting in Total-Based Invoice Acceptance Scenario

In total-based invoice acceptance, the system posts the difference amount into a non-operating expense or revenue account, as shown in Figure 6.37.

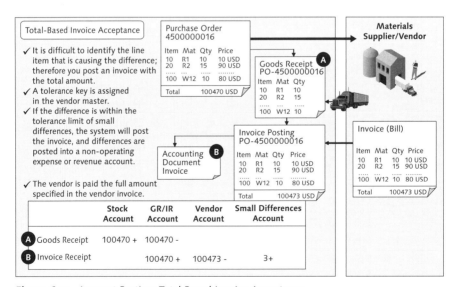

Figure 6.37 Account Posting: Total Based Invoice Acceptance

In total-based invoice reduction, the system posts the difference to a clearing account and generates a credit memo in a second document to clear this difference. In acceptance-based invoice reduction, the system automatically generates a difference line in an income or expense account.

Let's now take a look at how to post invoices with total-based reduction and total-based acceptance.

6.12.3 Process Steps

The process steps in total-based reduction and total-based acceptance are similar to the standard invoice verification process. Post an invoice via Transaction MIRO, and enter the invoice amount and PO number. The system will show the difference in the Balance field, and, if this difference is within the tolerance limits, the status will be green.

The system decides whether to proceed with total-based reduction or total-based acceptance by checking the relative tolerance differences. If an invoice difference is within acceptable limits (per the tolerance limit defined in the system), the invoice is posted using the total-based acceptance scenario. If the invoice difference is outside of these limits, the system checks the difference limits for total-based reductions. If the difference is within these limits, the system posts the invoice with total-based reduction. If, however, the difference exceeds these limits, the invoice cannot be posted with the difference amount. We'll discuss the setting of tolerance limits in the next section.

6.12.4 Configuration Steps

Follow these process steps for total- and acceptance-based invoice reductions:

4. **Define vendor-specific tolerances.**
   During configuration, you can create tolerance groups for each company code, which are then assigned to each vendor in the vendor master record. It's possible to define tolerances for both total-based acceptance and total-based invoice reduction. To do this, go to SAP IMG • MATERIALS MANAGEMENT • LOGISTICS INVOICE VERIFICATION • INCOMING INVOICE • CONFIGURE VENDOR-SPECIFIC TOLERANCES.

Enter the small difference limits for positive differences and negative differences, as shown in Figure 6.38. You can enter both absolute value limits and percentage limits. These limits are for total-based invoice acceptance. The last section in the screen is for Automatic Invoice Reduction (total-based invoice reduction) limit values.

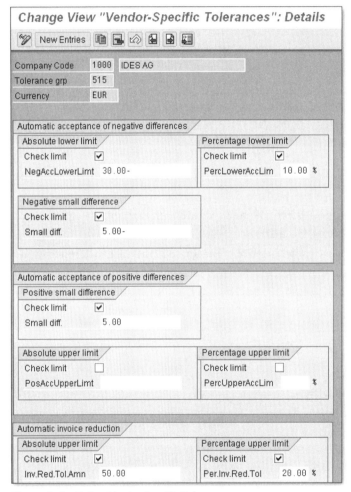

Figure 6.38 Define Vendor Specific Tolerances

5. **Assign tolerance groups in the vendor master record.**

Assign tolerance groups in the vendor master record via Transaction XK02. Go to the Payment Transaction view, and, in the Invoice Verification section, enter the Tolerance Group, as shown in Figure 6.39.

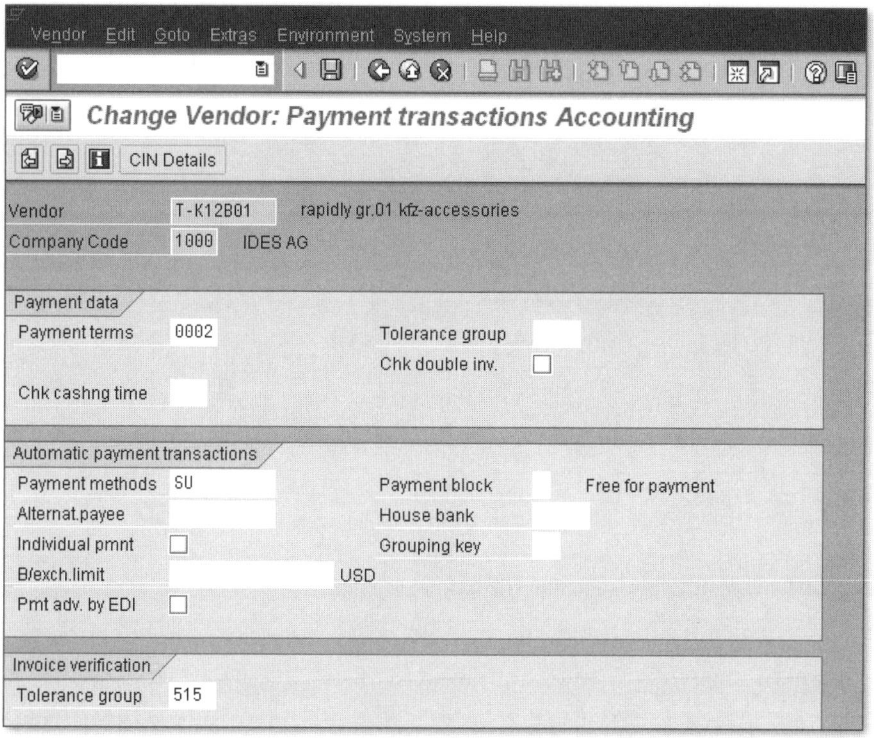

Figure 6.39 Assign a Tolerance Group in the Vendor Master Record

6.13   Taxes in Invoice Verification

Most invoices are taxable. This means that you need to verify that taxes can be entered for value-added tax (VAT) amounts, and according to a different tax procedure. During the purchase and sale of goods, taxes are calculated and paid to the vendor or charged to customers, respectively, as shown in Figure 6.40. For VAT, the tax is calculated on the difference between the purchase and sales price. The tax amounts collected from customers are paid to tax authorities.

In the following sections, we'll discuss the information you need to correctly handle taxes during invoice verification.

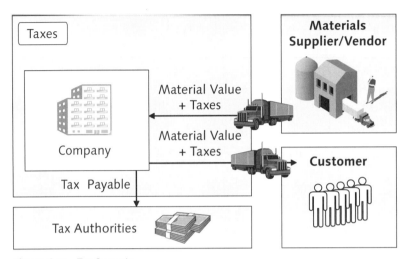

Figure 6.40 Tax Scenario

6.13.1 Entering Tax Data in an Invoice

When posting an invoice in the system, you can select the tax code and enter the tax amount. Alternatively, if you want the system to calculate the tax amount, you can select the Calculate Tax checkbox in the invoice transaction screen, as shown in Figure 6.41. The system calculates the tax based on the tax code defined for each line item. Tax codes are configured in the system for various types of taxes.

6.13.2 Configuration

Tax codes and tax procedures are configured by the person responsible for financial accounting. The SAP system also provides an option to link to an external tax calculation system, such as Taxware, which many customers find helpful.

MM allows you to maintain default values for tax codes. To do so, go to SAP IMG • MATERIALS MANAGEMENT • LOGISTICS INVOICE VERIFICATION • INCOMING INVOICE • MAINTAIN DEFAULT VALUES FOR TAX CODES. In this step, you can define the default tax codes for each company code. Click on the New Entries button and enter the company code, the default tax code, and the default tax code for unplanned delivery costs (Figure 6.42).

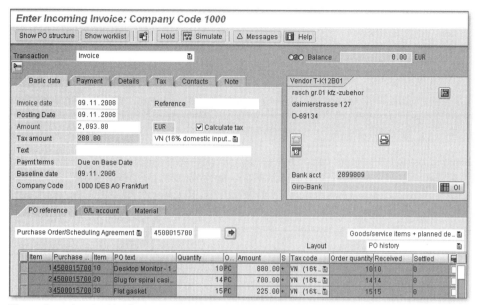

Figure 6.41 Invoice Verification via Transaction MIRO – Tax Entry

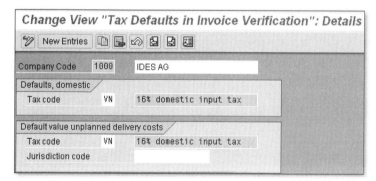

Figure 6.42 Maintain Default Tax Codes

6.14 Discounts in Invoice Verification

You may have a scenario where a vendor offers you discounts based on payment settlement dates. For example, the vendor may tell you that if you make payment within 10 days from the date of invoice, you get a discount of 5%; if you make payment within 15 days, you get a discount of 2%; and after 15 days, you don't get a discount. Such scenarios can be managed via the Payment tab in the SAP system.

You can define the payment terms in configuration, and these payment terms can be selected in the PO. When posting an invoice, the system copies the payment terms from the PO.

During invoice verification, you can enter the payment terms of fixed cash discount amounts, as shown in Figure 6.43. The Payment tab displays the payment terms that are supplied from the PO, which can be changed here.

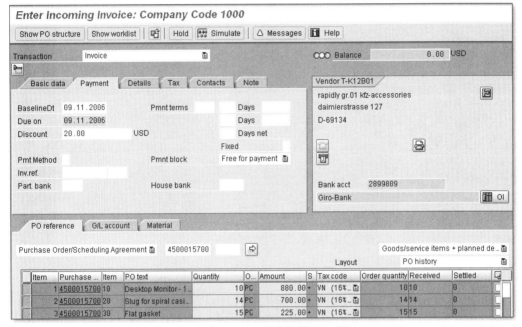

Figure 6.43 Invoice Posting via Transaction MIRO: Discount Entry

6.14.1 Account Postings

Cash discounts can be posted via either gross posting or net posting. We'll discuss both ways of posting in detail.

Gross Posting

In gross posting, the system ignores the cash discount amount at the time of the invoice posting and posts the cash discount amount into the cash discount G/L account at the time of payment. In this scenario, the cash discount amount isn't credited into stock accounts or cost accounts. Figure 6.44 shows an illustration of the gross-posting scenario.

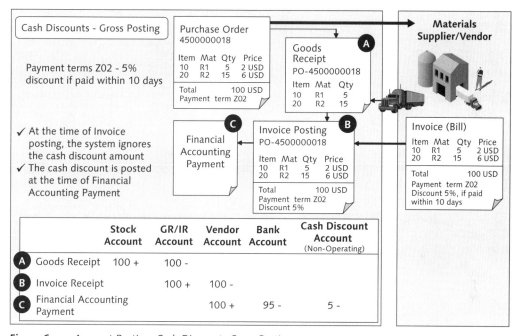

Figure 6.44 Account Posting: Cash Discounts Gross Posting

Net Posting

In net posting, the system posts the cash discount amount to the cash discount clearing account at the time of the invoice posting and the cash discount clearing G/L account is cleared at the time of payment. Figure 6.45 shows an illustration of the net posting scenario.

You can define whether postings should be gross or net for each document type in Customizing.

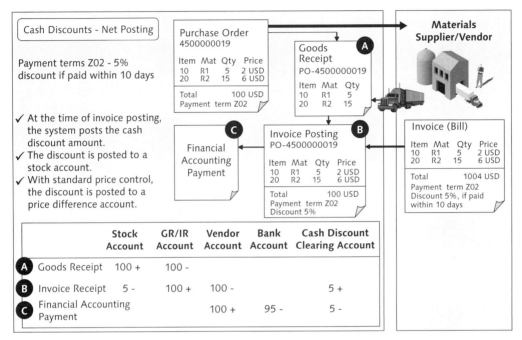

Figure 6.45 Account Posting: Cash Discounts Net Posting

6.14.2 Configuration of Gross/Net Posting

To configure gross or net posting for a document type, go to SAP IMG • Financial Accounting • Accounts Receivable and Accounts Payable • Business Transactions • Incoming Invoices/Credit Memos • Carry Out and Check Document Settings • Define Document Types. You will see a list of document types. Select the document type for invoice verification, and click on the Details button. If you want net posting, select the Net Document Type checkbox in the Control Data section. If you want gross posting, leave this checkbox blank (Figure 6.46).

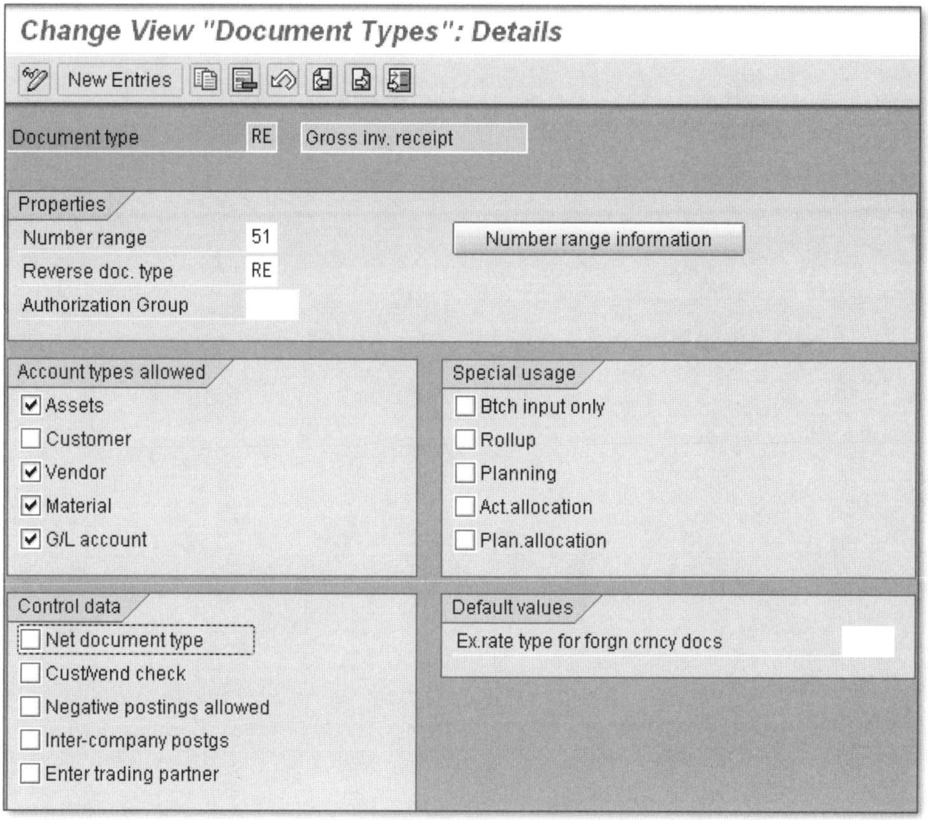

Figure 6.46 Document Type: Gross or Net Posting Configuration

6.14.3 Configuration of Payment Terms

To configure payment terms, go to SAP IMG • Financial Accounting • Accounts Receivable and Accounts Payable • Business Transactions • Incoming Invoices/ Credit Memos • Maintain Terms of Payment. You will see a list of payment terms defined by SAP (Figure 6.47). Here, you can change existing payment terms or define new payment terms.

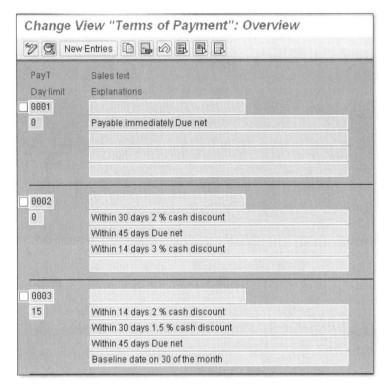

Figure 6.47 Defining Payment Terms

6.15 Invoice Blocking

After vendor invoices are verified and posted into the system, the finance department makes the payment to the vendor. However, there may be a scenario where you want to block the invoice for payment processing for a specific reason, such as quantity or price variance.

6.15.1 Business Scenario

For example, imagine a situation where an enterprise receives invoices for a higher amount than expected. As a result, the company wants to block the invoices for payment processing until the differences are resolved with the vendor. Invoices can be blocked manually or automatically due to a variety of different variance types, as follows:

- Blocking due to a quantity variance
- Blocking due to a price variance
- Blocking due to a quality inspection
- Blocking due to an amount
- Stochastic blocking

The SAP system allows you to define tolerance limits for each variance type. When posting an invoice, the system checks for different variances, and, if the variance is more than the tolerance limit, the system will automatically block the invoice for payment. Figure 6.48 shows an example of invoice blocking in the case of a price variance. The blocking reason is filled in the vendor line item in the Financial Accounting document. You can also select the blocking reason manually.

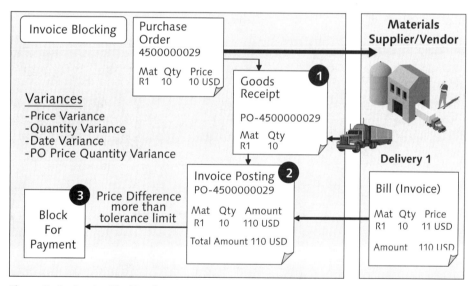

Figure 6.48 Invoice Blocking Scenario

Payment won't be released when invoices are blocked for payment. When the variances are resolved, you must indicate this by releasing the invoice for payment processing (discussed later in this section).

In the following sections, we'll discuss the most important variance types.

6.15.2 Quantity Variance

A quantity variance occurs if the invoice quantity is more than the goods receipt quantity. Invoices that are blocked because of a quantity variance can be released when you receive the balance quantity of the goods. Figure 6.49 shows a quantity variance example. A PO for 10 pieces of material R1 at $10/piece is issued to the vendor. However, the vendor delivers only 8 pieces of material R1. After the goods receipt, you receive an invoice for 10 pieces, and the invoiced quantity is more than the goods receipt quantity. This invoice can be blocked due to quantity variance. After some time, you receive the balance quantity and post another goods receipt. Now, the variance no longer exists and the invoice can be released for payment. All three documents (the goods receipt for 8 pieces, the invoice receipt for 10 pieces, and the goods receipt for 2 pieces) create accounting documents and post to different G/L accounts. Figure 6.49 shows the account postings for a quantity variance.

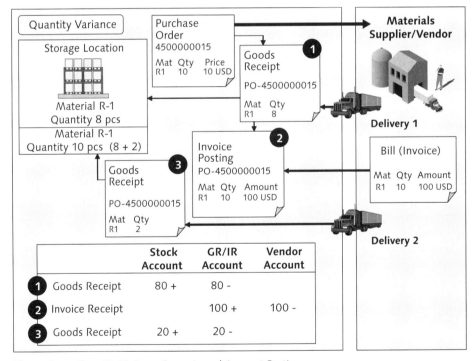

Figure 6.49 Quantity Variance Scenario and Account Posting

6.15.3 Price Variance

A price variance occurs if the invoice price is more than the PO price of an item. Figure 6.50 shows a price variance example. A PO for 10 pieces of material R1 at $10/piece is issued to the vendor. Goods are received against the PO, but the invoice received from the vendor has a price of $11/piece. In this case, the invoice should be blocked until the price variance is resolved.

The account postings for a price variance depend on the price control defined in material master record, and can be either posted with a standard price, or posted with a moving average price.

Account Posting

Figure 6.50 shows the account postings for standard price valuation. The price difference amount is posted to the price difference G/L account. In this case, the standard price, as defined in the material master, cannot be changed.

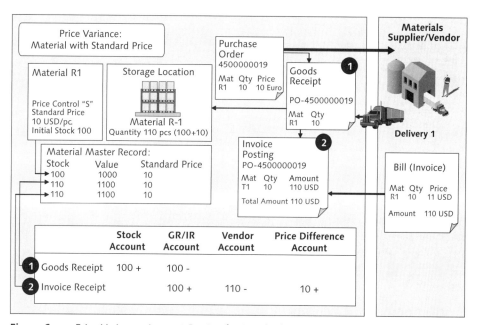

Figure 6.50 Price Variance: Account Posting for Standard Price Control

Account Posting with Moving Average Price

Figure 6.51 shows the account postings for a moving average price. In this case, the price difference amounts are posted into stock accounts, and the moving average price is changed. If there's insufficient stock quantity of the material, the system will post the price difference amount to the price difference G/L account.

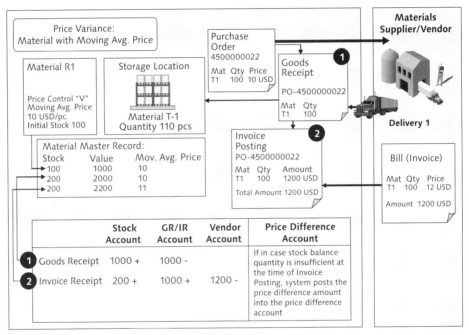

Figure 6.51 Price Variance: Account Posting for Moving Average Price Control

6.15.4 Stochastic Blocking

Stochastic blocking allows for the system to randomly check invoices, and then block invoices based on threshold values defined in the configuration. This blocking process is used to check that users are verifying and posting invoices accurately.

Stochastic blocking is configured in two steps:

1. **Activate stochastic blocking.**

   To activate stochastic blocking for a company, go to SAP IMG • MATERIALS MANAGEMENT • LOGISTICS INVOICE VERIFICATION • INVOICE BLOCK • STOCHASTIC

BLOCK • ACTIVATE STOCHASTIC BLOCK. Then select the checkbox next to the appropriate company code (Figure 6.52).

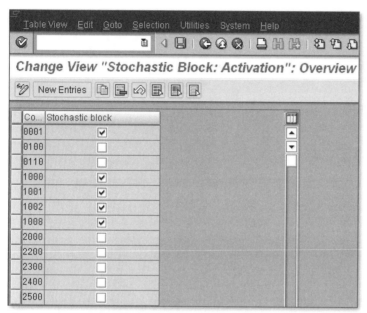

Figure 6.52 Activating Stochastic Block

2. **Set the stochastic block.**

In this step, you define the degree of probability that an invoice will be stochastically blocked. The degree of probability depends on the invoice value. For example, if for a particular company code, the threshold value is $2,000 and the probability is 50%, an invoice with a value of $2,000 would have a 50% probability of being blocked. An invoice with a value of $1,000 would have a 25% probability of being blocked.

> **Note**
>
> Probability percentages increase or decrease based on the threshold value and the value of the invoice.

To define threshold values and percentage probabilities for each company code, go to SAP IMG • MATERIALS MANAGEMENT • LOGISTICS INVOICE VERIFICATION • INVOICE BLOCK • STOCHASTIC BLOCK • SET STOCHASTIC BLOCK. Enter the threshold value and percentage probability for the company code, as shown in Figure 6.53.

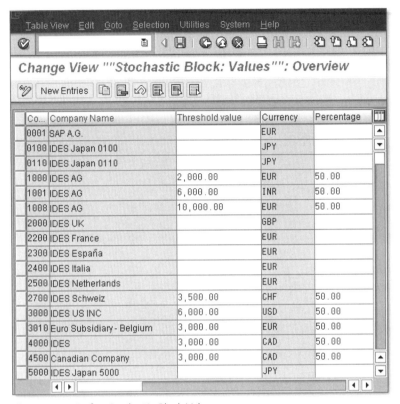

Figure 6.53 Define Stochastic Block Values

6.15.5 Manual Blocking

Users can manually block invoices at the time of the invoice posting via Transaction MIRO. This can be done at the header level, without reference to a particular line item. To do so, go to the Payment tab and select Blocked for Payment in the Pmnt Block dropdown list (Figure 6.54).

You can also block a particular line item during invoice posting. To do so, select the Manual Block checkbox, as shown in Figure 6.55 for the first line item.

We've now discussed the various blocking reasons and ways of blocking invoices such as automatic blocking and manual blocking. Furthermore, you must define tolerance limits to automatically block invoices. We'll now explain how these tolerances can be configured in the system.

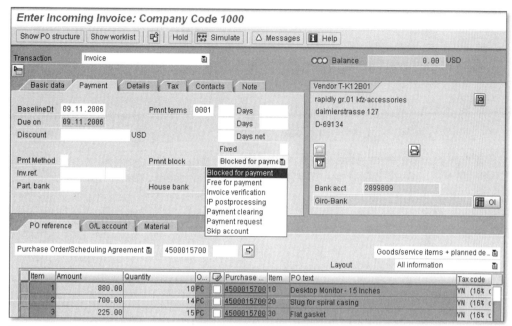

Figure 6.54 Invoice Posting via MIRO: Manually Blocking an Invoice

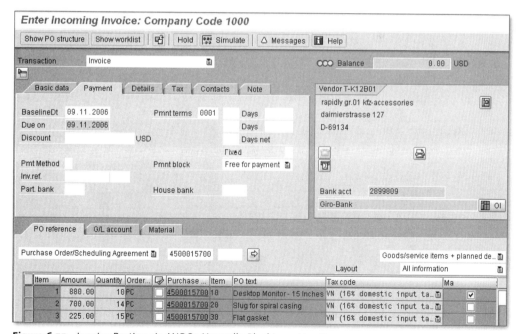

Figure 6.55 Invoice Posting via MIRO: Manually Blocking a Line Item

6.15.6 Tolerances

Tolerance limits can be defined for different variances, and can be absolute values or percentage limits. Reasons for blocking are defined as tolerance keys. The SAP-defined tolerance keys are as follows:

- AN: Amount for item without order reference
- AP: Amount for item with order reference
- BD: Form small differences automatically
- BR: Percentage order price quantity unit variance (invoice receipt before goods receipt)
- BW: Percentage order price quantity unit variance (goods receipt before invoice receipt)
- DQ: Exceeded amount — quantity variance
- DW: Quantity variance — goods receipt quantity equals zero
- KW: Variance from condition value
- LA: Amount of blanket PO
- LD: Blanket PO time limit exceeded
- PP: Price variance
- PS: Price variance of the estimated price
- ST: Date variance (value x days)
- VP: Moving average price variance

To configure tolerance limits, go to SAP IMG • MATERIALS MANAGEMENT • LOGISTICS INVOICE VERIFICATION • INVOICE BLOCK • SET TOLERANCE LIMITS. You will see a list of tolerance keys for each company code (Figure 6.56). To define the limit, select the tolerance key and company code combination, and click on the Details button.

You can define the lower and upper limits for the tolerance key, as shown in Figure 6.57. If you select the Do Not Check radio button, the system won't check the tolerance limit. You can also define absolute values and/or percentage values; if you define both, the system will check the lower value.

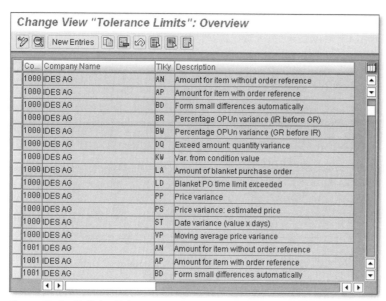

Figure 6.56 Defining Tolerance Limits

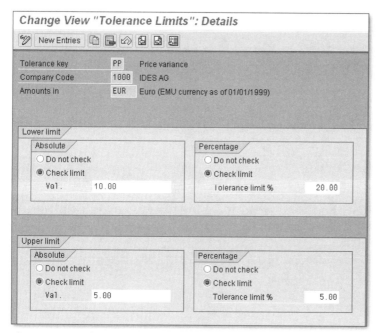

Figure 6.57 Defining Tolerance Limits: Details

Now that you understand how and why invoices are blocked, let's discuss how they can be released for payment processing.

6.15.7 Releasing Blocked Invoices

When the variance issue is resolved, you can release the invoice for payment processing. This can be done either automatically or manually. To release invoices, use Transaction MRBR and enter the selection criteria (Figure 6.58). Next, select the Processing option as Release Manually or Release Automatically. With manual release, the system displays the list of blocked invoices and allows you to select which ones you want to release (Figure 6.59).

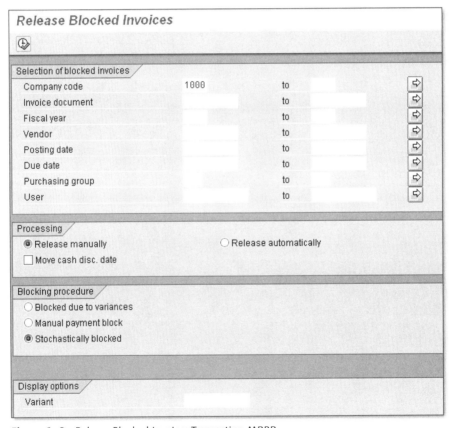

Figure 6.58 Release Blocked Invoice: Transaction MRBR

Doc. no.	Year	Crcy	TransIDate	Exch.r...	...	T...	Posting Date	CoCd	Invoicing pty.	Name	User name	Bline date	...	Dy...	Disc.1
5105607403	2006	EUR	20.02.2006	1.000...		RE	20.02.2006	1000	T-K12C01	C.E.B Berlin Gr.01	SAPUSER	22.02.2006		0	0.000
5105607403	2006	EUR	20.02.2006	1.000...		RE	20.02.2006	1000	T-K12C01	C.E.B Berlin Gr.01	SAPUSER	22.02.2006		0	0.000
5105607433	2006	EUR	21.03.2006	1.000...		RE	21.03.2006	1000	T-K12D01	Burohandel Leifritz Gr.01	SAPUSER	21.02.2006		0	0.000
5105607434	2006	EUR	21.03.2006	1.000...		RE	21.03.2006	1000	T-K12D01	Burohandel Leifritz Gr.01	SAPUSER	21.02.2006		0	0.000
5105607435	2006	EUR	21.03.2006	1.000...		RE	21.03.2006	1000	T-K12D01	Burohandel Leifritz Gr.01	SAPUSER	21.02.2006		0	0.000
5105607482	2006	EUR	10.05.2006	1.000...		RE	10.05.2006	1000	T-K515A01	Sapsota Company Limited	SAPUSER	10.05.2006		10	2.000
5105607522	2006	EUR	28.07.2006	1.000...		RE	28.07.2006	1000	T-L20C03	KAKE	SAPUSER	28.08.2006		0	0.000
5105607562	2006	EUR	02.09.2006	1.000...		RE	02.09.2006	1000	T-K10B01	kavita	SAPUSER	30.09.2006		0	0.000
5105607562	2006	EUR	02.09.2006	1.000...		RE	02.09.2006	1000	T-K10B01	kavita	SAPUSER	30.09.2006		0	0.000
5105607582	2006	EUR	06.09.2006	1.000...		RE	06.09.2006	1000	T-K12C01	C.E.B Berlin Gr.01	SAPUSER	06.09.2006		0	0.000
5105607602	2006	EUR	19.09.2006	1.000...		RE	19.09.2006	1000	T-K12B01	rasch gr.01 kfz -zubehor	SAPUSER	19.09.2006		0	0.000
5105607602	2006	EUR	19.09.2006	1.000...		RE	19.09.2006	1000	T-K12B01	rasch gr.01 kfz -zubehor	SAPUSER	19.09.2006		0	0.000
5105607622	2006	EUR	03.10.2006	1.000...		RE	03.10.2006	1000	T-K12C01	C.E.B Berlin Gr.01	SAPUSER	31.10.2006		0	0.000
5105607652	2006	EUR	17.10.2006	1.000...		RE	17.10.2006	1000	T-L15A01	T-L15A01	SAPUSER	18.10.2006		0	0.000
5105607652	2006	EUR	17.10.2006	1.000...		RE	17.10.2006	1000	T-L15A01	T-L15A01	SAPUSER	18.10.2006		0	0.000

Figure 6.59 Release Blocked Invoice Manually: Transaction MRBR

Note

You can also define a batch job via Transaction SM36 to execute the automatic release of blocked invoices. Use program RM08RELEASE.

6.16 GR/IR Account Maintenance

A goods receipt/invoice receipt (GR/IR) account is an intermediate account used for clearing goods receipt and invoices. A GR/IR clearing account is cleared for a PO item when the delivered quantity and the invoiced quantity are the same. The quantity differences between the goods receipt and invoice receipt for a PO result in a balance on the GR/IR account.

If an invoice quantity is more than the quantity delivered, this results in a balance amount on the GR/IR account, and the system expects additional goods receipts.

If the goods receipt quantity is more than the invoiced quantity, this results in a balance amount on the GR/IR account, and the system expects additional invoice postings.

If no additional goods invoice receipts are expected in the above scenario, you must manually clear the GR/IR account. Figure 6.60 shows an example of GR/IR account maintenance. 100 pieces of a material are delivered, as requested in the PO. However, an invoice is posted for only 80 pieces, and no additional invoices are expected from the vendor. The quantity difference of 20 pieces results in a balance of $200 in the GR/IR account. When you clear the GR/IR account with the GR/IR account maintenance transaction, the system will create an accounting document and clear the GR/IR difference of $200.

Account Posting

The GR/IR account clearing transaction posting will post an accounting document. Refer to Figure 6.60 for an example of a G/L account posting.

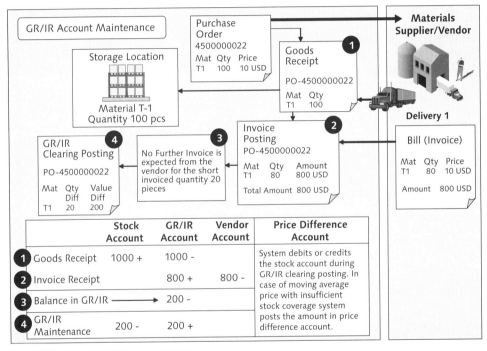

	Stock Account	GR/IR Account	Vendor Account	Price Difference Account
1 Goods Receipt	1000 +	1000 -		System debits or credits the stock account during GR/IR clearing posting. In case of moving average price with insufficient stock coverage system posts the amount in price difference account.
2 Invoice Receipt		800 +	800 -	
3 Balance in GR/IR ———→		200 -		
4 GR/IR Maintenance		200 -	200 +	

Figure 6.60 GR/IR Account Maintenance

We'll now look at the process steps used to clear a GR/IR account.

Process Steps

You can clear the GR/IR account via Transaction MR11, as shown in Figure 6.61. Enter the different selection criteria and execute the transaction. If the Prepare List processing option is selected, you will see a list of POs causing the balance in the GR/IR account (Figure 6.62). This list displays the PO number, line item number, quantity difference, value difference, and so on. Select the appropriate line and click on the Post button to clear the difference in the GR/IR account.

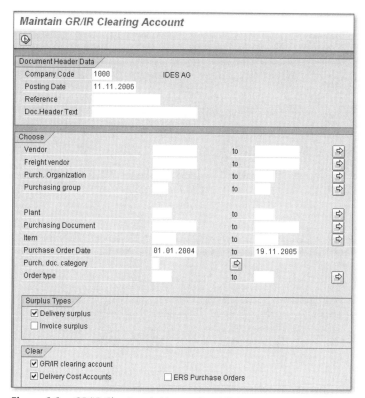

Figure 6.61 GR/IR Clearing via Transaction MR11

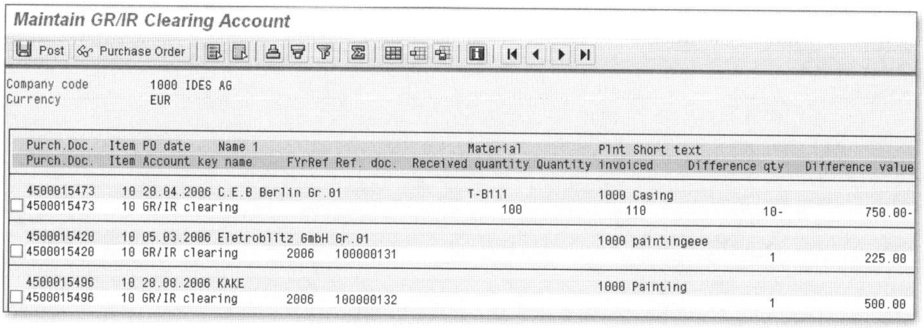

Figure 6.62 GR/IR Clearing: Process Manually from Purchase Order List

The GR/IR clearing document is updated in the PO history.

6.17 Duplicate Invoice Check

Imagine a scenario where a vendor mistakenly sends you an invoice twice, resulting in duplicate invoices being posted in your system. For this scenario, the SAP system provides the *duplicate invoice check* functionality that prevents incoming invoices being accidentally entered and paid more than once. To set up this functionality, go to SAP IMG • MATERIALS MANAGEMENT • LOGISTICS INVOICE VERIFICATION • INCOMING INVOICE • SET CHECK FOR DUPLICATE INVOICES. FOR EACH COMPANY CODE, select whether to activate or deactivate the check criteria for the company code, reference document number, and invoice date (Figure 6.63). The system will check for duplicate invoices only for the selected criteria. For example, if you've selected Check Reference for a company code, then posting two invoices in the same company code with the same reference number will result in a Duplicate Invoices Found message.

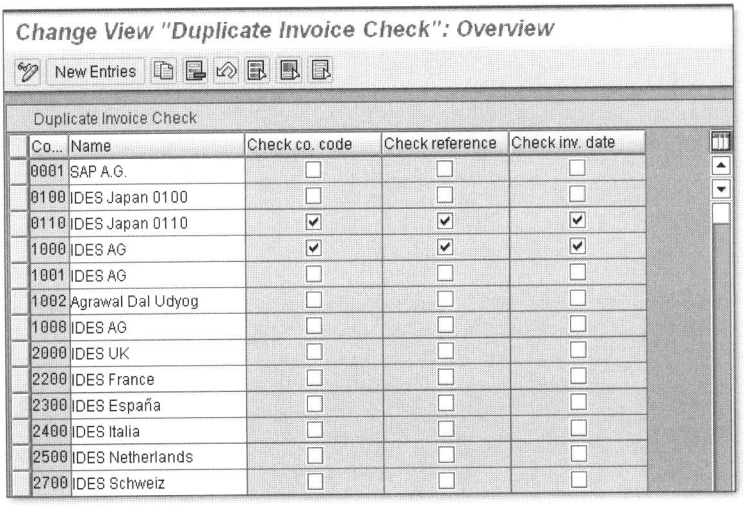
Change View "Duplicate Invoice Check": Overview

New Entries

Duplicate Invoice Check

Co...	Name	Check co. code	Check reference	Check inv. date
0001	SAP A.G.	☐	☐	☐
0100	IDES Japan 0100	☐	☐	☐
0110	IDES Japan 0110	☑	☑	☑
1000	IDES AG	☑	☑	☑
1001	IDES AG	☐	☐	☐
1002	Agrawal Dal Udyog	☐	☐	☐
1008	IDES AG	☐	☐	☐
2000	IDES UK	☐	☐	☐
2200	IDES France	☐	☐	☐
2300	IDES España	☐	☐	☐
2400	IDES Italia	☐	☐	☐
2500	IDES Netherlands	☐	☐	☐
2700	IDES Schweiz	☐	☐	☐

Figure 6.63 Settings for Duplicate Invoice Checking

6.18 Summary

This chapter explained the various invoice verification processes. You also learned how invoices are blocked for payment for variance in price or quantity and that subsequent debit/credit and invoice with reduction are very important processes in invoice verification. In this chapter, we also discussed the account postings in most of the scenarios. Furthermore, we showed that ERS and invoicing plans are very important processes that save a lot of time and reduce data entry errors.

The next chapter describes inventory valuation, which is very important for the financial book of accounts. Let's move on to learn about the various valuation methods and their impact in accounting.

In addition to quantity, inventory maintained in an organization has value attached to it. This inventory value is maintained in the company's book of accounts, and, unlike quantity, may fluctuate depending on market price.

7 Inventory Valuation

Whenever any valuated material is received into stock or issued from stock, the value of the total stock is changed and recorded in the financial accounts. This process is called *inventory valuation* and is the subject of this chapter. Inventory valuation in the SAP system is carried out based on the standard price or moving average price. Before we get into the details of each of the valuation methods, however, you need to understand the term valuation area, which we'll discuss first.

7.1 Valuation Area

A *valuation area* is the organizational level at which materials are valuated such as at the plant or company code level, as illustrated in Figure 7.1.

When the valuation area is at the plant level, you can valuate a material in different plants at different prices. When the valuation area is at the company code level, the valuation price of a material is the same in all of the plants of the company code.

> **Note**
>
> SAP recommends that you valuate materials at the plant level. Material valuation at the plant level is mandatory if your system is a retail system, or if you want to use either the production planning or product cost accounting components.

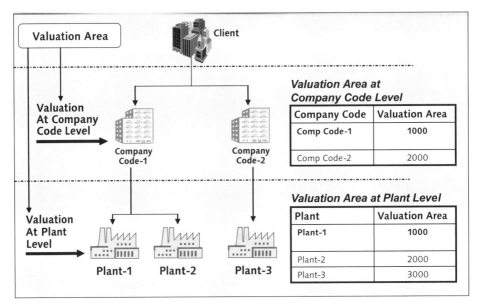

Figure 7.1   Valuation Area: Company Code or Plant Level

To define the valuation area at the company code or plant level, go to SAP IMG • Enterprise Structure • Definition • Logistics General • Define Valuation Level (Figure 7.2).

Select the valuation area level either at the plant or company code level as per your requirement, as shown in Figure 7.2.

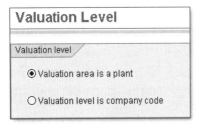

Figure 7.2   Define Valuation Area Level

Note

The valuation level is a fundamental setting and is very difficult to reverse after it's been selected.

In the following sections, we'll discuss the major concepts involved in inventory valuation, including valuation procedures, material price changes, and split valuation.

7.2 Valuation Methods: Moving Average Price and Standard Price

Material valuation is carried out according to the price controls set in the SAP system. In this section, we'll discuss the following valuation methods: Moving Average Price (Price Control V) or Standard Price (Price Control S) (Figure 7.3).

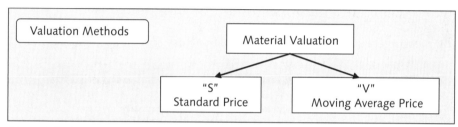

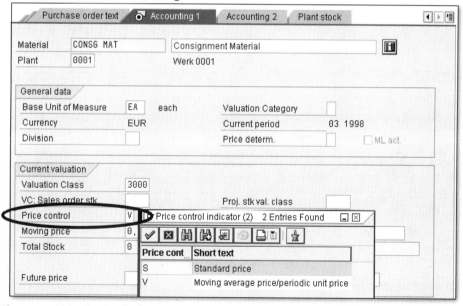

Figure 7.3 Valuation Methods

In the standard price procedure, the valuation price is defined and fixed in the material master record. If a PO price is different (either more or less) from the standard price, the difference amounts are posted into a price difference account.

Moving average price, on the other hand, is a weighted average price. The movements of materials such as goods issue or goods receipts may impact moving average prices.

The valuation method is defined in the accounting view screen of the material master as shown in Figure 7.3.

We'll discuss both valuation methods in detail in the next sections.

7.2.1 Moving Average Price "V"

The moving average price is the weighted average price of a material and will change regularly if PO prices of a material are changed regularly. This price is calculated based on total stock and total value using the following equation:

Moving average price = total stock value / total stock quantity

Consider, for example, a case where you have an initial stock of 100 pieces of material Mat-1 at a price of $8/piece (Figure 7.4). In the meantime, you've raised a PO for 100 pieces of Material Mat-1 at $10/piece. (Keep in mind that at the time of the PO an accounting document doesn't yet exist.) After you receive the 100 pieces from the vendor, you enter the goods receipt with reference to the PO.

When you post the goods receipt, an accounting document is created. The stock account is debited $1,000 (100 × 10), and the GR/IR account is credited $1,000, both according to the PO price. The total stock quantity becomes 200 pieces (100 + 100), and the total stock value becomes $1,800 ($800 + $1000). Plugging these numbers into the moving average price equation yields the following result:

Moving average price = total stock value/ total stock quantity.

= 1,800 / 200

= 9

As you can see, the moving average price for the stock is now $9.

If you post the invoice with the same price as in the PO, the GR/IR account will be debited with $1,000 and the vendor account will be credited with $1,000.

After the invoice posting, the moving average price will remain $9 each because there's no price difference between the PO and the invoice.

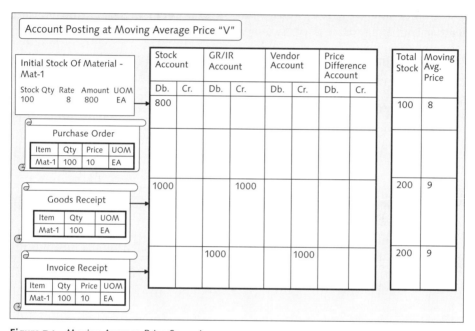

Figure 7.4 Moving Average Price Scenario

The material master record will always be updated with the current moving average price. You can check the price in the material master in the accounting view using Transaction MM03.

7.2.2 Standard Price "S"

A standard price is a fixed price defined in the material master record. Consider, for example, a case where you have an initial stock of 100 pieces of Material Mat-1. The standard price in the material master record is $8/piece (Figure 7.5). In the meantime, you've raised a PO for Material Mat-1 at a price of $10/piece. (Keep in mind that, at the time of the PO, the accounting document has not yet been created.)

After you receive the 100 pieces of Material Mat-1, you enter the goods receipt for the PO. When you post the goods receipt, an accounting document is created. In this case, the stock account is debited by $800 (100 × 8)—even though the PO lists a price of $10/piece. This is because the material uses a standard price valuation, which is $8. The GR/IR account, however, will be credited with *$1000*, because the GR/IR account is based on the PO and goods receipt, not the standard price. Because of the difference in costs, the price difference account is debited $200.

The bottom line is that the standard price is always fixed, and any difference between the standard price and the PO price is posted in the price difference account.

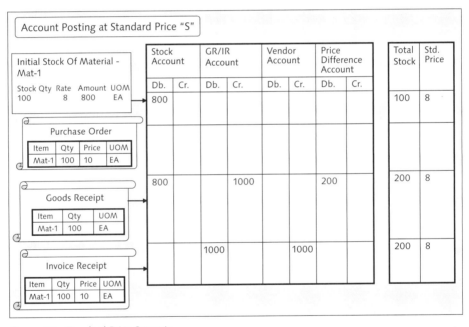

Figure 7.5 Standard Price Scenario

In the following sections, we'll discuss the configuration and process steps for standard prices and moving average prices.

7.2.3 Configuration Steps

Price control S (standard price) and price control V (moving average price) are both predefined in the SAP system. While creating the material master record, you must assign the valuation method in the accounting view. However, you can assign the price control to material types so that each time you create an accounting view of the material master, the price control is assigned automatically by the system. To do so, go to SAP IMG • LOGISTICS-GENERAL • MATERIAL MASTER • BASIC SETTINGS • MATERIAL TYPES • DEFINE ATTRIBUTES OF MATERIAL TYPES. The valuation method can be selected on the Valuation tab, as shown in Figure 7.6. It's then used as a default (proposed by the system) in the creation of the material master record but can be changed at the time of material master creation. You can make a particular valuation method mandatory by selecting the Price Control Mandatory checkbox in the Valuation section of Material Type, as shown in Figure 7.6. If the valuation method is made mandatory, the default valuation method cannot be changed in the material master record.

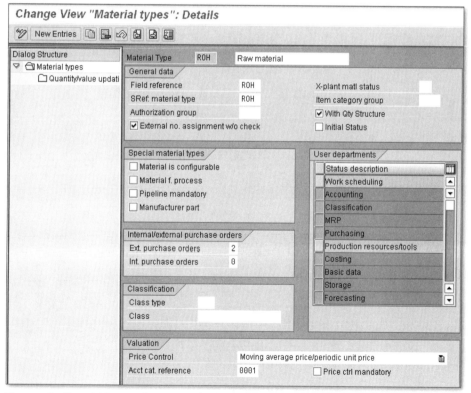

Figure 7.6 Material Type: Valuation Method Configuration

7.2.4 Process Steps

During the time of materials movement such as goods receipt, goods issue, and invoice posting, the system automatically posts the entries in the stock G/L account, and the valuation amount is calculated based on the valuation method defined in the material master.

You can view the total stock quantity, total value, and valuation method of a material in the material master accounting view. To do so, use Transaction MM03, as shown in Figure 7.7.

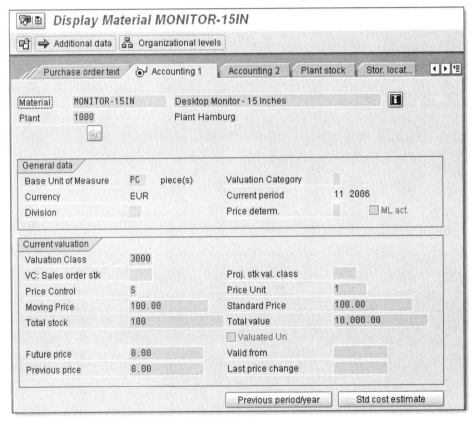

Figure 7.7 Valuation Price Details in Material Master

Valuation methods are directly related to the idea that materials experience price changes. In the following section, we'll discuss the concept of price changes in more detail.

7.3 Material Price Changes

Material prices can change over a period of time due to changes in the market price. The SAP system includes functionality to accommodate these changes and stock valuation is revaluated as per the current market price.

Let's understand this concept with the help of a business scenario.

7.3.1 Business Scenario

An enterprise engaged in computer hardware manufacturing wants to change the valuation price of a material (desktop monitor) due to a change in the market price.

For example, the company has a 100 pieces in stock with a stock value of $10,000. The material is maintained with the valuation method standard price, and the price is 100 $/piece. The market price of desktop monitors has since been reduced to 60 $/piece and the company would like to update their stock valuation as per the current market price.

Valuation prices can be changed based on business requirements for three scenarios:

- A price change during the current posting period
- A price change during the previous posting period and changes not carried over to the current period
- A price change during the previous posting period or year and changes carried over to the current period

> **Note**
>
> Keep in mind that changing the material price doesn't involve changing the material master record; it's an accounting transaction in which the total stock for a valuation area is revaluated.

Let's discuss these three different types of price changes.

▶ **Price change in the current posting period**
A material price change in the current posting period changes the material price and creates an accounting document. Figure 7.8 shows an example of a price change in the current period. Material Mat-1 has a stock balance of 100 pieces, a price of $12/piece, and a total stock value of $1,200. Now, the market price is changed from $12/piece to $20/piece, and to revaluate your stock valuation as per the current market price, you need to post a price change document. After you've posted the price change document in the system, an accounting document is created, the stock G/L account is debited $800 (the difference between the original value of $1,200 and the new value of $2,000), and the expense/revenue from revaluation G/L account is credited $800. The material price change is now complete, and the price stands at $20/piece.

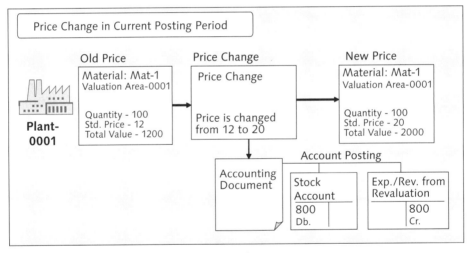

Figure 7.8 Material Price Change in Current Period

▶ **Price change in the previous period/year, with the change effective only in that period/year**
A material price change in the previous period or year changes the material price only in the previous period; i.e., the current price and valuation remain the same. In this scenario, the price change transaction creates two accounting documents: one for the previous year, and one for the current year.

Figure 7.9 shows an example of this process. When you change the price from $12 to $20 in the previous period or year, the previous period's stock account is debited $800, and revenue from the revaluation account is credited $800. To keep the price in the current valuation period the same, the system then posts one more accounting documents for the current period, the stock account is credited, and the expense from revaluation account is debited.

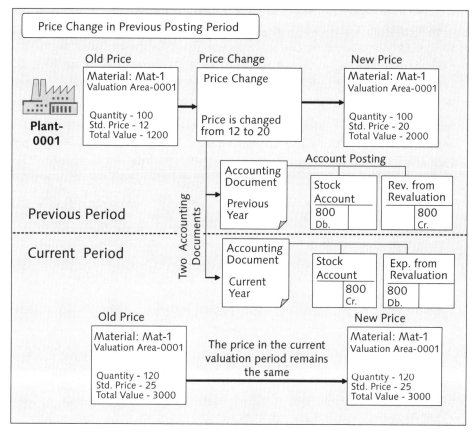

Figure 7.9 Material Price Change in Previous Posting Period/Year (Not Carried Over to Current Period)

▶ **Price change in the previous period/year with the change also effective for the current period**

In this scenario, the price change in the previous period or year is carried forward to the current period. Figure 7.10 shows an example where the material price is changed to $20. In the previous period, the material price was $12 and total stock was 100 pieces. In the current period, the material price is $15 and the total stock is 120 pieces.

As with the previous scenario, this transaction will create two accounting documents and the first accounting document is posted for the previous period and the second accounting document is posted for the current posting period. The following list details both of these documents:

1. **First Accounting Document (Posted for previous period)**
   The material price is increased by $8 (the new price is $20 – the old price was $12); therefore, the stock value will be increased in the previous period by $800 (increased price of $8 × stock quantity of 100 for the previous period). $800 Euro ($8 × 100) is debited to the stock G/L account, and $800 is credited to the revenue from the revaluation G/L account.

2. **Second Accouting Document (Posted for current period)**
   For the current posting period, the stock quantity is 120 pieces and the price is $15. Therefore, the calculation for the accounting posting will be as follows:

   ▸ **Reversal of price change in the current period**
   Reversal of the amount posted in the last posting period via the first accounting document:

   – Stock G/L account – $800 credit

   – Expense from revaluation account –$800 debit

   ▸ **Carry over price change into the current period**
   Because the new price needs to be carried over to the current period, the price difference amount results from the change in price from $15 per piece to $20 per piece in the current period:

   – Stock G/L account – $600 debit (120 pieces x $5 is the price difference)

   – Revenue from revaluation account – $600 credit

   ▸ **Net effect of the previous calculation**
   The net value is calculated from the previous two calculations and posted via the second accounting document:

   – Stock G/L account – $200 credit

   – Expense from revaluation account – $200 debit

As shown in Figure 7.10, the accounting document posted in the current posting period has credited $200 to the stock G/L account and debited $200 to the expense account from the revaluation account.

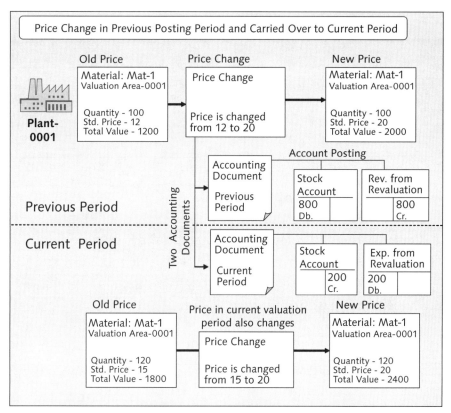

Figure 7.10 Material Price Change in Previous Posting Period/Year (Carried Over to Current Period)

Now that we've discussed the three possible price change scenarios, let's look at the process and configuration steps involved in prices changes.

7.3.2 Process Steps

You can change prices via Transaction MR21, as shown in Figure 7.11. Then, check the new valuation price and value of the stock in the material master accounting view via Transaction MM03. You can post a material debit/credit via Transaction MR22.

This scenario is required primarily when materials are valuated with standard price control.

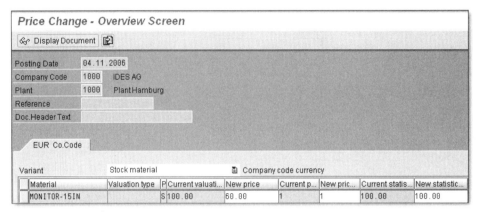

Figure 7.11 Price Change via Transaction MR21

7.3.3 Configuration Steps for Price Changes in the Previous Period/Year

For a price change in the previous period or year, you must define whether the change also applies to the current period. To do so, go to SAP IMG • MATERIAL MANAGEMENT • VALUATION AND ACCOUNT ASSIGNMENT • CONFIGURE PRICE CHANGE IN PREVIOUS PERIOD/PREVIOUS YEAR, and select the Price Carry Over checkbox to activate the price change carry over (Figure 7.12).

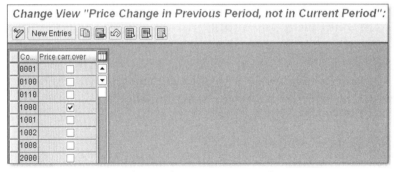

Figure 7.12 Previous Period Price Change Carryover Configuration

Now that we've covered two of the main topics in inventory valuation—valuation methods and material price changes—let's look at a specific type of inventory valuation called split valuation.

7.4 Split Valuation

Split valuation enables you to valuate sub-stocks (sub-stock means part of the total stock) of a material in different ways. There are a number of reasons you might want to valuate sub-stocks separately, such as:

▸ The material has different origins (i.e., comes from different countries)

▸ The material is acquired via different types of procurement (i.e., external procurement vs. internal procurement)

▸ The material has different categories of quality (i.e., damaged, poor quality, or good quality)

7.4.1 Business Scenario

As an example, imagine a car manufacturing organization that procures engine valves from both a domestic vendor and an overseas vendor. Naturally, the vendor prices for the material are different; therefore, the company wants to valuate the stock separately. Figure 7.13 shows an illustration of this concept.

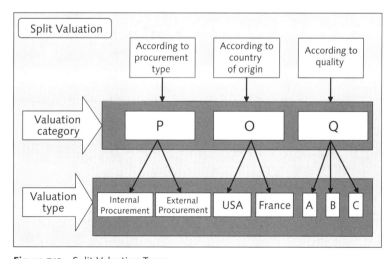

Figure 7.13 Split Valuation Types

> **Note**
>
> Split valuation is used only with moving average price control, and materials subjected to split valuation can be valuated only via the moving average price method.

Now, look closely at the example illustrated in Figure 7.14. Material Mat-1 is procured for Plant 0001 from Vendor-1 and Vendor-2, located in the US and France, respectively. The material is designated for split valuation based on the origin of material. From Vendor-1, Plant 0001 has procured 60 pieces of the material at a price of $10/piece. From Vendor-2, Plant 0001 has procured 40 pieces of the material at a price of $15/piece. While posting the goods receipt, the appropriate valuation type (either USA or France) needs to be selected for each vendor.

After this is done, you can see the total stock quantity and stock value at Plant 0001, and you can also see the material valuation based on the origin of the material. The stock value of the material procured from the US is $600, and the valuation price is $10/piece. The stock value of the material procured from France is $600, and the valuation price is $15/piece. The stock quantities and stock values of split-value materials are cumulated at the valuation area level.

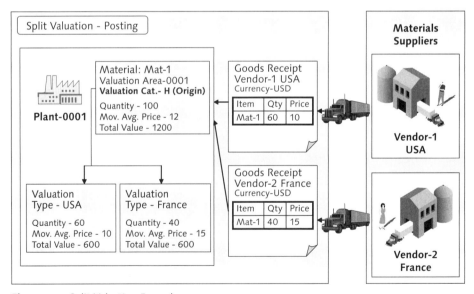

Figure 7.14 Split Valuation Example

This example introduces two essential concepts in split valuation: *valuation category* and *valuation type*. The valuation category indicates whether a material's stock should be valuated as one unit or in parts. It's also a key that indicates the criteria for defining partial stock, and determines which valuation type is allowed.

The *valuation type* is a key that identifies split-valuated stocks of a material and indicates the characteristic of a partial stock. The valuation category is assigned in the material master record, and selected during material transactions such as goods issues and goods receipts.

7.4.2 Configuration Steps

To configure split valuation, follow these steps:

1. **Activate split valuation.**
   To activate split valuation, go to SAP IMG CUSTOMIZING IMPLEMENTATION GUIDE • MATERIAL MANAGEMENT • VALUATION AND ACCOUNT ASSIGNMENT • SPLIT VALUATION • ACTIVATE SPLIT VALUATION (Figure 7.15). If you allow split valuation, this doesn't mean that you must only valuate material on a split valuation basis. Split valuation is used only when the valuation category is assigned in a material master record.

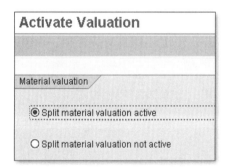

Figure 7.15 Activate Split Valuation

2. **Configure split valuation.**
   To configure split valuation, go to SAP IMG • MATERIAL MANAGEMENT • VALUATION AND ACCOUNT ASSIGNMENT • SPLIT VALUATION • CONFIGURE SPLIT VALUATION. You now have to define the global types and global categories.

First, click on the Global Types button. In this step, you create valuation types and define their attributes (Figure 7.16). To create a new valuation type, click on the New button and enter the valuation type. Define the following attributes:

▸ **External PO**
This indicates whether external POs are allowed.

▸ **Internal PO**
This indicates whether internal POs (i.e., production orders) are allowed.

▸ **Account Category Reference**
This is used to group valuation classes. Specify for which account category reference this valuation type is allowed.

Global Valuation Types

	Create	Change	Delete

Valuation Type	Ext. POs	Int. POs	ARef	Description
009	0	1	0001	Reference for raw materials
01	0	2	0001	Reference for raw materials
02	2	0	0001	Reference for raw materials
C1	2	2	0003	Reference for spare parts
C2	2	2	0003	Reference for spare parts
C3	2	2	0003	Reference for spare parts
EIGEN	0	2	0001	Reference for raw materials
FREMD	2	0	0001	Reference for raw materials
LAND 1	2	0	0001	Reference for raw materials
LAND 2	2	0	0001	Reference for raw materials
RAKTION	2	2	0005	Reference for trading goods
RNORMAL	2	2	0005	Reference for trading goods

Figure 7.16 Define Global Types: Valuation Types

Now, click on the Global Category button. In this step, you create global categories, as shown in Figure 7.17. To define a valuation category, click on the Create button. Enter the category code and description.

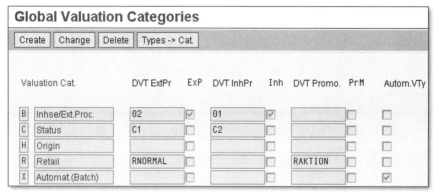

Figure 7.17 Define Global Category

You can define the following attributes for a valuation category (Figure 7.18):

▶ **Default External Procurement**
The valuation type selected in this field is proposed at the time of PO creation.

▶ **External Procurement Mandatory**
If you select this checkbox, the default valuation type is mandatory and cannot be changed in the PO.

▶ **Default In-house**
The valuation type selected in this field is proposed at the time of production order creation.

▶ **In-house Mandatory**
If you select this checkbox, the default valuation type is mandatory and cannot be changed in the production order.

▶ **Valuation Type Automatic**
If this checkbox is selected, the system will automatically determine the valuation type at the time of the goods receipt. This indicator is only useful for materials that are managed in batches. A valuation record is automatically created for each batch.

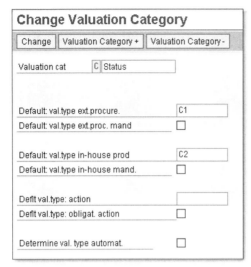

Figure 7.18 Valuation Category Details

You must activate valuation types for the valuation category by clicking on Types
• Cat or [F7]. As shown in Figure 7.19, valuation types LAND 1 and LAND 2 are
active for Valuation Category H (Origin).

Valuation Category H: Allocate Valuation Types

| Valuation Category + | Valuation Category - | Cat. -> OUs | Local Definitions | Local Definitions |

Valuation Cat.   [H] Origin

Assignment

Status	Valuation Type	Ex	In	ARef	Description
	009	0	1	0001	Reference for raw materials
	01	0	2	0001	Reference for raw materials
	02	2	0	0001	Reference for raw materials
	C1	2	2	0003	Reference for spare parts
	C2	2	2	0003	Reference for spare parts
	C3	2	2	0003	Reference for spare parts
	EIGEN	0	2	0001	Reference for raw materials
	FREMD	2	0	0001	Reference for raw materials
Active	LAND 1	2	0	0001	Reference for raw materials
Active	LAND 2	2	0	0001	Reference for raw materials
	RAKTION	2	2	0005	Reference for trading goods
	RNORMAL	2	2	0005	Reference for trading goods

Figure 7.19 Activate Valuation Types for Valuation Category

7.4.3 Process Steps

Follow these split valuation process steps:

1. **Assign a valuation category in the material master record.**
   After your configuration is complete, you must assign a valuation category to the material master record in the accounting view. Valuation Category H is assigned for the material shown in Figure 7.20.

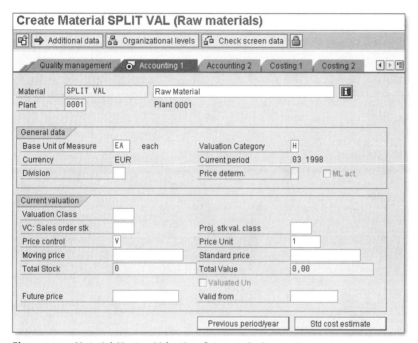

Figure 7.20 Material Master: Valuation Category Assignment

2. **Create a PO.**
   Create a PO via Transaction ME21N and enter the material, quantity, plant, vendor, and all other required data. As shown in Figure 7.21, the default valuation type is copied on the Delivery tab of the PO. You can change the default value and select the required valuation type.

3. **Post the goods receipt.**
   Post the goods receipt via Transaction MIGO. You can see the Valuation Type on the Material tab (Figure 7.22).

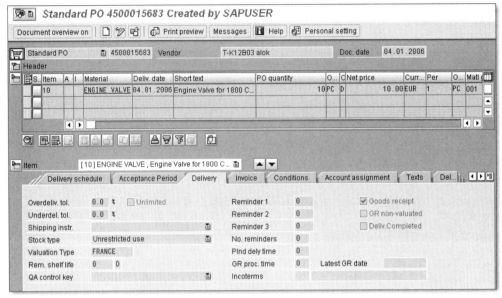

Figure 7.21 PO: Valuation Type in Delivery Tab

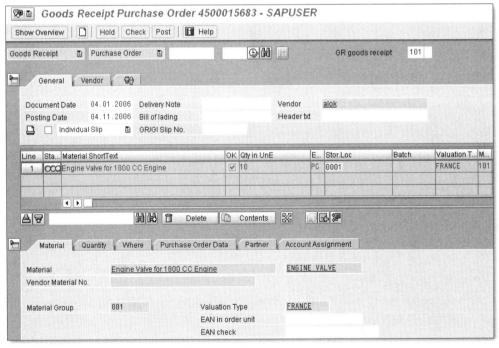

Figure 7.22 Goods Receipt: Split Valuated Material

4. **Display the valuation price in the material master record.**

   You can view the valuation price in the material master accounting view via Transaction MM03. This will show you the valuation price at the plant level. If you select a valuation type at the organizational level, the system will display the stock valuation for the selected valuation type.

   For example, for the material Engine Valve, the value is assigned for split valuation based on origin. Valuation Types France and USA are configured. In the material master record, the stock valuation for a plant will be the total valuation that's procured from both France and the USA (Figure 7.23). You can also display the valuation price for each valuation type.

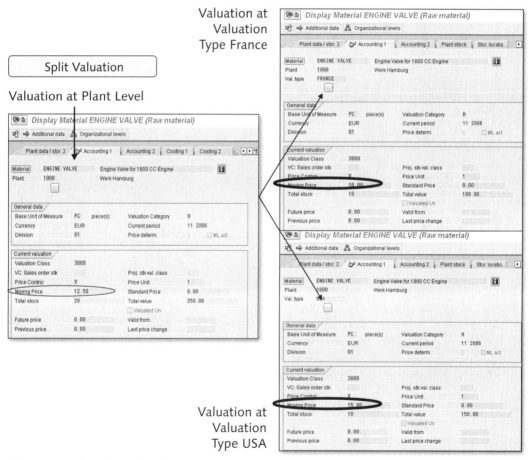

Figure 7.23 Split Valuation Price in Material Master

7.5 Summary

In this chapter, you've learned about valuation methods, material price changes, and how to configure split valuations. Now that you understand these concepts, you should be able to better meet the business requirements of your customers.

In the next chapter, we'll discuss some of the key configurations involved in MM.

There are a number of SAP system configurations that are common across business processes. This chapter explains these key configurations.

8 Key Configurations in SAP Materials Management

This chapter contains a discussion of the most common configurations required across business processes. The topics covered are:

- ▶ Release strategy
- ▶ Pricing procedure
- ▶ Automatic account determination
- ▶ Document type
- ▶ Version management
- ▶ Message determination

While implementing MM, you need to configure the pricing procedure and automatic account determination, which are required for all of the business processes.

The release strategy and version management may be implemented based on customer requirements.

We'll first discuss the topic of release strategy, including a business scenario where it can be implemented and the step-by-step configuration.

8.1 Release Strategy

Release procedures are approval procedures for purchasing documents such as purchase requisitions and POs. The manner in which you configure these procedures is called a *release strategy*. A release strategy involves a process whereby an approver verifies document data (such as material, quantity, and value), and then gives the authorization to purchase. The process takes place online, which saves time and is more efficient than a manual approval process.

8.1.1 Business Scenario

Say, for example, a manufacturing organization wants all external documents (such as POs, contracts, and scheduling agreements) to be approved by a manager and vice president based on their value, with low amounts requiring no approval, medium amounts requiring manager approval, and high amounts requiring both manager and vice president approval. To accomplish this, you can configure release strategies for both internal and external purchasing documents.

You can setup a scenario where purchase requisitions and POs need to be approved by certain people either by value limit or some other criteria such as document type, purchasing group, and so on.

For example, you may have a scenario where a purchase requisition needs to be approved by different levels of responsible people based on value limits such as:

▶ $0 – $1000: No approval required

▶ $1000 – $5000: Manager needs to approve

▶ More than $5000: Manager and vice president need to approve

Figure 8.1 shows the approval process flow for purchase requisitions and POs. When a release strategy is used, purchase requisitions must be approved before you can create any related documents (such as RFQs or POs). The system also prohibits circulation of the document via printouts, faxes, or email.

In the following sections, we'll provide an introduction to the concept of release strategy, and then explain the configuration and process steps involved.

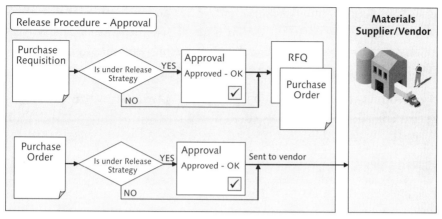

Figure 8.1   Release Procedure: Process Flow

8.1.2   Basic Concepts of Release Strategy

The SAP system provides two different types of release procedures:

▶ Release procedure without classification

▶ Release procedure with classification

For purchase requisitions, you can use either of these procedures. For POs and RFQs, you must use the release procedure with classification (Figure 8.2).

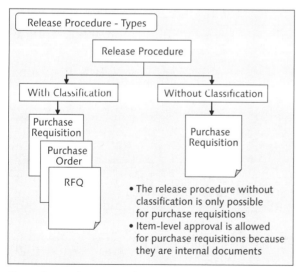

Figure 8.2   Release Procedure Types: With Classification and Without Classification

The release procedure without classification can be configured only for item-level release. Therefore, it can only be used for internal documents (such as purchase requisitions). This is because external documents (such as POs) must be sent to vendors, and therefore cannot be partially approved.

In the procedure without classification, you can set the release based on the following four criteria:

▶ Plant

▶ Value

▶ Material group

▶ Account assignment category

The procedure with classification offers many more criteria to define the release strategy. Before we get into the release procedure configuration steps, we'll define the key terms used in release procedures, as follows:

▶ **Release strategy**
Defines the entire approval process and consists of release conditions, release codes, and release prerequisites.

▶ **Release conditions/criteria**
Determines which release strategy applies for a particular purchasing document. For example, if the value of a requisition item is $1000, it may require a certain strategy; if the value of the item is $100,000, it may require a different strategy. If purchasing documents fulfill release conditions, they must be approved before they can be processed further.

▶ **Release code/point**
Two-character key that represents an individual or department that must give approval. Each person involved in the release procedure signifies approval in a release transaction using his release code.

▶ **Release prerequisite**
Sets the order in which approval must take place. For example, a manager must approve a document before the vice president approves it.

▶ **Release status/indicator**

Represents the current status of the item or document such as blocked and released. For example, if the document isn't fully approved, it may have a status of blocked.

Now that you have an understanding of the basic concepts of a release strategy, let's move on to the configuration steps involved. We'll discuss two types of configuration: without classification, and with classification.

8.1.3 Configuration Steps for Release Procedure without Classification

Follow the menu path SAP IMG • MATERIALS MANAGEMENT • PURCHASING • PURCHASE REQUISITION • RELEASE PROCEDURE • SET UP PROCEDURE WITHOUT CLASSIFICATION. This will display five activities, as shown in Figure 8.3. You need to select each activity, one by one, as follows:

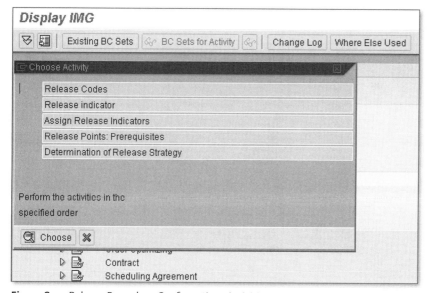

Figure 8.3 Release Procedure Configuration: Activities

1. **Select Release Codes.**
   The release code is used to approve the document. Click on New Entries and enter the two-digit Release Code key and Description, as shown in Figure 8.4.

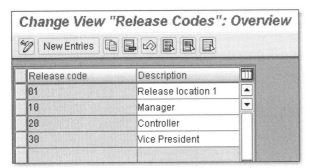

Figure 8.4 Release Procedure Configuration: Release Codes

2. **Select Release Indicator.**

   This specifies the release status of the purchase requisition. You can define the Release Indicator as shown in Figure 8.5. Click on New Entries and enter the one digit Release Indicator and Description (Figure 8.6).

Change View "Release Indicator": Overview

Release indicator	Description
1	Request for quotation
2	RFQ/purchase order
3	RFQ/PO no change of date
4	RFQ/PO no changes
A	Fixed RFQ
B	Fixed RFQ/purchase order
S	Blocked

Figure 8.5 Define Release Indicator

You also need to define controlling indicators and a field selection key for the release indicator, as shown in Figure 8.6. Let's discuss the impact of each indicator and selection key:

► **Fixed for MRP**

If you select this checkbox, the purchase requisition cannot be changed by MRP.

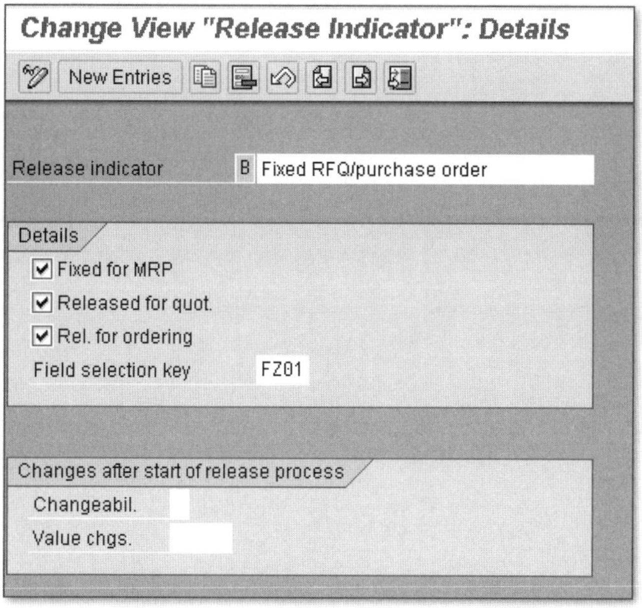

Figure 8.6 Release Indicator Details

▶ **Released for Quot.**
This indicator specifies that quotations and RFQs may be processed with reference to purchase requisitions. If you select this checkbox, it means that the purchase requisition is available for RFQ and quotation processing.

▶ **Rel for Ordering**
This indicator specifies whether POs can be generated with reference to purchase requisitions.

▶ **Field Selection Key**
When setting up a release strategy and release indicators, you can use the field selection key to determine whether certain fields in a purchase requisition may or may not be changed on approval. For example, you may have a requirement to configure the system in such a way that the requested quantity in the purchase requisition cannot be changed after this release indicator is set in the purchase requisition. For this requirement, you can configure the order quantity field as "display only" in the field selection key.

▶ **Changeabil.**
This defines how the system reacts if a purchasing document is changed after the start of the release procedure, as shown in Figure 8.7.

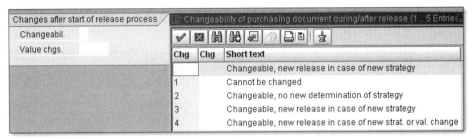

Figure 8.7 Changeable Option Selection

▸ **Value Chgs.**
Specifies the percentage by which the value of the purchase requisition can be changed after the release procedure has started. If the requisition is changed more than the specified limit entered here, it's again subjected to the release procedure.

3. **Select Assign Release Indicators.**
In this step, you assign the release indicators to a release strategy, as shown in Figure 8.8.

Rel.strat.	C1	C2	C3	C.	C.	C.	C.	C.	ReleaseInd	Description
R1	X							1		Request for quotation
R1	X	X						2		RFQ/purchase order
S1	X							2		RFQ/purchase order

Figure 8.8 Assign Release Indicators to a Release Strategy

This indicator specifies the release sequence; that is, which release point(s) must have a released requisition before the current individual or department is allowed to release that requisition. Look at Figure 8.8 for an example. For Release Strategy R1, Release Indicators 1 and 2 have been defined. If Release Indicator 1 is set, the RFQ can be created from the purchase requisition. Release Indicator 2 can be set only after Release Indicator 1 is set, and Release Indicator 2 means that RFQs or POs can be created.

4. **Select Release Points: Prerequisite.**

In this step, you configure the sequence of release codes and the prerequisites they must fill before they can be released. Look at Figure 8.9 for an example. For Release Strategy R1, there are two release codes, 10 and 20. Release Code 10 has no prerequisite, which means it can approve the purchase requisition. Release Code 20, however, does have a prerequisite, which means that it must be approved by Release Code 10 before it can be approved by Release Code 20. (Remember, release codes are references to specific people.)

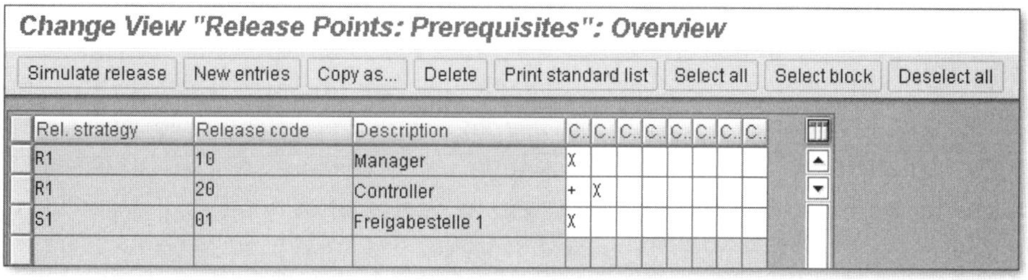

Figure 8.9 Select Release Points

You can test your sequence and prerequisites by clicking on the Simulate Release button, as shown in Figure 8.9. After clicking on this button, you see a popup window where you can test your release strategy (Figure 8.10).

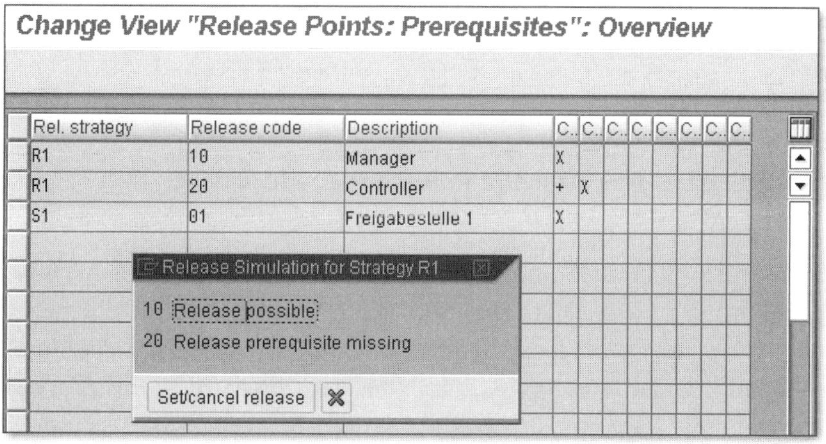

Figure 8.10 Release Strategy Simulation

Release Strategy R1 has two release indicators, which we assigned in Step 2. When Release Code 10 releases the purchase requisition, Release Indicator 1 is set. This means that you can create an RFQ even though the purchasing document hasn't yet been released by Release Code 20. When the document is released by Release Code 20, Release Indicator 2 is set. This allows the creation of POs.

5. **Select Determination of Release Strategy.**
In this step, you define when the purchase requisition is considered for a release procedure, and which release strategy is applicable. The without classification release strategy can be configured with only four criteria: account assignment category, material group, plant, and value. In Figure 8.11, you can see that for Account Assignment Category F, Material Group 011, Plant 3000, and Value 2,000.00 USD, Release Strategy R1 is applicable. When a purchase requisition is created with these attributes, the system will automatically assign Release Strategy R1, and will follow the approval process configured in this strategy.

	AcctAssCat	Matl group	Plnt	Value of purch. req.	Crcy	Release strategy	
	F	011	3000	2,000.00	USD	R1	
	K	007	1000	1,000.00	DEM	R2	
	K	007	1111	1,000.00	DEM	R2	
	K	007	2000	1,000.00	GBP	R3	

Change View "Determination of Release Strategy": Overview

Figure 8.11 Release Strategy Determination

8.1.4 Configuration Steps for the Release Procedure with Classification

A release procedure with classification can be defined for internal documents (purchase requisitions) and external documents (POs, RFQs, contracts, and scheduling agreements). For a release procedure with classification; you must define both characteristics and classes. We'll now discuss the steps involved in this process. Because some of these steps are fairly complex, we'll give each its own section.

Step 1: Edit Release Characteristics

In this step, you create classification characteristics for a release procedure. These characteristics are the criteria for a release condition; if the characteristics are satisfied, the associated release strategy is assigned to the purchasing document. For example, the release condition for release strategy S1 has the characteristic as defined in Table 8.1.

Characteristic	Characteristic Value
Total net value of PO	Over $1,000

Table 8.1 Characteristic

This means that if the total value of a PO exceeds $1000, release strategy S1 is assigned to the PO.

The SAP system provides the communication structures CEBAN for mapping characteristics for purchase requisitions, and CEKKO for mapping characteristics for POs. In communication structure CEKKO, you'll find all of the fields that can be used as characteristics for a release condition. (For example, BSART is used for the order type, and GNETW is used for the total order value.)

Note
To check the fields that can be used as characteristics for your release strategy, go to Tools • ABAP Workbench • Development • ABAP Dictionary. Or, via Transaction SE11, enter CEKKO in Database Table, and select Display.

To define a characteristic, go to SAP IMG • Materials Management • Purchasing • Purchase Order • Release Procedure for Purchase Order • Edit Characteristic. (The menu paths will be slightly different for each purchasing document; select the appropriate document from the Purchasing menu.) Click on New and enter the characteristic name and validity start date. On the Basic Data tab, enter the Description and set the Status, as shown in Figure 8.12. In the Value Assignment section, select Single Value or Multiple Value. In the Format section, enter the Data Type and the number of characters. (The data type will depend on the field you're selecting from the CEKKO table.)

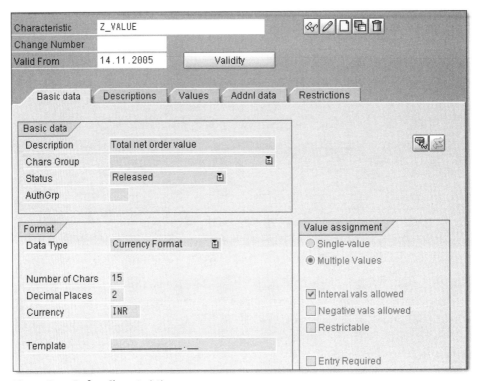

Figure 8.12 Define Characteristic

On the Addnl Data tab, enter table name CEKKO (if configuring for POs) or CEBAN (if configuring for purchase requisitions). Also enter the field name from the purchasing document (e.g., GNETW means total value in POs).

On the Values tab, you can define a list of different values for the characteristic. Alternatively, you can leave this blank; in this case, values can be defined in the release strategy.

Step 2: Edit Classes

In this step, you create classes for a release procedure. Classes are used to group together characteristics that constitute a release condition for a release strategy. To define a class, go to SAP IMG • Materials Management • Purchasing • Purchase Order • Release Procedure for Purchase Order • Edit Class. Click on Create and enter the class name. Also enter the class type, which is always 032. (This is the class type used for release procedures.) On the Basic Data tab, enter the

Description, Status, and Validity, as shown in Figure 8.13. On the Char. tab, select the different characteristics that should be grouped in this class.

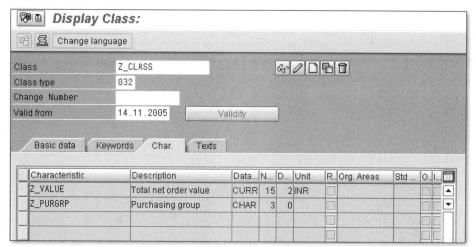

Figure 8.13 Define Class

Step 3: Define the Release Procedure for Purchase Orders

In this last step, you define the release procedure for POs. To do so, go to SAP IMG • MATERIALS MANAGEMENT • PURCHASING • PURCHASE ORDER • RELEASE PROCEDURE FOR PURCHASE ORDER • DEFINE RELEASE PROCEDURE FOR PURCHASE ORDERS. You'll see a list of five activities; select each activity, one by one, as follows:

1. **Select Release Groups.**

   A release group contains one or more release strategies. You can define different release strategies with the same key for different release groups. For example, release group 01 is defined for purchase requisitions, and release group 02 is defined for POs. You can define a release strategy for both release groups 01 and 02 with the same key: in our example S3 is used. Click on New Entries and enter the Release Group code and Release Object (1 for purchase requisitions and 2 for POs). Enter the Class name and Description, as shown in Figure 8.14.

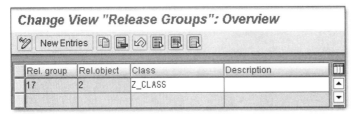

Figure 8.14 Define Release Groups

2. **Select Release Codes.**
   In this step, you define different release codes. These can be defined however you choose. In the example in Figure 8.15, three release codes have been defined: AA, AB, and AC.

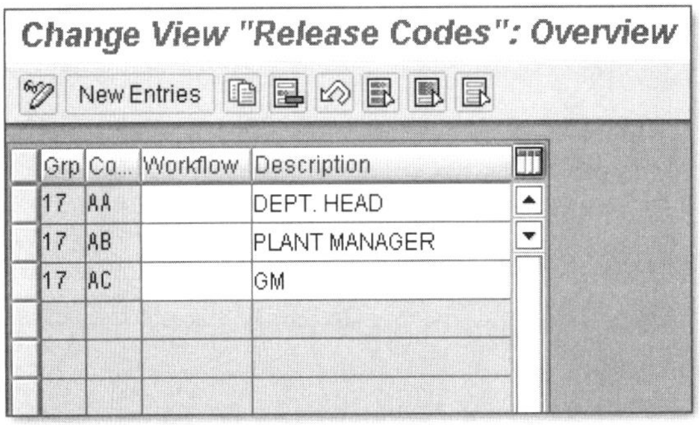

Figure 8.15 Define Release Codes

3. **Select Release Indicator.**
   The release indicator specifies whether the purchasing document can be processed or is blocked. Click on New Entries and enter the Release Indicator, Released status checkbox (which indicates whether the document is released or not), Changeable option, Value Change Percent, and Description (Figure 8.16).

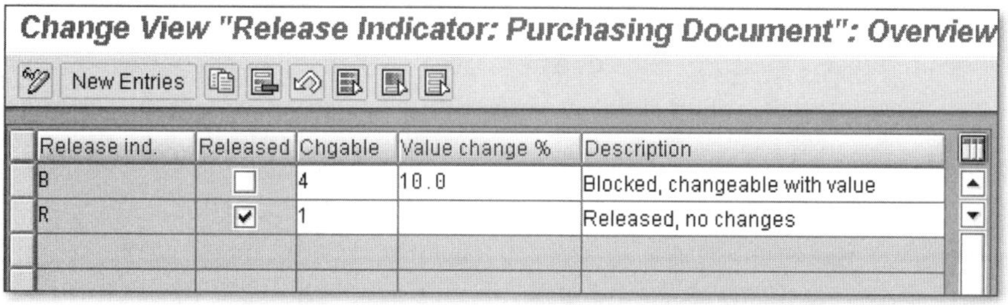

Figure 8.16 Define the Release Indicator

4. **Select Release Strategies.**

In this step, you configure the different release strategies. Click on New Entries and select the Release Group (which we created in Step 1). Enter the Release Strategy key and description, and select the Release Codes applicable for the release strategy. As shown in Figure 8.17, there are four options in the bottom of the screen: Release Prerequisites, Release Statuses, Classification, and Release Simulation.

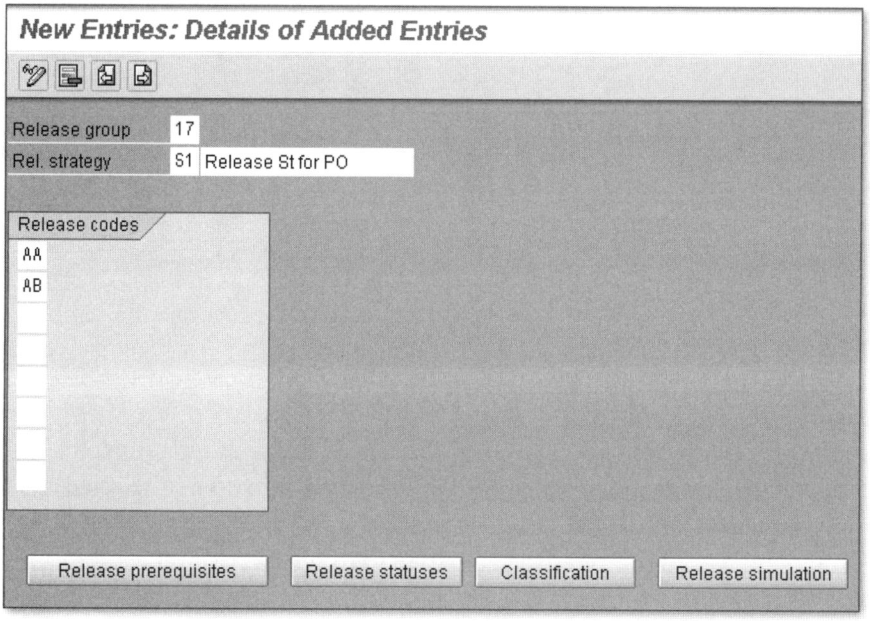

Figure 8.17 Define the Release Strategy

First, click on Release Prerequisites. If you have multiple release codes, you need to define the release prerequisite for each code. For example, Release Code AB can approve only if Release Code AA has approved.

Next, click on Release Statuses. Here, you define the different release indicators at different statuses of the release procedure. For example, Figure 8.18 shows that Release Indicator B is set until it's been approved by both release codes, whereas Release Indicator R is set only when it's been approved by both release codes.

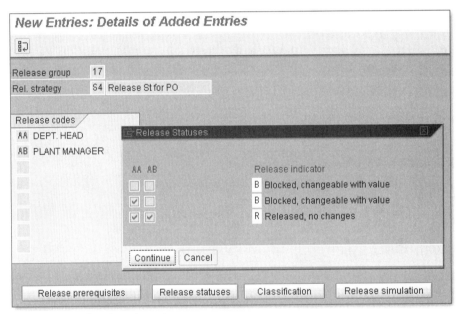

Figure 8.18 Define the Release Status

Next, click on Classification and enter the characteristics values. Based on these values, this release strategy will be picked up in the appropriate purchasing documents. For example, in Figure 8.19, two characteristics are selected. The first characteristic, Total Net Order Value, has a value of greater than 2,000 USD, and the second characteristic, Purchasing Group, has two values, Purchase Group 1 and Purchase Group 2. Therefore, if a PO is created with a value of more than $2000 and Purchasing Group 1 or Purchase Group 2, Release Strategy S1 will be assigned to the PO.

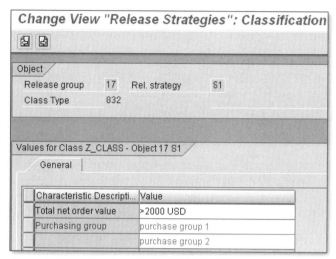

Figure 8.19 Define Characteristics Values

Finally, click on the Release Simulation button (Figure 8.18) to test whether your release strategy is working in the correct sequence. This will display a screen with the release codes and status.

5. **Select Workflow.**

You can also define a workflow for release procedures. Employees involved in the approval process are defined as agents. Define the agent for each release code, and this agent will be configured in the workflow. This step is optional.

This completes the configuration steps for release procedures with classification. Before we move on to the process steps, however, there's one last topic we must cover: item-level release procedures.

Item-Level Release for Purchase Requisition

Releasing each line item separately is called *item-level release*. A purchase requisition may contain one or more line items. With item-level release, a particular line item can be released while other line items may be pending for approval or rejection. It isn't possible to perform item-level release procedures using a release procedure with classification for external documents because external documents are always released or blocked as a whole document. However, for internal documents, you can configure line item-level approval or complete document approval using the release procedure with classification.

To configure item-level release for a purchase requisition, go to SAP IMG • MATE-
RIALS MANAGEMENT • PURCHASING • PURCHASE REQUISITION • DEFINE DOCUMENT
TYPES. Select the OverReqRel checkbox to enable overall release of a purchase
requisition. If you want item-level approval, don't select this checkbox. In Figure
8.20, document Type NB has OverReqRel selected; therefore, any purchase requisition created with document Type NB will be released as a whole document.

Type	Doc. type descript.	Item...	NR int.as.	No.rng.ext	Field sel.	Cont...	OverReqRel	Variant
EC	Purch.requis. EBP	10	01	RQ	NBB		☐	
F0	Framework requisn.	10	01	02	FOF		☐	SRV
IN	Purch.requis. I-Comm	10	01	02	NBB		☐	
MV	Model specification	10	01	02	RVB	R	☐	
NB	Purch.requis. Stand.	10	01	02	NBB		☑	
RV	Outl. agmt. requisn.	10	01	02	RVB	R	☐	

Figure 8.20 Item-Level Release Configuration

8.1.5 Process Steps

When you create a purchasing document, the system will automatically assign
the relevant release procedure. Figure 8.21 shows a PO that has been assigned to
Release Strategy S4. This PO cannot be sent to the vendor, because it's in a blocked
state (Release Indicator B means blocked). This PO requires two levels of approval:
from the plant manager (release Code AB) and the department head (release Code
AA).

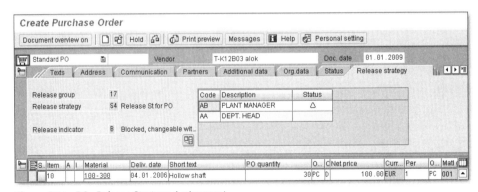

Figure 8.21 PO: Release Strategy Assignment

You can release purchasing documents individually or collectively. In individual release, one document is released at a time. Go to Transaction ME29N for the individual release of POs, and Transaction ME54N for the individual release of purchase requisitions. Click on the Release button, which you'll find on the Release Strategy tab (Figure 8.22). After a PO is approved by all of the approvers, it can be sent to the vendor.

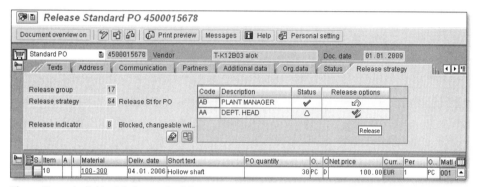

Figure 8.22 Individual Release of a PO

You can also release purchasing documents collectively, which means that documents are released as a group instead of individually. The following transaction codes are used for collective release:

- ME28: PO release
- ME55: Purchase requisition release
- ME35K: Contract release
- ME35L: Scheduling agreement release

8.2 Pricing Procedure

A *pricing procedure* is used to determine the price of a material in a PO. The net price of a material depends on discounts, surcharges, taxes, freight, and so on.

8.2.1 Business Scenario

A purchasing department in an enterprise calculates the net price based on the gross price, discounts, taxes, freight charges and so on. These values are referred while creating a PO and contracts.

In the SAP system, the price, discounts, surcharges, freight costs, and so on are represented in the form of *condition types*. Condition types are used in the determination of net and effective prices in POs. Each condition type has condition records (i.e., values), and these records are defined in condition tables. The sequence in which condition records are referred is defined in the access sequence, and this sequence is assigned to condition types.

Various condition types are grouped in a sequence in a *calculation schema*. A calculation schema is assigned for a combination of vendor schema groups and purchasing organization schema groups.

> **Note**
>
> Conditions can be time-dependent or time-independent. Time-dependent conditions are defined for a certain validity period; time-independent conditions don't have a validity period. Conditions in info records and contracts are always time-dependent conditions. Conditions in POs are always time-independent.

In the following sections, we'll discuss the process and configuration steps for the pricing procedure.

8.2.2 Process Steps

As shown in Figure 8.23, the pricing procedure begins with Step 1 and ends with Step 9. Using this figure, we'll go through each of the steps and explain how the price for Material Mat-1 was determined in the PO created with Vendor ABC and Purchasing Organization 1000.

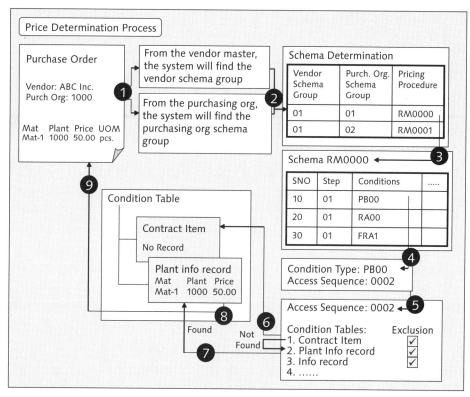

Figure 8.23 Pricing procedure: Price Determination in a PO

1. **Determine the vendor schema group and the purchasing organization schema group.**

   The system determines this information from the vendor master record and the purchasing organization. In this example, it's Vendor Schema Group 01 and Purchasing Organization Schema Group 01.

2. **Determine the calculation schema.**

   In this step, the system determines the relevant calculation schema. This is based on a combination of the vendor schema group and the purchasing organization schema group. In this example, the calculation schema is RM0000.

3. **Determine the condition type.**

   The calculation schema consists of various condition types listed in a sequence. Here, Condition Type PB00 is defined for the material price.

4. **Determine the access sequence.**
   In this step, the system uses the calculation schema to determine the access sequence (in this example, 0002) assigned to the condition type (in this example, PB00).

5. **Determine the condition tables.**
   In this step, the system determines the condition tables assigned to the access sequence (in this example, 0002).

6. **Determine the condition record (Part I).**
   The condition table of access sequence 0002 consists of many condition records of which Contract Item has the highest priority. A system search yields no value for this condition record.

7. **Determine the condition record (Part II).**
   In the previous step, the system search yielded no result for the highest priority condition record, which is Contract Item. Therefore, the system moves to the next condition record, which is Plant Info Record.

8. **Determination of material price.**
   The system search yields a value of $50.00 for Plant Info Record. This value for Condition Type PB00 is assigned to the material as the price in the PO.

> **Note**
>
> Material-specific discounts and surcharges are supplementary conditions linked to the gross price (condition type PB00). No access sequence is assigned to supplementary conditions and no separate price determination is carried out for them. They're found using the condition records for the gross price.

Settings made in Customizing determine the details of these pricing elements and how the price is computed.

8.2.3 Configuration Steps

Follow these steps for pricing procedure configuration:

1. **Define condition types.**
   The condition types are used to represent pricing elements such as prices, discounts, surcharges, taxes, or delivery costs in the SAP system. For example, for gross price, the condition type is PB00. These are stored in the system in the form of condition records. Condition types have control parameters, and

are differentiated by condition class. For condition types for which you wish to maintain records with their own validity period, you must specify an access sequence. The access sequence is used to search valid condition records.

To configure condition types, go to SAP IMG • MATERIALS MANAGEMENT • PURCHASING • CONDITIONS • DEFINE PRICE DETERMINATION PROCESS • DEFINE CONDITION TYPES. Here, you'll see a list of condition types provided by the SAP system (Figure 8.24). You can create new condition types by clicking on New Entries or by copying from existing SAP-provided condition types.

> **Note**
>
> If you define your own condition types, the key should begin with the letter Z because SAP keeps these name slots free in the standard system. You shouldn't change the condition types that are included in the standard SAP system.

Change View "Conditions: Condition Types": Overview

CTyp	Condition Type	Condition class	Calculation type
A001	Rebate	Expense reimbursement	Percentage
A002	Material Rebate	Expense reimbursement	Quantity
A003	Hierarchy Rebate	Expense reimbursement	Percentage
A004	Hierarchy rebate/mat	Expense reimbursement	Quantity
AK01	Customer Rebate	Expense reimbursement	Percentage
AM01	Internal Amort. %	Discount or surcharge	Percentage
AM02	Internal Amort./Qty	Discount or surcharge	Quantity
CU00	Gross price cust.sim	Prices	Quantity
CUAC	Antidumping cus.qty	Discount or surcharge	Quantity
CUAD	Anti-dumping cust %	Taxes	Percentage
CUAE	Antidumping cust.wt	Discount or surcharge	Not weight
CUAS	Customs exemption %	Taxes	Percentage
CUDC	3rd country cust qty	Discount or surcharge	Quantity
CUDE	3rd country weight	Discount or surcharge	Net weight
CUDL	3rd country cust %	Taxes	Percentage
CUFR	Freight qty customs	Discount or surcharge	Quantity
CUIN	Insurance customs	Discount or surcharge	Quantity
CUP1	Preference qty cust	Discount or surcharge	Quantity
CUP2	Preference wt cust.	Discount or surcharge	Net weight

Figure 8.24 Define Condition Types

Figure 8.25 shows the details of the condition types. In the Control Data 1 section, you can see the Condition Class, Calculation Type, Condition Category, Rounding Rule, and Plus/Minus fields.

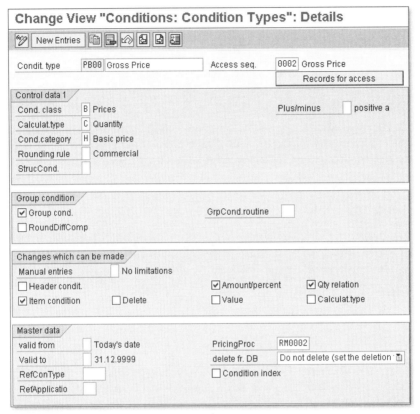

Figure 8.25 Define Condition Types: Details

The *condition class* is used for grouping similar condition types; for example, condition class A is used for discounts and surcharges, and condition class B is used for prices. The *calculation type* determines how the condition value should be calculated; that is, whether it's based on quantity, weight, or volume. *Plus/minus* controls whether the condition results in an amount that's negative (a discount), positive (a surcharge), or whether both positive and negative amounts are possible.

Based on your requirements, you need to define all of the control data for the condition type you want to create.

2. **Define an access sequence.**

An access sequence is a search strategy the SAP system uses to search for valid condition records of a certain condition type. For example, when supplying a price, you can stipulate that the SAP system first searches for the price for a specific plant, and then for a generally-applicable price. For condition types for which you wish to maintain records with their own validity period, you must assign an access sequence. With this, you define which fields the SAP system checks when searching for a valid condition record.

To define an access sequence, go to SAP IMG • MATERIALS MANAGEMENT • PURCHASING • CONDITIONS • DEFINE PRICE DETERMINATION PROCESS • DEFINE ACCESS SEQUENCE. The system will list the SAP-provided access sequence, as shown in Figure 8.26.

> **Note**
>
> Access sequence is a cross-client setting; that is, each change you make will have an effect on all other clients in the system.

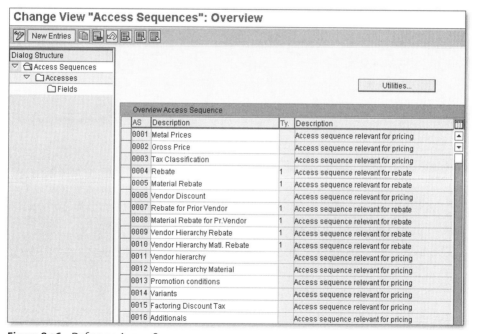

Figure 8.26 Define an Access Sequence

If you define your own access sequence, the key should begin with the letter Z because SAP keeps these name slots free in the standard system. You shouldn't change the access sequences that are included in the standard SAP system.

Select the access sequence and then select Accesses, located in the left tree menu. This will open the sequence of condition tables for an access sequence, as shown in Figure 8.27.

Change View "Accesses": Overview

New Entries

Dialog Structure
▽ ☐ Access Sequences
  ▽ ☐ Accesses
    ☐ Fields

Access sequence 0002 Gross Price

Overview Accesses

No.	Tab	Description	Requiremnt	Exclusive	
5	118	"Empties" Prices (Material-Dependent)	43	☑	▲
10	68	Outline Agreement Item: Plant-Dependent		☑	▼
13	16	Contract Item		☑	
15	16	Contract Item		☑	
20	67	Plant Info Record per Order Unit	36	☑	
25	17	Material Info Record (Plant-Specific)	35	☑	
30	66	Info record per order unit	34	☑	
35	18	Material Info Record		☑	
40	25	Info Record for Non-Stock Item (Plant-Specific)	38	☑	
45	28	Info Record for Non-Stock Item	11	☑	
60	67	Plant Info Record per Order Unit	37	☑	
65	17	Material Info Record (Plant-Specific)	37	☑	
70	66	Info record per order unit	37	☑	
75	18	Material Info Record	37	☑	

Figure 8.27 Define Access Sequence: Condition Tables

For example, if for the gross price condition PB00, you've defined access sequence 0002, the system will search the valid condition record in this sequence. The system will pick the lowest number table first and search for condition record. If it isn't found, the system will search in the next table and so on.

The Exclusive checkbox controls whether the system stops searching for a record after a successful result has been obtained.

3. **Define the calculation schema or pricing procedure.**
   In a *calculation schema*, you define the complete structure of different price components (i.e., conditions) with a sequence and control parameters. While cre-

ating a PO, the system finds the calculation schema and, based on the schema system, finds the value of each condition defined in that schema.

To define a calculation schema, go to SAP IMG • MATERIALS MANAGEMENT • PURCHASING • CONDITIONS • DEFINE PRICE DETERMINATION PROCESS • DEFINE CALCULATION SCHEMA. SAP-provided calculation schemas can be used, or you can create your own. To create your own, click on New Entries, or copy an existing calculation schema (Figure 8.28).

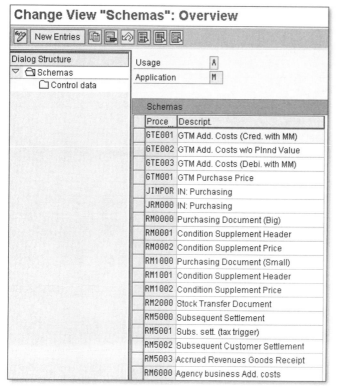

Figure 8.28 Define a Calculation Schema

Select the calculation schema and then select Control Data in the left tree menu. The system will display the screen shown in Figure 8.29.

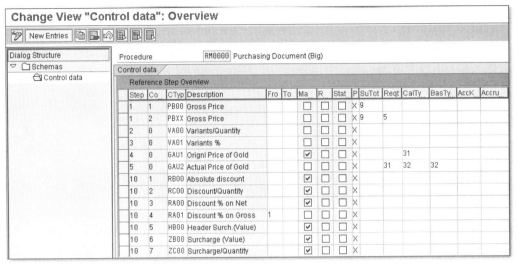

Figure 8.29 Calculation Schema Control Data

The following list provides an explanation of the different controlling fields in calculation schemas:

▶ **Step**
Determines the sequence of the condition types.

▶ **Counter**
This is the access number of the conditions within a step in the pricing procedure.

▶ **Condition Type**
Defines the condition type you want to include in the pricing procedure.

▶ **From and To**
From and To is defined to calculate the number of condition types based on which the amount needs to be calculated for that condition. For example, to calculate the surcharge on the gross price, you need to define the sequence number of the gross price in the From field. The system will then calculate the surcharge based on the gross price.

▶ **Manually**
This is defined for manually entered conditions.

▶ **Required**

This is defined for mandatory conditions.

▶ **Statistical**

This indicator is set for the conditions that are required for some other calculation. The value of this condition isn't directly included in the pricing.

4. **Define schema group.**

A company may have multiple calculation schemas that are used based on the purchasing organization or vendor. Defining a *schema group* helps you keep track of this by grouping together the purchasing organizations or vendors that use the same calculation schemas.

To define a schema group, you need to do the following:

▶ Define a vendor schema group

▶ Define a purchasing organization schema group

▶ Assign a purchasing organization schema group to the purchasing organization

▶ Assign a vendor schema group in the vendor master record

To define a vendor schema group, go to SAP IMG • Materials Management • Purchasing • Conditions • Define Price Determination Process • Define Schema Group • Schema Group: Vendor (Figure 8.30).

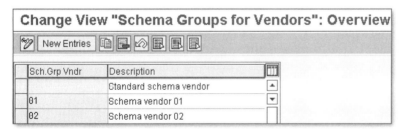

Figure 8.30 Define Schema Groups for Vendors

To define a purchasing organization schema group, go to SAP IMG • Materials Management • Purchasing • Conditions • Define Price Determination Process • Define Schema Group • Schema Groups for Purchasing Organizations (Figure 8.31).

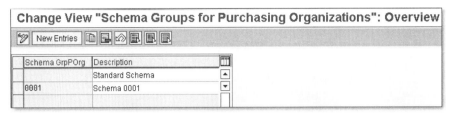

Figure 8.31   Define Schema Groups for Purchasing Organizations

To assign a purchasing organization schema group to a purchasing organization, go to SAP IMG • Materials Management • Purchasing • Conditions • Define Price Determination Process • Define Schema Group • Assignment of Schema Group to Purchasing Organization (Figure 8.32).

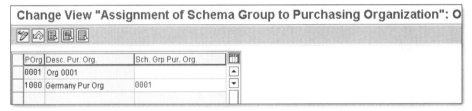

Figure 8.32   Assign a Purchasing Organization Schema Group to a Purchasing Organization

When creating the vendor master record, assign the schema group to that vendor in the Purchasing view via Transaction XK01 or MK01 (Figure 8.33).

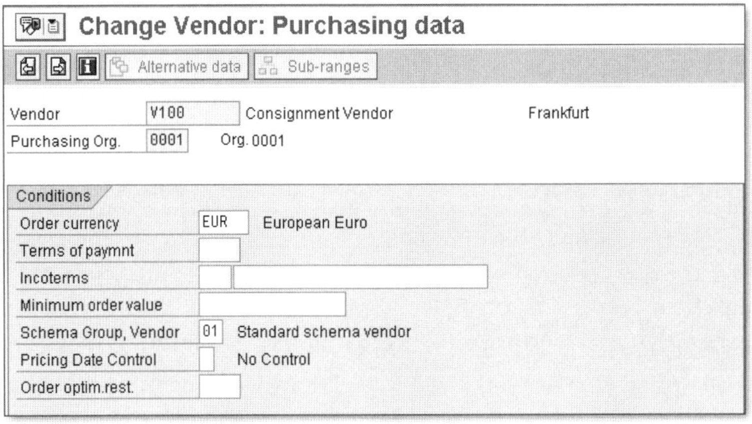

Figure 8.33   Assign a Vendor Schema Group to the Vendor Master

5. **Define the schema determination.**

   To define the schema determination, go to SAP IMG • MATERIALS MANAGEMENT • PURCHASING • CONDITIONS • DEFINE PRICE DETERMINATION PROCESS • DEFINE SCHEMA DETERMINATION • DETERMINE CALCULATION SCHEMA FOR STANDARD PURCHASE ORDERS. Here, you can define the calculation schema determination for standard POs and stock transport orders:

6. **Standard POs**

   The calculation schema is assigned for a combination of vendor schema group and purchasing organization schema group (Figure 8.34).

7. **Stock transport orders**

   The calculation schema is assigned for a combination of supplying plant and purchasing organization schema group.

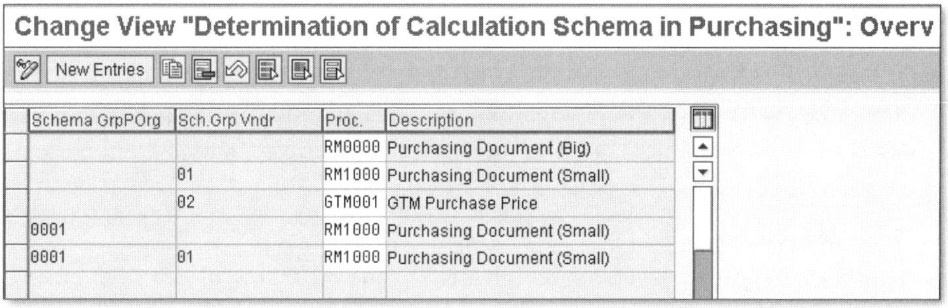

Schema GrpPOrg	Sch.Grp Vndr	Proc.	Description
		RM0000	Purchasing Document (Big)
	01	RM1000	Purchasing Document (Small)
	02	GTM001	GTM Purchase Price
0001		RM1000	Purchasing Document (Small)
0001	01	RM1000	Purchasing Document (Small)

Figure 8.34 Calculation Schema Determination

8.3 Automatic Account Determination

Various transactions in MM are relevant for accounting, such as goods receipts, goods issues, and invoice receipts. In such cases, the system always creates an accounting document and posts the amount in the appropriate G/L accounts. G/L accounts are automatically determined with the help of *automatic account determination* settings.

8.3.1 Business Scenario

Consider, for example, a manufacturing enterprise that stores stock materials purchased from vendors. Whenever the material is received in a storage location with reference to a PO, the company wants their system to automatically determine and update the stock G/L account. Similarly, whenever an invoice is posted, the system should automatically determine the vendor G/L account and post the liability.

The SAP system provides automatic G/L account posting via the automatic account determination process. When you post a goods receipt against a PO, the system creates an accounting document (along with the material document) and G/L account postings are made. The system determines which G/L accounts should be debited and credited based on configuration settings for automatic account determination.

Before we discuss these configuration settings, let's cover the definitions of a few essential terms.

- ▶ **Valuation area**
  A valuation area is an organizational unit that subdivides an enterprise for the purpose of uniform and complete valuation of material stocks. The valuation area can be at the company code or plant level. If the valuation area is at the plant level, each plant will have a valuation area assigned and materials are valuated at the valuation area level. (For more information about valuation areas, see the beginning of Chapter 7, Inventory Valuation.)

- ▶ **Chart of accounts**
  A chart of accounts provides a framework for the recording of values to ensure an orderly rendering of accounting data. The G/L accounts it contains are used by one or more company codes. For each G/L account, the chart of accounts contains the account number, the account name, and technical information.

- ▶ **Valuation class**
  A valuation class is used to determine the G/L account for the materials stock account. In automatic account determination, you must create valuation classes and assign them to material types. While creating material master records, you must select the appropriate valuation class in the Accounting view. The valuation class list in the material master record will depend on the material type. For example, in the standard SAP system, material type ROH (raw material) has three valuation classes: 3000, 3001, and 3002.

- ▶ **Transaction key**
  Transaction keys are used to determine accounts or posting keys for line items that are automatically created by the system. They're defined in the system and cannot be changed by the user.

Now that you understand the key terms in automatic account determination, we'll move on to describe the configuration and process steps involved.

8.3.2 Configuration with the Automatic Account Determination Wizard

Automatic account determination can be configured either with or without the automatic account determination wizard, a tool provided by SAP to help users with automatic account determination functionality. To configure automatic account determination with the help of the wizard, go to SAP IMG • MATERIALS MANAGEMENT • VALUATION AND ACCOUNT ASSIGNMENT • ACCOUNT DETERMINATION • ACCOUNT DETERMINATION WIZARD.

The wizard asks you a number of questions and, based on your answers, finds the correct settings and saves them in the corresponding SAP tables. With the exception of a few restrictions (these are documented in the wizard), the wizard undertakes the following steps:

1. Defining valuation control.
2. Grouping valuation areas.
3. Defining valuation classes.
4. Defining account grouping for movement types.
5. Managing purchase accounts.
6. Configuring automatic postings.

8.3.3 Configuration without the Automatic Account Determination Wizard

Account determination without the wizard enables you to create a more complex configuration. In the sections that follow, we'll discuss each step involved in this configuration process.

Step 1: Define Valuation Control

To define valuation control, go to SAP IMG • MATERIALS MANAGEMENT • VALUATION AND ACCOUNT ASSIGNMENT • ACCOUNT DETERMINATION • ACCOUNT DETERMINATION WITHOUT WIZARD • DEFINE VALUATION CONTROL. For account determination, you can group together valuation areas by activating the valuation grouping code. This makes the configuration of automatic postings much easier. As shown in Figure 8.35, the valuation grouping code can be made active or inactive.

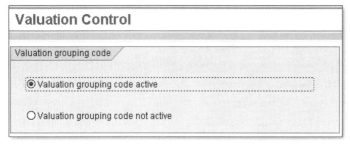

Figure 8.35 Valuation Control: Valuation Grouping Code Active

Step 2: Assign Valuation Grouping Codes to Valuation Areas

To assign valuation grouping codes to valuation areas, go to SAP IMG • Materials Management • Valuation and Account Assignment • Account Determination • Account Determination without Wizard • Group together Valuation Areas (Figure 8.36). The valuation grouping code makes it easier to set automatic account determination. Within the chart of accounts, you assign the same valuation grouping codes to the valuation areas you want to assign to the same account. As shown in Figure 8.36, Valuation Grouping Code 0001 is assigned to Valuation Area 0001 and Company Code 0001. If another valuation area is using the same set of G/L accounts as Valuation Area 0001, you can assign Valuation Grouping Code 0001 to that valuation area.

Step 3: Define Valuation Classes

In this step, you define the valuation classes allowed for material types. First define the account category reference and then the valuation class for each account category reference. After that, assign the account category reference to the material type.

Change View "Acct Determination for Val. Areas": Overview

Val. Area	CoCode	Company Name	Chrt/Accts	Val.Grpg Code
0001	0001	SAP A.G.	INT	0001
1000	0001	SAP A.G.	INT	0002

Figure 8.36 Valuation Grouping Code

As shown in Figure 8.37, Account Category References 0001 and 0002 are defined, and for each account category reference, one or more valuation classes are assigned. Account Category Reference 0001 is assigned to Material Type ROH, and Valuation Classes 3000, 3001, and 3002 are assigned to Account Category Reference 0001. Consequently, Valuation Classes 3000, 3001, and 3002 are assigned to Material Type ROH. While creating the material master record for material type ROH, you can select any one of these valuation classes. Similarly, for Material Type HALB, you can select Valuation Classes 7900 or 7901.

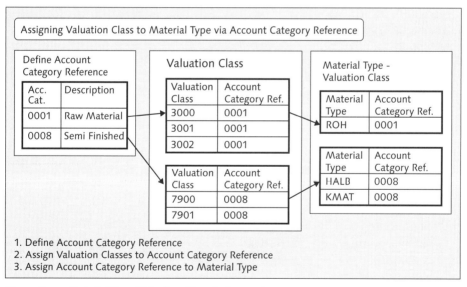

Figure 8.37 Material Type: Valuation Class Assignment

To define which valuation classes are allowed for a material type, go to SAP IMG • MATERIALS MANAGEMENT • VALUATION AND ACCOUNT ASSIGNMENT • ACCOUNT DETERMINATION • ACCOUNT DETERMINATION WITHOUT WIZARD • DEFINE VALUATION CLASSES. In this screen, you'll see three options: Account Category Reference, Valuation Class, and Material Type/Account Category Reference. Follow the below steps:

1. **Click Account Category Reference.**

   Click on Account Category Reference and define the code and description as shown in Figure 8.38. The account category reference is used to group valuation classes.

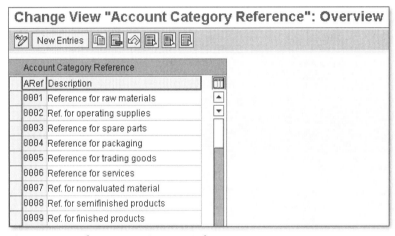

Figure 8.38 Define Account Category Reference

1. **Click on Valuation Class.**

   In this step, you assign valuation classes to account category references, as shown in Figure 8.39.

2. **Click on Material Type/Account Category Reference.**

   In this step, you assign material types to account category references, as shown in Figure 8.40.

Change View "Valuation Classes": Overview

New Entries

Valuation Classes

ValCl	ARef	Description	Description
0710	0001	Equipment 1	Reference for raw materials
0720	0001	Equipment 2	Reference for raw materials
1210	0002	Spec.complex fixed assets	Ref. for operating supplies
3000	0001	Raw materials 1	Reference for raw materials
3001	0001	Raw materials 2	Reference for raw materials
3002	0001	Raw materials 3	Reference for raw materials
3003	0001	Raw materials 4	Reference for raw materials
3030	0002	Operating supplies	Ref. for operating supplies
3031	0002	Operating supplies 2	Ref. for operating supplies
3040	0003	Spare parts	Reference for spare parts
3050	0004	Packaging and empties	Reference for packaging
3100	0005	Trading goods	Reference for trading goods
3200	0006	Services	Reference for services
3300	0007	Nonvaluated material	Ref. for nonvaluated material
7900	0008	Semifinished products	Ref. for semifinished products
7920	0009	Finished products	Ref. for finished products

Figure 8.39 Assign Valuation Classes to Account Category References

Change View "Account Category Reference/Material Type": Overview

Account Category Reference/Material Type

MTyp	Material type descr.	ARef	Description
ABF	Waste	0007	Ref. for nonvaluated material
CH00	CH Contract Handling	0006	Reference for services
CONT	Kanban Container		
COUP	Coupons	0005	Reference for trading goods
DIEN	Service	0006	Reference for services
EPA	Equipment Package	0004	Reference for packaging
ERSA	Spare Parts	0003	Reference for spare parts
FERT	Finished Product	0009	Ref. for finished products
FGTR	Beverages	0005	Reference for trading goods
FHMI	Production Resource/Tool	0008	Ref. for semifinished products
FOOD	Foods (excl. perishables)	0005	Reference for trading goods
FRIP	Perishables	0005	Reference for trading goods
HALB	Semifinished Product	0008	Ref. for semifinished products
HAWA	Trading Goods	0005	Reference for trading goods

Figure 8.40 Assign Account Category Reference to Material Types

Step 4: Define Account Grouping for Movement Types

In this step, you assign an account grouping to movement types. The account grouping is a finer subdivision of the transaction/event keys for account determination. For example, during a goods movement, the offsetting entry for the inventory posting (Transaction GBB) can be made to different accounts, depending on the movement type, as shown in Table 8.2.

Movement Type	Description	Account Grouping Code	Account
561	Initial entry of stock balance	BSA	399999
201	Goods issue to cost center	VBR	400000

Table 8.2 Account Grouping for Movement Types

The account grouping is provided for the following transactions:

▸ GBB (offsetting entry for inventory posting)

▸ PRD (price differences)

▸ KON (consignment liabilities)

> **Note**
>
> The account grouping in the standard system is only active for Transaction key GBB (offsetting entry for inventory posting).

To define account grouping for movement types, go to SAP IMG • MATERIALS MANAGEMENT • VALUATION AND ACCOUNT ASSIGNMENT • ACCOUNT DETERMINATION • ACCOUNT DETERMINATION WITHOUT WIZARD • DEFINE ACCOUNT GROUPING FOR MOVEMENT TYPES. Define the account grouping code, the movement type, and the transaction/event key combination, as shown in Figure 8.41.

Change View "Account Grouping": Overview

MvT	S	Val.Update	Qty update	Mvt	Cns	Val.strng	Cn	TEKey	Acct modif	C
101	Q	☐	☑	B	P	WE06	1	KBS		☑
101		☑	☐	B	A	WE06	1	KBS		☑
101		☑	☐	B	V	WE06	1	KBS		☑
101		☑	☑	B	A	WE06	1	KBS		☑
101		☑	☑	B	V	WE06	1	KBS		☑
101		☑	☑	F		WF01	2	GBB	AUF	☑
101		☑	☑	F		WF01	3	PRD	PRF	☐
101	E	☑	☑	B		WE01	3	PRD		☐
101	E	☑	☑	B	E	WE06	1	KBS		☑
101	E	☑	☑	B	P	WE06	1	KBS		☑
101	E	☑	☑	F		WF01	2	GBB	AUF	☑
101	E	☑	☑	F		WF01	3	PRD	PRF	☐
101	Q	☑	☑	B		WE01	3	PRD		☐
101	Q	☑	☑	B	P	WE06	1	KBS		☑
101	Q	☑	☑	F		WF01	2	GBB	AUF	☑
101	Q	☑	☑	F		WF01	3	PRD	PRF	☐
102		☐	☐	B	A	WE06	1	KBS		☑
102		☐	☐	B	P	WE06	1	KBS		☑

Figure 8.41 Account Grouping for Movement Types

Step 5: Configure Automatic Posting

In this step, you enter the system settings for inventory management and invoice verification transactions that result in automatic posting to G/L accounts. To assign G/L accounts to transaction/event keys, go to SAP IMG • MATERIALS MANAGEMENT • VALUATION AND ACCOUNT ASSIGNMENT • ACCOUNT DETERMINATION • ACCOUNT DETERMINATION WITHOUT WIZARD • CONFIGURE AUTOMATIC POSTING.

To assign the G/L account, click on Account Assignment. You will see a list of transaction keys; double-click on the key for which you want to set the G/L accounts. You need to define the valuation grouping code (also known as the *valuation modifier*), valuation class, and G/L account, as shown in Figure 8.42. You can then check your settings using the simulation function.

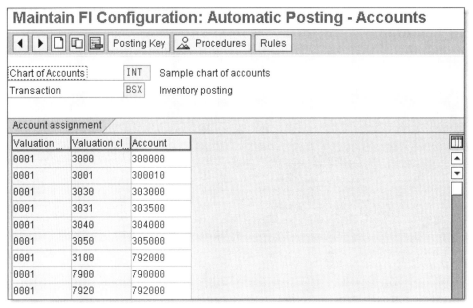

Figure 8.42 Account Assignment

8.3.4 Process Steps

Now, let's discuss the G/L account determination as they relate to goods receipt and goods issue postings.

Goods Receipt

Post a good receipt with reference to a PO via Transaction MIGO. Then, display the goods receipt document and go to the Document Info tab. Click on the FI Documents button; this will display a list of financial documents created for the goods receipt document (Figure 8.43). Select the accounting document to see the details of that accounting document (Figure 8.44). You can see the G/L account postings, which are determined based on the automatic account determination configuration.

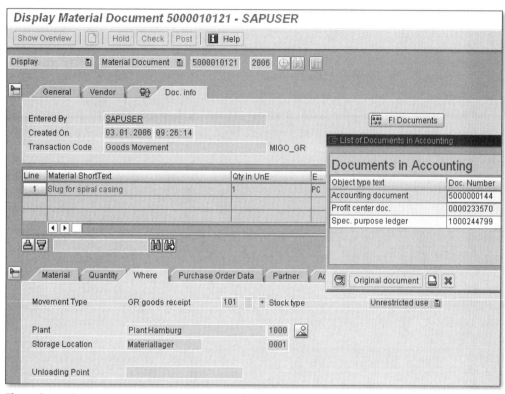

Figure 8.43 Accounting Documents List in a Goods Receipt

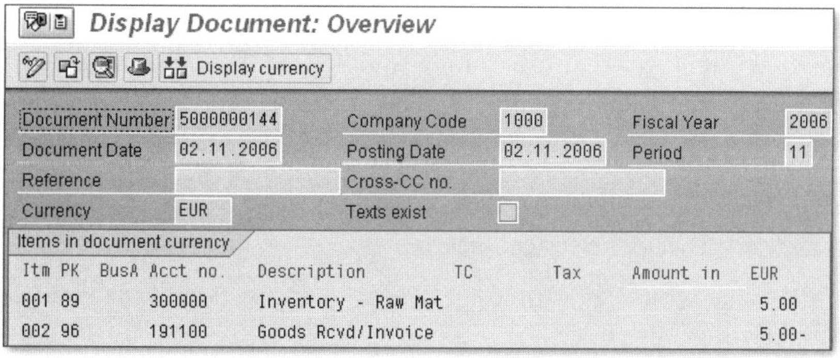

Figure 8.44 Accounting Document: Goods Receipt Transaction

As shown in Figure 8.44, G/L Account 300000 (Inventory Raw Material Stock Account) is debited, and GR/IR Account 191100 is credited.

Goods Issue

Similarly, when you issue goods to production, the respective G/L accounts are automatically determined. Go to Transaction MB1A or MIGO_GI, and use movement type 201 (goods issue to cost center). Select the cost center, plant, storage location, material, and quantity, and post the transaction. Display the material document and open the accounting document, as shown in Figure 8.45. Here, you can see that G/L Account 300000 is credited, and Account 400000 is debited.

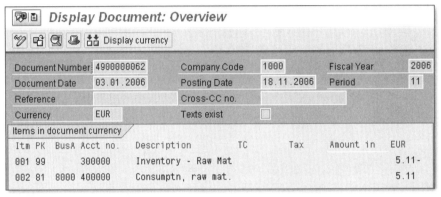

Figure 8.45 Accounting Document: Goods Issue to Cost Centre

G/L account determination depends on various parameters such as plant, material, business transaction, and movement type. As shown in Figure 8.46, a goods issue to cost center transaction is posted, which automatically creates an accounting document with the appropriate G/L account postings. Read the following steps to learn about the determination process:

1. Based on the business transaction, the system determines the value string. From there, you can take the following steps:

    ▸ From the value string, the system determines the account modifier.

    ▸ From the value string, the system gets a list of transaction/event keys, as shown in Figure 8.46.

2. From the plant, the system determines the valuation area. (If you've defined the valuation area at the company code level, the system will determine the valuation area from the company code.)

   ▶ From the valuation area, the system determines the valuation grouping code.

3. From the material master record, the system determines the valuation class, price control, and valuation price.

   After the system has determined the transaction key, account modifier, valuation grouping code, and valuation class, it will find the respective G/L account for the combination of these factors.

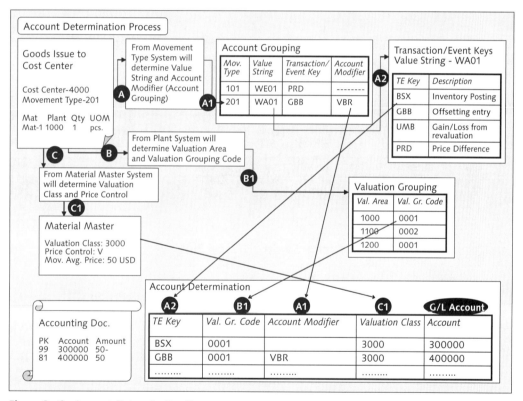

Figure 8.46 Account Determination Process

8.4   Document Type

You can define separate document types for each purchasing document category, such as PO, purchase requisition, RFQ, and so on (Figure 8.47).

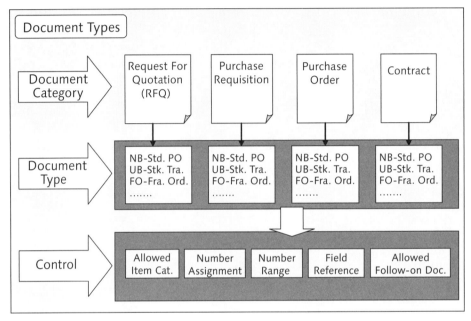

Figure 8.47   Document Types

8.4.1   Business Scenario

Consider, for example, a manufacturing enterprise that requires two different number ranges for stock material procurement to identify POs issued to local vendors and POs issued to overseas vendors (also known as import POs). In this case, document types will be very helpful. The SAP system includes preconfigured document types for each document category; however, you can create new document types based on your requirements.

The essential fields of document types are as follows:

▶ **Allowed Item Category**
You can define allowed item categories for document types.

▶ **Number Assignment**
You can define number assignments for document types; that is, internal or external numbers. Internal numbers are automatically assigned by the system when creating documents. External numbers are manually assigned by the user when creating documents.

▶ **Number Range**
For each document type, you can assign number ranges for internal and external assignments. For internal number assignments, number ranges can be numeric only. For external number assignments, number ranges can be numeric or alphanumeric.

▶ **Field Selection Key**
You can define field selection keys for each document type. Field selection keys identify the field attributes such as hidden, display, optional, and mandatory.

▶ **Allowed Follow-on Documents**
You can define allowed follow-on documents for each document type.

Now that we've discussed the essential features of document types, let's move on to the configuration and process steps involved.

8.4.2   Configuration Steps

You can configure document types for POs, purchase requisitions, RFQs, contracts, and scheduling agreements. The configuration steps for these documents are all quite similar; therefore, we'll focus only on the PO. You can follow the same steps for defining document types for other document categories.

1. **Define document types.**
   To define document types for a PO, go to SAP IMG • PURCHASING • PURCHASE ORDER • DEFINE DOCUMENT TYPES. You can start either by clicking on the New Entries button, or by copying an existing document type. Using the copy function will save time.

   Enter the document type key, document type description, item interval, internal number range, external number range, and field selection key, as shown in Figure 8.48.

Type	Doc. type descript.	Item...	NR int.as.	No.rng.ext	No.r...	Updat...	Field sel.	Cont...	SlIn
ECDP	Electronic commerce	10	45	DM		SAP	NBF		
FO	Framework order	10	45	41		SAP	FOF		
IN	Internet commerce	10	45	41		SAP	NBF		
NB	Standard PO	10	45	41		SAP	NBF		
OB	Overseas PO	10	91	41		SAP	NBF		
UB	Stock transport ord.	10	45	41		SAP	UBF	T	
ZA	RAW PO	10	ZA			SAP	NBF		
ZB	Test PO	10		ZB		SAP	NBF		
ZS	Test Transport Req	10							

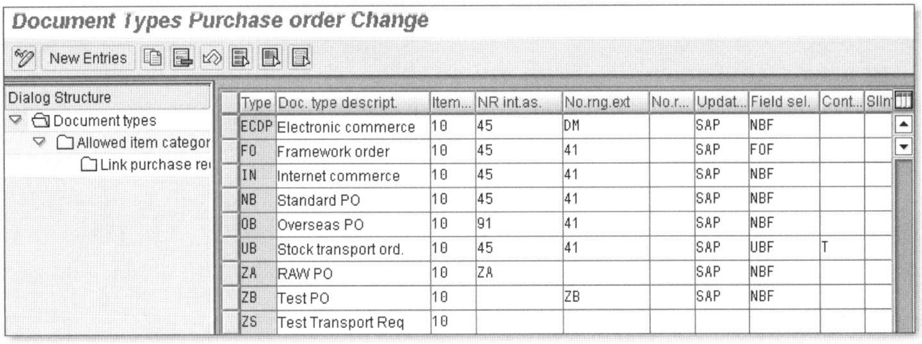

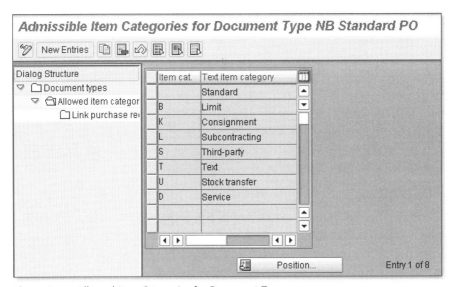

Figure 8.48 Define Document Types for PO

Note

Standard document types are preconfigured by SAP. These include document type NB (standard PO), document type UB (stock transport PO), and document type FO (framework order).

To define allowed item categories, select Document types (in the left tree menu) and then double-click on Allowed Item Categories (again in the left tree menu) (Figure 8.49).

Item cat.	Text item category
	Standard
B	Limit
K	Consignment
L	Subcontracting
S	Third-party
T	Text
U	Stock transfer
D	Service

Figure 8.49 Allowed Item Categories for Document Type

You can define allowed item categories based on the document type.

2. **Define a number range.**

   Every purchasing document type will have a number range, which can be internal, external, or both. To define the number range, go to SAP IMG • PURCHASING • PURCHASE ORDER • DEFINE DOCUMENT TYPES. Click on the Change Intervals button. This will show you the existing number ranges; you can add a new number range by clicking on the Insert Number Range button (Figure 8.50).

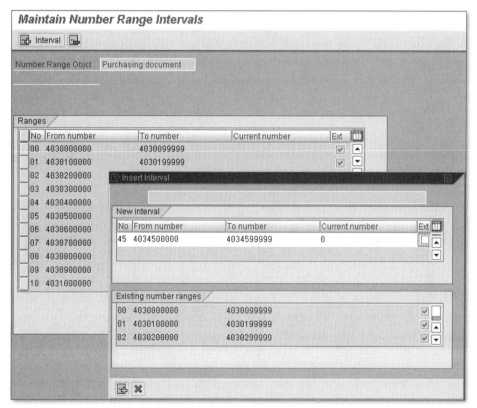

Figure 8.50 Define a Number Range Interval

Enter the Number Range key, the From Number, and the To Number. To make a number range external, select the External Number Range checkbox; to make it internal, leave this checkbox unchecked.

3. **Assign a number range to the document type.**
   Number range intervals are assigned when defining document types, as we saw in Step 1.

> **Note**
>
> Number range intervals cannot overlap each other, and, in MM, number ranges are year-independent.

8.4.3 Process Steps

When you create a purchasing document such as a PO, you can select the document type. Based on the field selection key assigned to the document type, different fields of the PO will either be displayed, hidden, optional, or mandatory. The PO number will be created based on the number range assigned to the document type.

8.5 Version Management

You can control and manage purchasing document changes via SAP's version management functionality, which can be activated for both internal and external purchasing documents.

8.5.1 Business Scenario

Consider an enterprise that has a requirement that they want to track any changes made to POs. If changes are made on a PO, the new version of the PO should be issued to the vendor.

SAP provides version management functionality to control and track changes in purchasing documents such as purchase requisitions, POs, contracts, scheduling agreements, and RFQs.

If version management is active for a document category and document type, the system will automatically create the first version at the time of document creation. Subsequent changes in the document will then create a new version of that document. As shown in Figure 8.51, a PO labeled Version 0 is issued to the vendor by the purchasing department. However, the buyer then changes the order price, which updates the PO, and creates Version 1. The revised PO is then sent to the vendor.

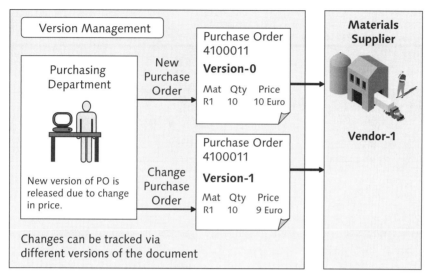

Figure 8.51 Version Management Scenario

In the following sections, we'll discuss the configuration and process steps involved in this process.

8.5.2 Configuration Steps

Follow these steps to configure version management:

1. **Setup version management.**
   There are two ways to do this, depending on whether you're working with internal or external documents. First, we'll look at internal documents (i.e., purchase requisitions).

   You can activate version management for a combination of document category and document type. After version management is active, changes made to a purchase requisition are managed in versions.

To setup version management for purchase requisitions, go to SAP IMG • MATE-RIALS MANAGEMENT • PURCHASING • VERSION MANAGEMENT • SET UP VERSION MANAGEMENT FOR PURCHASE REQUISITION. You need to set up control data for version control, as shown in Figure 8.52.

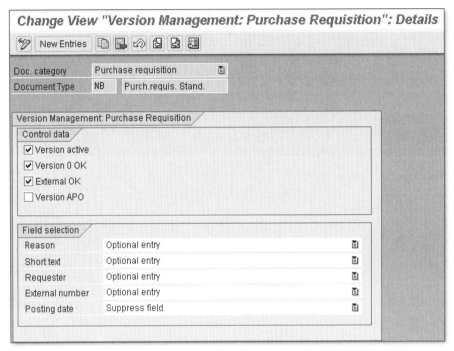

Figure 8.52 Version Management Setup for Purchase Requisitions

The following is a list and description of the important fields in this screen:

▶ **Version Active**
This indicator enables the version control functionality for a particular document type.

▶ **Version 0 OK**
If this indicator is active, version 0 (a brand new purchase requisition) will be automatically completed. If you haven't selected this indicator, version 0 must be manually flagged as completed.

▶ **External OK**

If this indicator is active, externally-generated versions of purchase requisitions (e.g., those created via BAPI) will be completed automatically. If you haven't selected this indicator, the versions must be manually marked as completed.

▶ **Version APO**

If this indicator is active, version management for purchase requisitions transferred from an APO system will be enabled. If you haven't selected this indicator, the system doesn't create a version.

▶ **Field Selection**

You can set up the field selection as Display, Optional, Required, or Suppress for the following fields: Reason, Short Text, Requester, External Number, and Posting Date. If not suppressed, these fields will be available On the Version Data tab of the purchase requisition header.

We'll now discuss this same process (setting up version management) for external purchasing documents. In external purchasing documents, you can activate version management for a combination of purchasing organization, document category, and document type. To configure this, go to SAP IMG • MATERIALS MANAGEMENT • PURCHASING • VERSION MANAGEMENT • SET UP VERSION MANAGEMENT FOR EXTERNAL PURCHASING DOCUMENTS.

A list of the document categories and document types will be displayed, as shown in Figure 8.53. Click on the New Entries button, and enter the Document Category, Document Type, and Purchasing Organization, as shown in Figure 8.54. Then configure the control data as follows:

▶ **Version Active**

Select this to activate version management.

▶ **Version 0 OK**

If this indicator is active, a new purchasing document will automatically be created as version 0, and marked as completed. If you haven't selected the indicator, version 0 must be manually flagged as completed.

▶ **Field Selection**

You can set up field selection as Display, Optional, Required or Suppressed for the following fields: Reason, Short Text, Requester, External Number, and Posting Date. If not suppressed, these fields will be available on the Version Data tab of the purchasing document header.

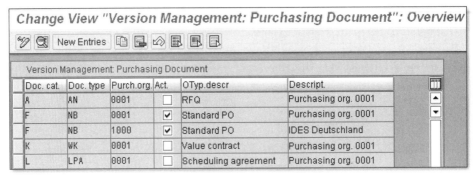

Figure 8.53 Version Management for External Purchasing Document

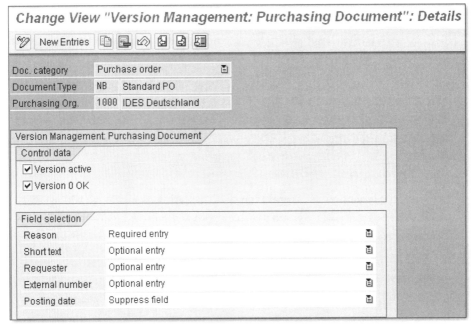

Figure 8.54 Version Management: Details

2. **Define reasons for changes.**

In this step, you can define reasons for changes to both internal and external purchasing documents. To do so, go to SAP IMG • MATERIALS MANAGEMENT • PURCHASING • VERSION MANAGEMENT • DEFINE REASONS FOR CHANGE. Enter the reason code and description, as shown in Figure 8.55.

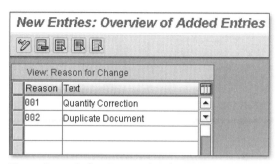

Figure 8.55 Define Reasons for Change

3. **Set up change displays.**

   In this step, you can define fields that should be displayed in the PO change history via the Display Changes button. This button is available on the Version Control tab of the document header.

   To set up change display, go to SAP IMG • MATERIALS MANAGEMENT • PURCHASING • VERSION MANAGEMENT • SET UP CHANGE DISPLAYS. Click on the New Entries button and enter the document type, change table name, and field name. Select the checkboxes No Output and Version, per your requirements. If No Output is selected, the corresponding field isn't included in the display. If Version is selected, the corresponding field won't be included in the change history that you can invoke via the Change icon on the Versions tab.

4. **Define version-relevant fields for purchase requisitions.**

   In this step, you can specify whether changes to a field are version-relevant. If a field is *version-relevant*, a change to that field causes a new version to be created. To define version-relevant fields, go to SAP IMG • MATERIALS MANAGEMENT • PURCHASING • VERSION MANAGEMENT • VERSION RELEVANT FIELDS OF PURCHASE REQUISITIONS. Click on the New Entries button and enter the document type, table name, and field name.

8.5.3 Process Steps

After you activate version management for a document category and document type, you can see the Versions tab in the purchasing document header (Figure 8.56). Purchasing document output (messages such as printout, fax, email, etc.) will be triggered only if you set the Completed indicator.

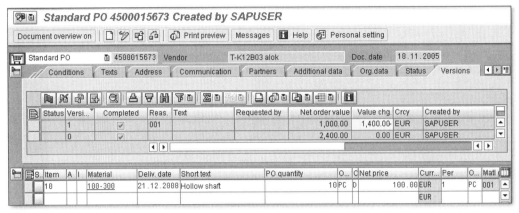

Figure 8.56 PO: Version Management

External purchase documents such as POs, RFQs, contracts, and scheduling agreements are sent to vendors in the form of printouts, faxes, EDI, or email. These outputs are called *messages* in the SAP system. Let's move on to learn how messages are configured in the system.

8.6 Message Determination

External purchasing documents generate output—or, in other words, a message. This message is information sent to a vendor using a variety of media such as printers, EDI, fax, or email (Figure 8.57). The variety of media will depend on each vendor; that is, some may prefer faxes whereas others may prefer email, and so on. While generating output for a vendor, it's difficult for the user to remember the type of media acceptable to the vendor. For this reason, the SAP system provides message determination functionality where you can define the output media for vendors. The system then automatically proposes the output media during document creation.

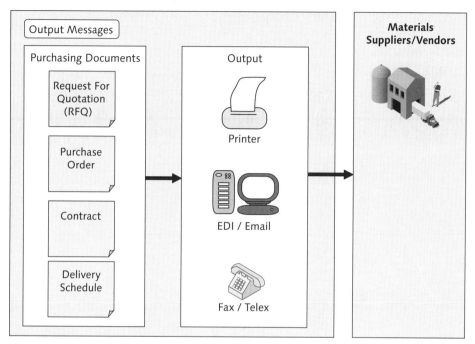

Figure 8.57 Output Messages for Purchasing Documents

8.6.1 Business Scenario

For example, consider an enterprise that wants the system to output messages upon creation of or changes to purchasing documents such as POs, contracts, and so on.

For each purchasing transaction, you can define whether the system should use message determination.

When you're not using message determination, the system can generate output for SAP-defined messages such as message NEU for POs. However, you can change the proposed parameters in the individual documents. For printout messages, the system needs to determine the printer. This is done via the following sequence:

▶ Printer defined for the purchasing group

▶ Printer defined in user parameter PRI

▶ Printer defined in user defaults

For messages *with* message determination, the SAP system uses the condition techniques discussed in Section 8.2, Pricing Procedure. Messages are determined based on predefined criteria such as document type and vendor.

8.6.2 How Message Determination Works

Let's learn how the system determines messages, using the help of an example (Figure 8.58).

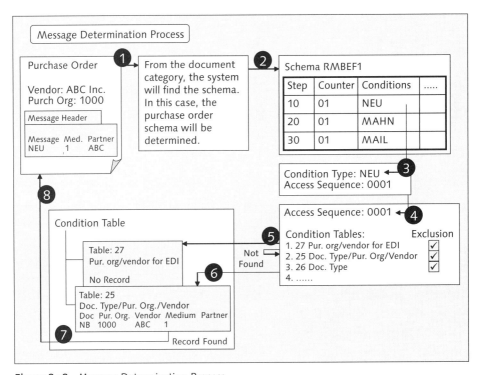

Figure 8.58 Message Determination Process

Message determination begins with Step 1 and ends with Step 8. The PO is created with Vendor ABC, Purchasing Organization 1000, and Purchasing Document Type NB. Let's see how the message is determined for this PO:

1. **Determination of the message schema.**
   The system determines the schema from the document category. In this example, the document category is Purchase Order, and the schema is RMBEF1. For each document category, the schema is defined in the system in Customizing (SAP IMG).

2. **Determination of the condition type.**
   The calculation schema consists of various condition types listed in a sequence. In this example, Condition Type NEU is determined.

3. **Determination of the access sequence and condition table.**
   In this step, the system determines the Access Sequence (0001) assigned to Condition Type (NEU).

4. **Determination of the condition record.**
   In this step, the system determines the Condition Tables assigned to Access Sequence 0001. A condition table consists of condition records in a sequence that defines priority. In this example, the system first determines Condition Table 27 and searches for a valid condition record in this table. Because the system doesn't find the condition record, it moves to the next condition table, which is Condition Table 25.

5. **Determination of the next condition record.**
   Condition Table 25 consists of condition records for the combination of document type, purchase organization, and vendor. In this example, the system determines the condition record for Document Type NB, Purchase Organization 1000, and Vendor ABC. The condition record consists of Medium, Partner Function, and Partner. Medium 1 (Printout) is found in this example. Partner is blank in the condition record; therefore, the output partner will be the PO vendor.

6. **Message details are copied into the document.**
   The system copies all of the details such as medium, partner, and printer into the document. If required, you can change the print parameters for a specific document.

8.6.3 Configuration Steps

In this section, we'll discuss message determination configuration for POs. However, you can use the same configuration steps for all other external purchasing documents.

1. **Define the condition table.**

    In a condition table, you define the combination of fields for which you want to create message records. To define new condition tables, or to check existing condition tables, go to SAP IMG • MATERIALS MANAGEMENT • PURCHASING • MESSAGES • OUTPUT CONTROL • CONDITION TABLE • DEFINE CONDITION TABLE FOR PURCHASE ORDER.

    You can define a new table by copying an existing condition table. For example, Condition Table 025 has three fields assigned to it (Figure 8.59): Purchasing Document Type, Purchasing Organization, and Vendor. The condition record is maintained for the combination of these selected fields. Condition records are maintained via Transaction MN06.

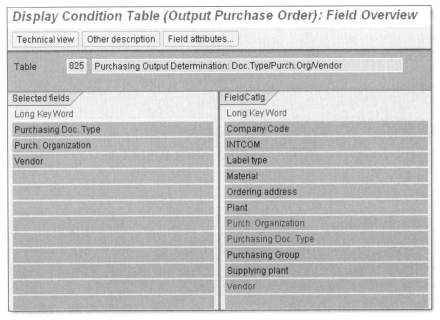

Figure 8.59 Define Condition Table

> **Note**
>
> The condition tables included in the standard SAP system shouldn't be changed. If you want to make changes, you should create new condition tables by copying a similar, already existing condition table and then making the necessary changes. New condition tables can be created with table numbers 501 to 999.

2. **Define the access sequence.**

In this step, you define the access sequence. This is a search strategy by which the SAP system searches for valid message records. We recommend using the access sequence provided by the SAP system. To define the access sequence, go to SAP IMG • Materials Management • Purchasing • Messages • Output Control • Access Sequence • Define Access Sequence for Purchase Order. You can define the access sequence by clicking on the New Entries button, or by copying a SAP-provided access sequence (Figure 8.60).

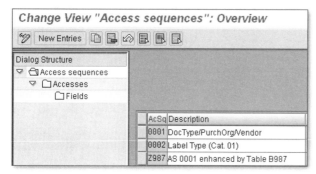

Figure 8.60 Define Access Sequence

To make changes to the access sequence provided by the SAP system, select the sequence and double-click on Accesses on the left tree menu. Here, you can define the access sequence number, table number, and Exclusive indicator, as shown in Figure 8.61.

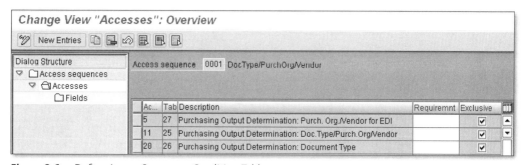

Figure 8.61 Define Access Sequence: Condition Tables

3. **Define the message type.**

In this step, you define the message types for a PO. To define a message type, go to SAP IMG • MATERIALS MANAGEMENT • PURCHASING • MESSAGES • OUTPUT CONTROL • MESSAGE TYPES • DEFINE MESSAGE TYPES FOR PURCHASE ORDER. You can define a message type by clicking on the New Entries button, or by copying a standard message type provided by the SAP system (Figure 8.62).

An access sequence is assigned to a message type, and you can define the processing routines (Figure 8.63). For different mediums of output type, you can define the Form and FORM Routine, as shown in Figure 8.63. Forms can be realigned per customer requirements, or you can create new forms.

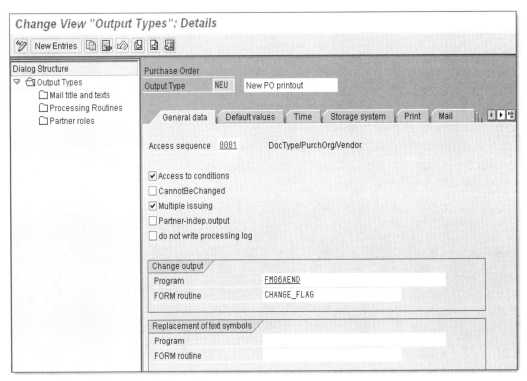

Figure 8.62 Define Message Type

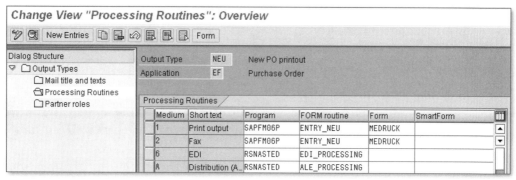

Change View "Processing Routines": Overview

Medium	Short text	Program	FORM routine	Form	SmartForm
1	Print output	SAPFM06P	ENTRY_NEU	MEDRUCK	
2	Fax	SAPFM06P	ENTRY_NEU	MEDRUCK	
6	EDI	RSNASTED	EDI_PROCESSING		
A	Distribution (A...	RSNASTED	ALE_PROCESSING		

Figure 8.63 Define Message Type: Processing Routines

4. **Define the message schema.**

In this step you define the message schema for purchasing documents. The allowed message types are stored in the message schema. To define message schemas, go to SAP IMG • MATERIALS MANAGEMENT • PURCHASING • MESSAGES • OUTPUT CONTROL • MESSAGE DETERMINATION SCHEMAS • DEFINE MESSAGE SCHEMA FOR PURCHASE ORDER. Define the sequence of the conditions for which you want the system to search for condition records (Figure 8.64). The defined schema needs to be assigned to a PO.

Change View "Control data": Overview

Procedure   RMBEF1 Purchase Order

Step	Cntr	CTyp	Description	Requiremnt	Manual only
10	1	NEU	New PO printout	101	☐
20	1	MAHN	Dunning	103	☐
30	1	AUFB	Dunning Ord Confirm	107	☐
40	1	ACE1			☐
50	1	NEUS	New PO printout	101	☐
60	1	MAIL	New PO printout	101	☐

Figure 8.64 Define Message Schema

Note

Only one schema and one message type can be assigned to each purchasing document.

5. **Define partner roles.**

   In this step, you define the allowed partner roles for the message types. To do so, go to SAP IMG • MATERIALS MANAGEMENT • PURCHASING • MESSAGES • OUTPUT CONTROL • PARTNER ROLES PER MESSAGE TYPE • DEFINE PARTNER ROLES FOR PURCHASE ORDER. You can define the partner roles for each output type and medium type combination by clicking on the New Entries button (Figure 8.65).

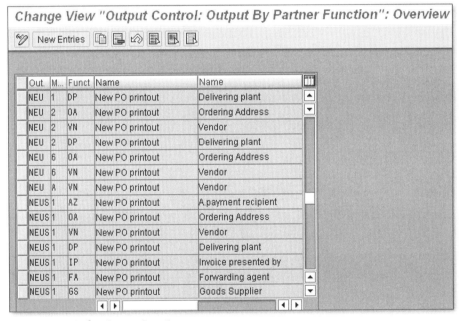

Figure 8.65 Define Partner Function

6. **Assign output devices to purchasing groups.**

   In this step, you assign output devices to purchasing groups via SAP IMG • MATERIALS MANAGEMENT • PURCHASING • MESSAGES • ASSIGN OUTPUT DEVICES TO PURCHASING GROUPS. Assign the output device (such as a printer) to the purchasing group, as shown in Figure 8.66.

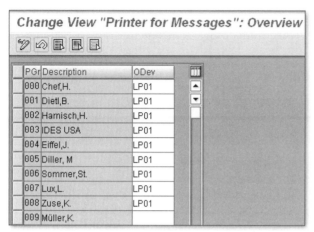

Figure 8.66 Assign Output Devices to Purchasing Groups

8.6.4 Process Steps

It's necessary to maintain the condition records for the condition tables configured for message determination. To define condition records, go to Transaction MN04 and select the key combination for which you want to maintain the condition records (Figure 8.67).

Create Output - Condition Records : Purchase Order

Key combination

Output Type   NEU   New PO printout

Key Combination

- ● Purchasing Output Determination: Purch. Org./Vendor for EDI
- ○ Purchasing Output Determination: Doc.Type/Purch.Org/Vendor
- ○ Purchasing Output Determination: Document Type

Figure 8.67 Maintain Condition Records: Select Key Combination

For the selected key combination, enter the condition record, as shown in Figure 8.68. Fill in the Vendor (number), Partner Function, Medium, and Date/Time fields. If the Partner Field is left blank, the system will assign the ordering vendor to the output partner in the purchasing document. After you've maintained the condition records, the system will automatically determine the message condition in POs.

Create Condition Records (New PO printout): Fast Entry

| Communication | | |

| Purchasing Doc. Type | NB | |
| Purch. Organization | 1000 | IDES Deutschland |

Condition Recs.

Vendor	Name	PartF	Partner	Medium	Date/Time	Language
T-K12B03	alok	VN		1	4	
T-K12B05	rasch05	VN	T-K12B05	1	4	

Figure 8.68 Maintain Condition Records

Create a PO via Transaction ME21N. Enter the vendor, purchasing organization, purchasing group, company code, and line item details. If you click on the Message button, you can see the message determined by the system (Figure 8.69). The printer is determined from the purchase group. Changes to the print parameters are made in a document.

Create Pur. order :: Output

| | Communication method | Processing log | Further data | Repeat output | Change output |

Pur. order.........

Output

Sta...	Outpu...	Description	Medium		Par...	Partner	La...	C...	Pro
OOO	NEU	New PO print..	Print output		VN	T-K12B03	EN	☐	▲

Figure 8.69 Create PO: Messages Tab

8.7   Summary

In this chapter, you learned the key configurations involved in MM release strategies, pricing procedures, automatic account determination, document types, version management, and message determination.

In the next chapter, we'll discuss classification and variant configuration.

Classification is a powerful tool used to organize master data objects in a way that allows you to find them more easily, as well as enhance master data by adding additional information.

9   Material Classification

A *classification system* is an organized and structured way to arrange objects such as material and vendor master data. For example, a company may have several thousand materials, thus it becomes difficult to search for a specific material. A classification system is used to classify materials based on characteristics; with the help of this, you can search for a material based on its characteristic values.

Such classification is used in almost all SAP components, including MM, SD, Production Planning, and others. This chapter will focus on material classification as it relates to MM, where it is used for release procedures and batch management.

In the following sections, we'll first provide an introduction to material classification and a review of key terms. We'll then cover the process and configuration steps required to configure this function.

9.1   Introduction to Material Classification

Material classification is used to find materials, as shown in Figure 9.1.

One of the most useful aspects of classification is that it can be used to search for a specific material number. Figure 9.1 shows the process flow for searching for a material master record via the classification functionality, illustrating the search options via both class and characteristic values. To do so yourself, first, click on the material search and enter or select the class name. A list of characteristics will be displayed for the selected class. Then, based on the values of the characteristics you enter, the system will search for the materials that are assigned these values.

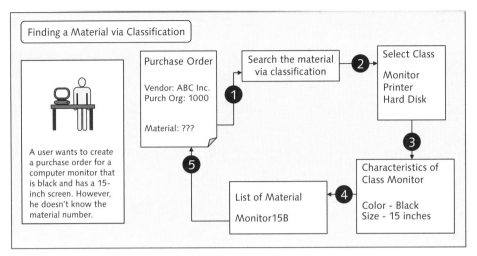

Figure 9.1 Finding a Material via Classification

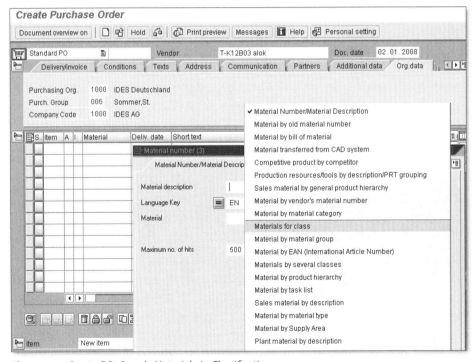

Figure 9.2 Create PO: Search Material via Classification

As an example, let's say you want to create a PO for a computer monitor that is black and has a 15-inch screen. Even if you don't know the material number for this type of monitor, you can search for it using the classification system. To do so, go to the transaction used to create POs (Transaction ME21N). Enter the vendor number and purchasing organization details. To find the material, press ⎡F4⎤, or click on the Search icon in the Material field (Figure 9.2). In the material search options, select Materials for Class. The system will then open the Find Objects in Classes screen (Figure 9.3).

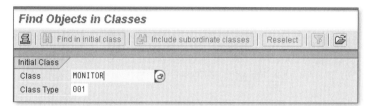

Figure 9.3 Finding an Object via Classification: Select Class

Enter the Class name, or select it from the dropdown list. Then, enter 001 (material class) as the Class Type. Press ⎡Enter⎤. The system will display the characteristics of the class; in this example, size and color. You can select the size of the monitor and its color, and click on the Find button, as shown in Figure 9.4. The system will find the material number that has the selected characteristics (Figure 9.5). If you click on the material number, it will copy into the PO screen.

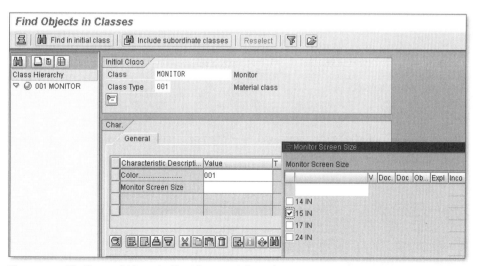

Figure 9.4 Finding an Object via Classification: Select Characteristics Value

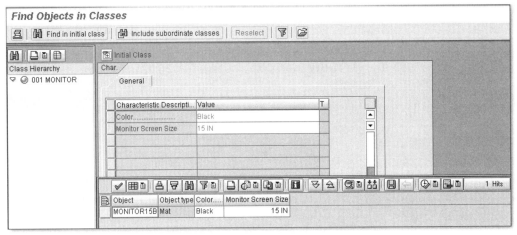

Figure 9.5 Finding an Object via Classification: Select Required Material

This example demonstrates how easily you can find a specific material master record from within thousands of master data records.

9.2   Key Terms of the Classification System

Before we discuss the technical configuration of material classification, you must have a good understanding of the different components involved in the process. The following key terms are essential to this subject:

- Objects
- Class type
- Classes
- Characteristics
- Values

Objects consist of three different types—vendor, material, and batch—and are assigned to classes based on their characteristics.

The *class type* has central control functions in class maintenance because it determines which object types you can assign to a class. Preconfigured class types are provided in the SAP system but you can also create your own, if necessary. The following are examples of the standard class types:

► Material class type: 001

► Vendor class type: 010

► Release strategy: 023

► Variant classification: 300

A *class* is a group of characteristics. For example, computer hardware trading companies define material classes for monitors, laser printers, and hard disk drives.

Characteristics are properties of objects. In the case of material classification, the characteristics are material properties. For example, a computer monitor material class might have characteristics that include color and size.

Characteristics have their own *values*. For example, for a computer monitor class with a color characteristic and a size characteristic, the values of the former might be white and black, and the values of the latter might be 15 inches, 17 inches, and 21 inches.

9.3   Configuration Steps

Figure 9.6 illustrates the process flow for setting up a material classification system. First, you define the characteristics and allowed values for each characteristic. Next, you maintain classes and assign the characteristics to these classes. Finally, you assign objects (such as materials) to the classes, and use the characteristics to describe the objects.

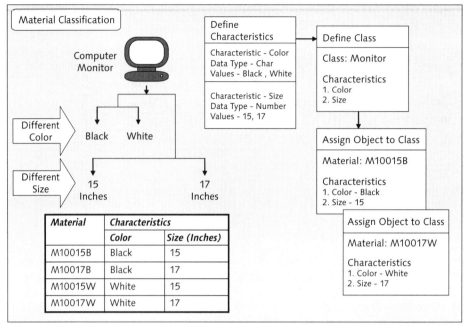

Figure 9.6 Material Classification Flow

In the following sections, we'll describe each of these steps in more detail.

9.3.1 Step 1: Define Characteristics

In the SAP system, characteristics and classes are both types of master data. You can define characteristics via the following menu path: SAP MENU • CROSS-APPLICATION COMPONENTS • CLASSIFICATION SYSTEM • MASTER DATA • CHARACTERISTICS. Alternatively, you can use Transaction CT04.

In the resulting screen, enter the Characteristic name and click on Create. Enter a Description and the Characteristics Group, as shown in Figure 9.7. In the Status field, you have three options: In Preparation, Locked, and Released. A status of Released means that the characteristic can be used; a status of Locked or In Preparation means that it cannot be used.

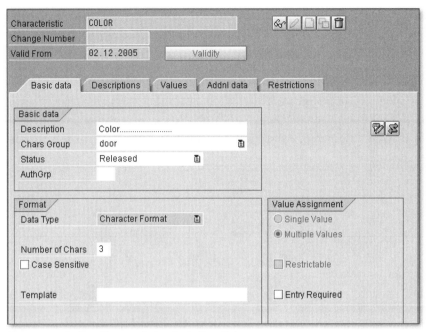

Figure 9.7 Define Characteristics: Basic Data Tab

In the Format section, select the *Data Type*, which is used to define the format of the characteristic's values. You can select any of the following predefined data types:

▶ **Character Format (CHAR)**
Used for values that consist of a character string. For example, if one of the characteristics is color, it needs to be defined with the Character Format, because its values are written as words (black, blue, white, etc.).

▶ **Numeric Format (NUM)**
Used for numeric characteristic values.

▶ **Date Format (DATE)**
Used for characteristic values that represent a date.

▶ **Time Format (TIME)**
Used for characteristic values that represent a time.

▶ **Currency Format (CURR)**
Used for characteristic values that represent a currency.

363

In the Value Assignment section, select either Single Value or Multiple Values. The Single Value indicator specifies that only one value can be assigned to this characteristic; the Multiple Values indicator is used when more than one value is possible.

Select the Values tab and enter the possible values for this characteristic, as shown in Figure 9.8. The Additional Values indicator allows you to enter characteristic values that aren't defined. After you've defined the values, you can save the characteristic.

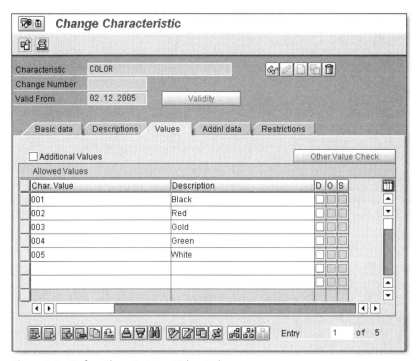

Figure 9.8 Define Characteristics: Values Tab

9.3.2   Step 2: Define Class

To define a class, go to SAP MENU • CROSS-APPLICATION COMPONENTS • CLASSIFICATION SYSTEM • MASTER DATA • CLASSES, or use Transaction CL02. Enter the Class Type as 001 (Material Class), and fill in the appropriate Class name. Then click on New (Figure 9.9). Enter a Description and set the Status as Released. Enter the validity dates.

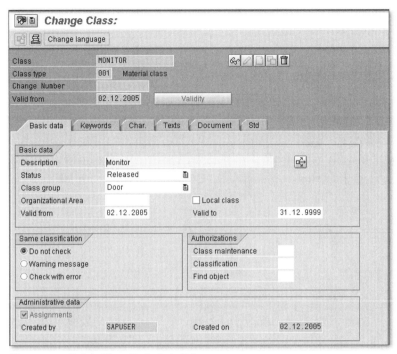

Figure 9.9 Define Class: Basic Data Tab

On the Char. tab, assign the characteristics to the class, as shown in Figure 9.10.

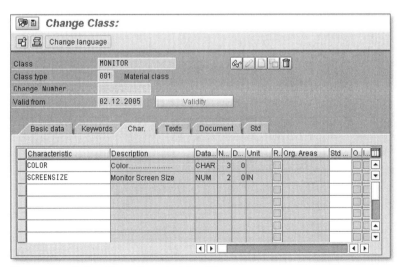

Figure 9.10 Define Class: Characteristics Tab

You've now defined the class and assigned characteristics to the class. You're now ready to assign objects to the class.

9.3.3   Step 3: Assign Objects to Classes

To assign objects to classes, go to SAP MENU • CROSS-APPLICATION COMPONENTS • CLASSIFICATION SYSTEM • ASSIGNMENT • ASSIGN OBJECT TO CLASSES, or use Transaction CL20N. Enter the Material number and Class Type 001. Then enter the class in which you want this material to be assigned. The characteristics of the class will be displayed, as shown in Figure 9.11. Select the values for each of the characteristics.

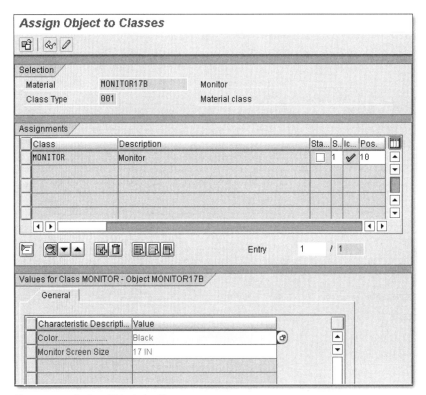

Figure 9.11   Assign Objects to Classes

You can classify a material while creating material master records via Transaction MM01. Enter the material number, industry type, and material type to see a list of material views, as shown in Figure 9.12. Select the Classification View and the class. After you've selected the class, display the list of characteristics. Enter the characteristic values and save the material master record.

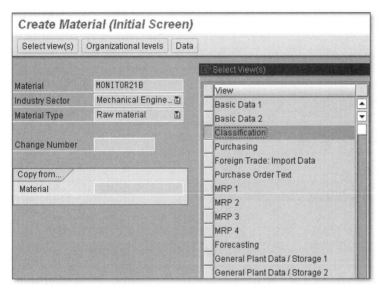

Figure 9.12   Create Material Master: Classification View

9.4   Summary

In this chapter, you learned about the key terms and configuration steps involved in material classification. Although it's a useful tool, remember that it can be used efficiently only when materials are properly classified.

In the next chapter, we'll conclude the book with a brief summary, a review of the chapters, and additional resources.

In this chapter, we'll review the lessons learned from this book.

10   Conclusion

MM is the heart of supply chain management, which makes this book essential for SAP components such as Warehouse Management, Quality Management, Sales & Distribution, and Production Planning. In the following sections, we'll review what you've learned in each chapter of this book.

Chapter 1

Chapter 1 explained the concept of ERP and discussed how the SAP system is integrated with various different functional areas of an enterprise. This is an important topic because SAP system architecture and landscape knowledge are very important for SAP consultants and SAP users.

Chapter 2

Organizational structure is the key for successful SAP system implementation. This chapter explained a variety of possible organizational structures, as well as the step-by-step procedures used to configure them. The organizational elements discussed in this chapter—including client, company code, plant, storage location, and purchasing organization—are fundamental concepts essential to understanding MM.

Chapter 3

This chapter described the different types of master data, including material master data, vendor master data, info records, and source lists. Material master data is the most important of these because it's used by almost all of the functional areas of the SAP system.

Chapter 4

Procurement processes are extremely important for material management consultants and users. This chapter explained most of the procurement processes used in industry. Each section covered the process and configuration steps for its respective procurement process.

Chapter 5

Inventory management is important not only for materials management, but also for financial accounting, production planning, and materials requirement planning. This chapter described the importance of movement types in stock keeping as well as in account determination. It also explained various physical inventory management processes and how to configure physical inventory.

Chapter 6

This chapter described the various processes in invoice verification, including the account postings for each of these processes. Invoice verification is very important from both a purchasing and financial accounting perspective because it generates liability and facilitates vendor payment.

Chapter 7

MM is tightly integrated with FI and this chapter explained the importance of stock valuation and its methods. This chapter also covered split valuation and discussed how you can use this functionality to meet customer requirements.

Chapter 8

Release strategies, pricing procedures, automatic account determination, document types, version management, and message determination are all very important aspects of MM. This chapter provided introductions to these topics, including detailed configuration steps.

Chapter 9

This chapter described the concept of material classification, which is used to search for materials and which is a very important feature for enterprises with large numbers of material master records. The topics discussed included how to define characteristics and classes, and how to assign objects.

Appendices

A   The Author

Akash Agrawal has over 14 years of experience in SAP Supply Chain Management. He has worked extensively on SAP system support, rollouts, and upgrade and implementation projects and has managed large global SAP projects in both the U.S. and Europe. His experience includes working with SAP 4.0B, SAP 4.6C, SAP 4.7 Enterprise Edition, SAP ECC 5.0, SAP SRM 5.0 , SAP IS Utilities and other ERP products.

In terms of industries, he has worked with the continuous process chemical, batch process, discrete manufacturing (telecom & media), utilities, and banking and insurance industries.

Akash has received many awards such as the best SAP Architect Award from IBM and the best Quality and Delivery Award. He is an engineer and has an MBA from a premier educational institute. Akash can be reached at *akasherp@gmail.com.*

B   List of Important Transaction Codes

B.1   Material Master & Service Master

Transaction Code	Description
MM01	Create Material
MM02	Change Material
MM03	Display Material
MM06	Flag for Deletion
AC03	Service Master
AC06	Service List
MMNR	Define Number Range for Material Master

Table B.1   Material Master Transaction Codes

B.2   Vendor Master

Transaction Code	Description
MK01	Create Vendor – Purchasing
MK02	Change Vendor – Purchasing
MK03	Display Vendor – Purchasing
XK01	Create Vendor – Centrally
XK02	Change Vendor – Centrally
XK03	Display Vendor – Centrally
XK05	Block Vendor – Centrally
XK06	Flat for Deletion – Centrally
XKN1	Define Number Range for Vendor Accounts

Table B.2   Vendor Master Transaction Codes

B.3 Other Master Records

Transaction Code	Description
ME11	Create Info Record
ME12	Change Info Record
ME13	Display Info Record
ME15	Flag for Deletion – Info Records
MEMASSIN	Mass Maintenance – Info Records
ME01	Maintain Source List
ME03	Display Source List
ME07	Delete Info Record
MEQ1	Maintain Quota Arrangement
MEQ3	Display Quota Arrangement
OMEO	Define Number Range for Purchasing Info Records

Table B.3 Info Records, Source List & Quota Arrangement Transaction Codes

B.4 Inventory Management

Transaction Code	Description
MMBE	Stock Overview
MB51	Material Document List
MIGO	Goods Movement (Receipts/Issues/Transfers)
MIGO_GI	Goods Issue
MIGO_GR	Goods Receipt
MIGO_TR	Transfer Posting
MIGO_GS	Subcontracting – Subsequent Adjustment
MBST	Cancel/Reverse Material Document
MBRL	Return Delivery
MB90	Process Output – Messages

Table B.4 Inventory Management – Material Movements Transaction Codes

B.5 Physical Inventory

Transaction Code	Description
MI01	Create Physical Inventory Document
MI02	Change Physical Inventory Document
MI03	Display Physical Inventory Document
MI04	Enter Inventory Count
MI05	Change Inventory Count
MI06	Display Inventory Count
MI09	Enter Inventory Count without Reference to Document
MI11	Recount

Table B.5 Inventory Management – Physical Inventory Transaction Codes

B.6 Purchasing & Invoicing Transactions

Transaction Code	Description
ME51N	Create Purchase Requisition
ME52N	Change Purchase Requisition
ME53N	Display Purchase Requisition
ME59N	Automatic Creation of PO
ME41	Create RFQ
ME42	Change RFQ
ME43	Display RFQ
ME47	Maintain Quotation
ME48	Display Quotation
ME49	Price Comparison – Quotations
ME21N	Create PO
ME22N	Change PO
ME23N	Display PO

Table B.6 Purchasing Transaction Codes

Transaction Code	Description
ME29N	Individual Release PO
ME28	Collective Release PO
ME31K	Create Contract
ME32K	Change Contract
ME33K	Display Contract
ME31L	Create Scheduling Agreement
ME32L	Change Scheduling Agreement
ME33L	Display Scheduling Agreement
ME38	Maintain Delivery Schedule
ME81N	Maintain Service Entry Sheet
MIRO	Enter Invoice
MIR7	Park Invoice
MIRA	Enter Invoice Verification in Background
MIR4	Display Invoice Document
MRRL	ERS Settlement
MRKO	Consignment and Pipeline Settlement
MRIS	Invoicing Plan Settlement
MR11	GR/IR Account Maintenance
MR21	Material Price Change
MR22	Debit/Credit Material

Table B.6 Purchasing Transaction Codes (Cont.)

B.7 Configuration

Transaction Code	Description
OX10	Define Plant (Copy, Check and Delete)
OX14	Define Valuation Level
OX09	Maintain Storage Location
OX08	Define Purchase Organization
OX17	Assigning Plant to Purchasing Organization
OX18	Assigning Plant to Company Code
OMS2	Define Material Types

Table B.7 MM Configuration Transaction Codes

C   List of Important Tables

C.1   Material Master Tables

Table	Description
MARA	General Data
MAKT	Short Texts, Descriptions
MARM	Conversion Factors
MVKE	Sales Org, Distribution Channel
MLAN	Sales Data, Tax Indicator, Tax
MARC	Classification
MBEW	Plant Planning Data
MLGN	Valuation Data
MLGT	Warehouse Management Inventory Data
MVER	Warehouse Management Storage Type
MARD	Consumption Data
MCHB	Storage Location Data with Stock Balances

Table C.1   Material Master Tables

C.2   Other Important Tables

Table	Description
EINA	Purchasing Info Record – General Data
EINE	Purchasing Info Record – Purchasing Organization Data
EBAN	Purchase Requisition
EBKN	Purchase Requisition Account Assignment
EKAB	Release Documentation
EKBE	History per Purchasing Document

Table C.2   MM Tables

Table	Description
EKET	Scheduling Agreement Schedule Lines
EKKN	Account Assignment in Purchasing Document
EKKO	Purchasing Document Header
EKPO	Purchasing Document Item
IKPF	Header – Physical Inventory Document
ISEG	Physical Inventory Document Items
LFA1	Vendor Master General Data
LFB1	Vendor Master Company Code Data
NRIV	Number Range Intervals
T161T	Texts for Purchasing Document Types
T023	Material Groups
T024	Purchasing Groups

Table C.2 MM Tables (Cont.)

Index

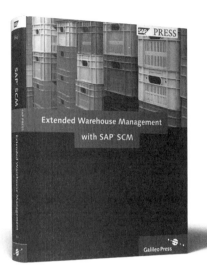

Provides the only complete reference to SAP SCM EWM

Covers everything from a general overview of the capabili-ties to detailed system set-up and configuration guidelines

Explains the difference between ERP EWM and SCM EWM

M. Brian Carter

Extended Warehouse Management with SAP SCM

This is the definitive guide to SAP EWM with SCM covering everything from a general functional overview to detailed system set-up and configuration guidelines. You'll learn about the key capabilities of the EWM solution; explore the configuration elements available in the standard solution; discover the methods used to solve common business process requirements; and find out how to extend the solution to meet your more complex or unique business requirements.

approx. 560 pp., 79,95 Euro / US$ 79.95
ISBN 978-1-59229-304-9, Nov 2009

>> www.sap-press.com

Learn how to implement and use variant configuration in SAP ERP and SAP CRM

Discover how to set up, customize, and maintain a complete product model

Review customer experiences, third-party extensions, and industry-specific features

Uwe Blumöhr, Manfred Münch, Marin Ukalovic

Variant Configuration with SAP

This is a complete resource that teaches users how to implement, set up, and use variant configuration functionality with SAP ERP 6.0 and CRM 2007. Consultants, managers, and even business decision leaders will learn about the business processes and integration issues, details of configuration in SAP CRM, special features of industry solutions, extensions of SAP customers and partners, and the selected challenges of using variant configuration. This is the one-stop resource to mastering Variant Configuration with SAP.

approx. 450 pp., 79,95 Euro / US$ 79.95
ISBN 978-1-59229-283-7, Oct 2009

>> www.sap-press.com

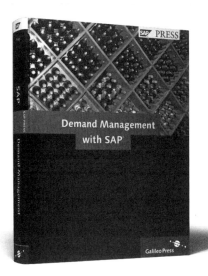

Teaches what demand management is and how to use it effectively

Describes how to configure SAP solutions, such as APO, SNC, DSR, etc., to support demand management

Provides case studies, real-world examples, and best practices throughout

Up-to-date for ERP 6.0

Christopher Foti, Jessie Chimni

Demand Management with SAP

This is the first resource that managers and business leaders need to understand and effectively use SAP's demand management tools. Each chapter begins with a general description of a business strategy or a process in Demand Management from the SAP perspective, and then teaches how SAP's solution is designed to work and teaches readers how to configure and customize the solutions. After reading this book, users will understand demand management, and will know how to configure and use the SAP solutions.

approx. 450 pp., 69,95 Euro / US$ 69.95
ISBN 978-1-59229-267-7, Oct 2009

>> www.sap-press.com

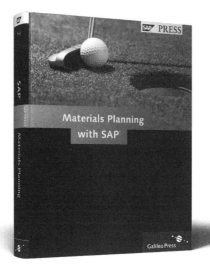

Provides details on implementing, customizing, and using MRP procedures with SAP APO and SAP ERP

Teaches users how to integrate MRP with existing SAP systems

Covers all relevant SAP MRP parameters and their interactions

Up-to-date for SAP ERP 6.0 and SCM 5.1

Marc Hoppe, Ferenc Gulyassy, Martin Isermann, Oliver Köhler

Materials Planning with SAP

With this comprehensive reference users will learn how to implement, optimize, and use SAP ERP and APO for effective material planning. They'll learn about cross-component material planning with SAP ERP 6.0 (MM, PP, SD) and SAP SCM 5.1 (APO), and review modern MRP procedures. And they'll discover how to configure and use the different SAP ERP applications and integrate them with an existing SAP system. In addition, the topics of how to optimize the tools and determine which settings are useful and how they affect other settings are covered.

approx. 564 pp., 79,95 Euro / US$ 79.95
ISBN 978-1-59229-259-2, Aug 2009

>> www.sap-press.com

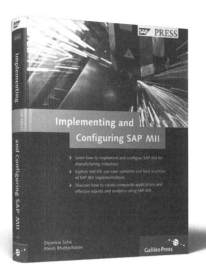

Learn how to implement and customize SAP MII for manufacturing

Explore real-life implementation scenarios of SAP MII in different industries

Discover how to create composite applications and effective reports using SAP MII

Abesh Bhattachargee, Dipankar Saha

Implementing and Configuring SAP MII

Implementing and Customizing SAP MII is your guide to the product features of SAP MII, how to implement it, and how to configure and customize it for different manufacturing tasks and issues. The book will help manufacturing teams get processes and systems working together by showing how to create composite applications that connects them. Once the systems are linked and generating comprehensive and accurate data, the book details how to use MII tools to generate accurate reports for analysis and planning.

approx. 468 pp., 79,95 Euro / US$ 79.95
ISBN 978-1-59229-256-1, July 2009

>> www.sap-press.com

Interested in reading more?

Please visit our Web site for all
new book releases from SAP PRESS.

www.sap-press.com

SAP PRESS